My Life *with* TRAINS

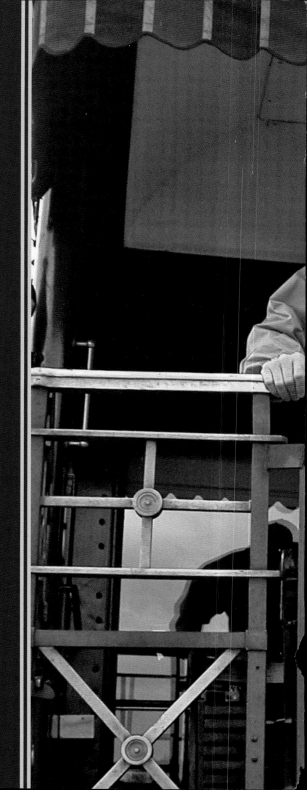

RAILROADS PAST & PRESENT

George M. Smerk and H. Roger Grant, Editors

INDIANA UNIVERSITY PRESS

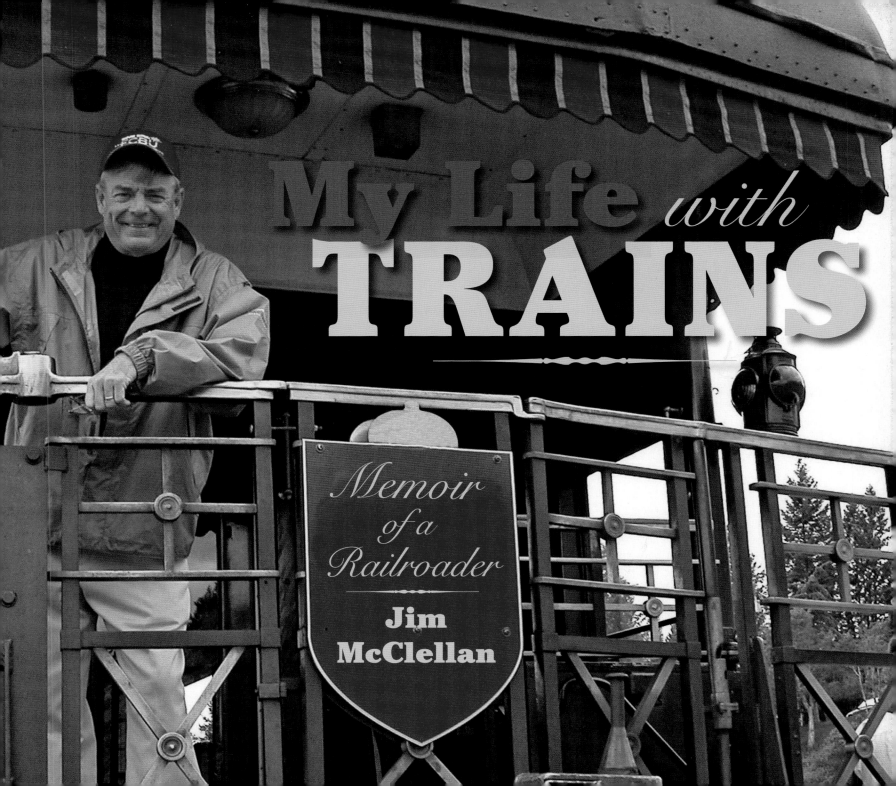

My Life with TRAINS

Memoir of a Railroader

Jim McClellan

This book is a publication of

INDIANA UNIVERSITY PRESS
Office of Scholarly Publishing
Herman B Wells Library 350
1320 East 10th Street
Bloomington, Indiana 47405 USA

iupress.indiana.edu

Manufactured in China

Library of Congress Cataloging-in-Publication Data

Names: McClellan, Jim (James W.), [date], author.
Title: My life with trains : memoir of
    a railroader / Jim McClellan.
Description: Bloomington : Indiana
    University Press, [2017] | Series: Railroads
    past and present | Includes index.
Identifiers: LCCN 2016045754 (print) | LCCN
    2017001480 (ebook) | ISBN 9780253024008
    (cl) | ISBN 9780253024084 (ebook)
Subjects: LCSH: McClellan, Jim (James
    W.), 1939-2016. | Railroads—United
    States—Biography. | Executives—United
    States—Biography. | Railroads—United
    States—Employees—Biography. | Railroads—
    United States—Management—History. |
    Railroads—Canada—Management—History.
Classification: LCC HE2754.M33 A3 2017
    (print) | LCC HE2754.M33 (ebook)
    | DDC 385.092 [B] —dc23
LC record available at https://
    lccn.loc.gov/2016045754

1 2 3 4 5   22 21 20 19 18 17

This book is dedicated to my wife, Joanne. We have been married for more than fifty-five years. She is my best friend and has been an understanding companion through the good times and the bad. Marrying Joanne was the best decision that I ever made.

Contents

Preface

I HAVE BEEN A RAILROADER FOR MORE THAN FOUR decades and a railfan for more than six decades. Riding trains, photographing trains, modeling trains—all were passions of mine at a very early age. During my railroad career I was involved in some of the major events of the past fifty years, so my experiences got a lot of attention in Rush Loving Jr.'s book *The Men Who Loved Trains*.

When I wrote this book, railroads were clearly on a roll: profits were up and it looked like clear sailing. Tony Hatch and others declared that it was a "rail renaissance." Now, thanks to the decline in coal traffic, the future seems more uncertain. Railways are in great physical condition but they will need a new business model that is less dependent on coal. Perhaps the best assessment of where we are today comes from Jim Hagen, who, as the president of both the US Railway Association and later Conrail, was one of the heroes of the rail renaissance: "The railroads went through a long and difficult transition. The surviving railroads have prospered. But prosperity does not last. Certainly, coal traffic, an important source of both revenues and profits, is declining rapidly. The railroads need to develop a plan to focus on other markets and how to match their assets to a new reality." The rail renaissance was real and it saved an important industry. But clearly the renaissance is taking a rest right now, and how things turn out will depend on a new team of railroad leaders.

That said, the prospects are far better than they were when I started railroading in 1962. With a few exceptions (most notably the Southern Railway, where I started my career), railroads were in decline and were written off as something akin to the wagon train—perhaps important at one time but irrelevant in a modern world. In a sense, I came to the party just as the lights were dimming for what most thought would be the last dance.

Still, I wanted to be a railroader. By high school my mind was set; I even wrote to several railroads seeking career advice. I went to Wharton to get a degree in transportation economics, served as a naval officer, and went on to work for a number of railroads and government agencies, including the Southern Railway, the New York Central, the Penn Central, the Federal Railroad Administration, Amtrak, the Federal Railroad Administration once again, the US Railway Association, and the Association of American Railroads. In 1978 I returned to Southern, which later became Norfolk Southern. There, my job focused on strategic planning, rail mergers and acquisitions, and network management—essentially adding routes and capacity to reach new markets and shedding what was no longer needed. I retired from NS in 2003 as senior vice president for planning.

Often I was in the middle of the decision processes that reshaped the industry. I had a role in the creation of Amtrak and was one of its first employees, though I was fired after a few years. I participated in both the creation of Conrail and its subsequent dismemberment by CSX and Norfolk Southern.

Since my retirement I have traveled the world, still chasing trains, albeit in more exotic locations such as Kazakhstan and Malaysia. For a couple of years I missed being an "important railroad official," but touring the world has turned out to be an interesting and satisfying substitute.

When I started railroading, there were a lot of railroad companies. Most of them operated a variety of services, from passenger trains to mail trains, main-line freight trains to branch-line and local trains. Now there are just a handful of major railroads and they are freight only. Passenger services reside in the public sector, either Amtrak or state or local agencies. Much of the feeder network was transferred to lower-cost regional and short-line carriers. It took decades but the railroad industry of today is a far different beast than it was when I started my career.

In the first part of this book, as a backdrop to the detailed accounts I give of my career, I have sketched out some of the major changes in the industry, with a chapter dedicated to each major region and Canada. This is a cursory, Cliffs Notes version of the postwar era; for more details, consult the many great histories of railroading during this era of change, most notably *American Railroads: Decline and Renaissance in the Twentieth Century* by Robert E. Gallamore and John R. Meyer. In the book's second part, I recount some of my varied experiences, focusing first on my days with the Southern and the New York Central, and then moving on to my tours in government at Amtrak, my stint at the Association of American Railroads, and my return to the Southern.

I came out of the closet early: at my first railroad job at Southern I was tagged as a railfan. But I was a "realistic railfan." I loved the industry but always tried to be honest about the economics of the business; in my career, economics necessarily trumped aesthetics. Nostalgia is nice but it doesn't pay the rent.

Throughout my career, I spent a lot of time riding trains and otherwise observing the North American rail network. After all, how could I advise the NS board of directors about, say, the issues involved with a merger with Burlington Northern Santa Fe or Conrail without knowing how trains operated in the Powder River Basin or into and out of Chicago? My work on mergers gave me the perfect cover to go out and explore railroading in both the United States and Canada.

Since retiring, I have had a lot more time to explore the railroad scene both in North America and around the world. Wherever they run, trains remain a fascination.

Acknowledgments

THEY SAY IT TAKES A VILLAGE TO RAISE A CHILD. Well, it takes a village to produce a book as well. A lot of folks have helped this project, but I owe special thanks to Eileen Ridge, my "computer tutor" for years, without whom I simply would not have been able to produce all of these pictures and all of this text; to my sister-in-law, Jane Valtin, who spent weeks of her life scanning thousands of my slides; and to M. D. Ridge, who undertook the critical task of line editing.

Tom Hoback was supportive of this project from beginning to end. Fred Frailey was my "über-editor," whose knowledge of the industry and editorial skills were indispensable. Linda Oblack, Sarah Jacobi, and Eric Levy provided invaluable guidance as this project worked its way through Indiana University Press.

My informal board of directors, or jury of my peers, included Rod Case, Jim Dietz, Dave DeBoer, Bob Gallamore, Jim Hagen, Ed King, Rush Loving Jr., Don Phillips, and Bill Schafer. They were all participants in and keen observers of railroading in the years covered in this volume. Their assistance, too, was invaluable.

We have all endeavored to keep the story moving and as accurate as possible but obviously any mistakes are my responsibility. I hope this book gives the reader a feel for what it was like to participate in what Tony Hatch has dubbed "the rail renaissance."

PART I. RAILROADS: 1950–2014

The Pennsylvania Railroad's westbound Gotham Limited leaves Pittsburgh, bound for Chicago, 1958. Like most trains on the Pennsylvania main line, this train carried a heavy load of mail and express traffic.

THE NORTHEAST

How the once-dominant northeastern rail network fell from grace and is now run from Jacksonville and Norfolk, and how the northeastern railroad crisis forced a basic change in the structure of railroading.

VANTAGE POINT

Growing up in south Texas in the mid-1950s, I was fascinated by stories about northeastern railroading. At the time, south Texas was a railroad backwater. Single-tracked lines handled between eight and ten trains a day. The Northeast, as I learned from *Trains* magazine and *Railroad* magazine, was a land of multiple-tracked main lines that often saw as many trains in an hour as a railroad serving San Antonio did in a day. A trip to Washington, DC, in 1955 let me see northeastern railroading firsthand. It lived up to its advance billing, so much so that I decided to attend the University of Pennsylvania, lured largely by its proximity to big-time northeastern railroading (30th Street Station was a short walk from the Penn campus).

The Northeast would also loom large in my career, with jobs at the New York Central and the Penn Central after the merger. Early into that merger it was obvious to me that it would fail and I left for the public sector, with tours at the Federal Railroad Administration, Amtrak, and the US Railway Association. I returned to the private sector and ultimately landed back at the Southern (later Norfolk Southern). There, my work focused on rail mergers and line rationalization, including the merger of the Southern and the Norfolk & Western (to create NS) and the acquisition of over half of Conrail to create the current NS system (the largest northeastern railroad). Years of chasing trains around the Northeast gave me knowledge of the network that was invaluable when it was time to redraw the northeastern rail map: once while in government (creating Conrail), and again at NS (splitting Conrail).

SIXTY YEARS OF CHANGE

The railroad industry has undergone monumental change, and the epicenter of much of that change was the Northeast. In the 1950s, it was the home of the power players in the rail industry: the Pennsylvania Railroad and the New York Central, with the Baltimore & Ohio and a host of lesser players filling in behind them. All carriers of any size operated passenger, mail, and express trains as well as a spiderweb of feeder lines. It was quite a show.

Sixty years later, all of that had changed. Declining traffic and profits led to bankruptcies, mergers, abandonments, and new ways of organizing the railroad business. Passenger services became the ward of federal, state, and local governments, and much of the freight feeder network was abandoned or transferred to new low-cost, short-line operators. Control of the northeastern freight network moved from Philadelphia, New York, and Baltimore to Norfolk, Virginia, and Jacksonville, Florida. The only major railroads now based in the Northeast are Amtrak and Genesee and Wyoming. The northeastern rail crisis redefined the relationship between the government and the rail industry and led to the creation of Amtrak and Conrail (CR) and the passage of the Staggers Act, a law that fundamentally changed how railroads related to their customers.

THE VIEW FROM 1950

In 1950 northeastern railroads were the busiest and richest in North America. Manufacturing was king, requiring the movement of huge volumes of coal, iron ore, steel, automobiles, and a host of other industrial products. That traffic volume supported what were the most profitable railroads in the nation for more than one hundred years. Heavy traffic density required a robust infrastructure: the Northeast hosted the most miles of multiple-tracked routes as well as the most sophisticated signal systems. Significant segments of the network were electrified. (Electrification was a rarity elsewhere in North America.)

The Pennsylvania Railroad (PRR) was the largest railroad in the nation in terms of revenues, passenger-miles, and ton-miles: it accounted for a full 10 percent of rail industry activity in 1950. With more than a little arrogance, it called itself the "Standard Railroad of the World"—not the United States, not North America, but the world. The PRR stretched from Manhattan to Chicago and St. Louis via Philadelphia, Harrisburg, and Pittsburgh. It did not serve New England and relied on the New Haven (NYNH&H or NH) for access to that market. The PRR operated an extensive network of intercity passenger trains, led by the all-Pullman Broadway Limited between New York and Chicago. The PRR operated what was and remains the busiest intercity rail passenger line in the nation—New York and Washington—and had major commuter services in New York and Philadelphia as well as some minor markets.

The New York Central (NYC) was, in terms of volume and revenues, the second-largest railroad in both the region and the nation and actually had more route-miles than the PRR. At a time when there were many great trains, its flagship passenger train, the 20th Century Limited, was probably the most famous passenger train in the world. New York Central operated extensive commuter services out of Grand Central Terminal in New York. Like the PRR, the NYC served virtually all of the important northeastern markets, linking the East Coast to the Midwest through its main line through upstate New York and Cleveland. However, it did not reach Philadelphia, Baltimore, or Washington.

The third major carrier in the region was the Baltimore & Ohio (B&O), which mimicked the route structure of the PRR but with its heart in Baltimore rather than Philadelphia. It was a more modest and friendly (and less arrogant) version of its competitor to the north. While it reached most important markets in the region, it had to rely on connecting railroads—the Reading and the Central of New Jersey—to reach

A Northeast Corridor train from Washington approaching 30th Street Station, 1958. Note the freight train on the bridge in the background. This is the Pennsylvania Railroad "high line," which allowed freight traffic to bypass 30th Street Station.

An east–west train, en route to New York, pauses at North Philadelphia, 1958. An eastbound freight behind P5 electric engines blasts by on an adjacent track. The Pennsylvania Railroad was "infrastructure intense" and most of what was built early in the twentieth century remains in use today, albeit predominately by Amtrak and commuter authorities.

Left: **Westbound New York Central freight train west of Batavia, New York, 1961.** This had been a four-track main line until New York Central president Alfred E. Perlman installed centralized traffic control and reduced the number of tracks in the process.

Facing: **Baltimore & Ohio passenger power gets a bath at Baltimore, 1959.** The B&O had a lot of pride in its passenger service, but as riders dwindled and losses mounted, scenes such as this became increasingly rare.

the greater New York and New England markets. The B&O infrastructure was adequate, if not great, and its main routes were double-tracked. But it was built early and the alignment reflected that fact; unlike the PRR, it never had the financial resources for a major "do-over" of its track structure. It also operated extensive passenger service led by its premier train, the Capitol Limited, as well as commuter services in Baltimore/Washington and Pittsburgh.

These three railroads were the dominant players in the Northeast in 1950. They do not survive as corporations, but portions of their main-line network continue to be important. Surprisingly, the line survival rate has been higher for both the NYC and the B&O; much of the mighty PRR main-line network has been transferred to regional carriers or to Amtrak.

And while PRR's Harrisburg-to-Cleveland route remains a busy freight route, its once busy lines to Chicago and St. Louis have largely fallen by the wayside.

The "big three" were supplemented by a number of secondary carriers, including the Erie-Lackawanna, the Reading, the New Haven, the Boston & Maine, the Maine Central, the Western Maryland, the Nickel Plate, the Delaware & Hudson, and the Wabash. They all shared a common trait: they lacked the market coverage of the major carriers. All northeastern railroad carriers faced daunting obstacles as the economy of the region declined. Starting in the 1950s, heavy industry, such as steel, declined in both relative and absolute importance. Some of these changes reflected new technology (such as aluminum replacing steel) and

An Erie-Lackawanna westbound freight leaving Port Jervis, New Jersey, 1967. After the Pennsylvania, the New York Central, and the Baltimore & Ohio, the Erie-Lackawanna was the fourth carrier in an overcrowded market. Its lines were abandoned or downgraded with the coming of Conrail.

An eastbound Boston & Maine freight train near Concord, Massachusetts, 1962. The decline in New England railroads came early as industry left for the South and an improved highway network decimated most short-haul business.

A Shore Line express from New York arriving at South Station with—miracle of miracles—a clean New Haven unit up front, 1962.

The Delaware & Hudson's southbound Laurentian, the day train between Montreal and New York, has picked up a second locomotive unit and is ready to depart from Rouses Point, New York, 1961.

A westbound Maine Central freight arriving at St. Johnsbury, Vermont, where the Maine Central connected with the Canadian Pacific, 1962. The train crossed the White Mountains through Crawford Notch, New Hampshire. Much of the line has been abandoned but the scenic trip through Crawford Notch remains, thanks to a tourist railroad.

The eastbound Pocahontas, one of three Norfolk & Western trains between Cincinnati and Norfolk, departing Roanoke, Virginia, behind a J Class 4-8-4, 1955. To the left, train number 8, a Roanoke-to-Norfolk local making all stops, sits behind a K Class Mountain. It would follow the Pocahontas twenty minutes later.

The westbound Sportsman, bound for Cincinnati and Detroit, about to depart Alexandria, Virginia, 1963. An Amtrak triweekly train, the Cardinal, still plies the former Chesapeake & Ohio main line, one of the most scenic in the East.

some the relocation of manufacturing to places with lower labor costs, lower taxes, and less regulation. Most of this relocation was to the south and the west; shifts to Mexico and China would come decades later. And with the building of limited access highways (toll roads and then the Interstate System), trucks took an increasing share of the freight market. Smaller roads, at least the ones that did not find a "sugar daddy" (think the Nickel Plate being acquired by the Norfolk & Western), faced an especially bleak future. Nowhere was the pain more intense than in New England where short hauls, intense passenger operations, and a lack of significant coal traffic combined to create a recipe for failure.

The southern flank of the Northeast was protected by two of the most profitable railroads in the land. The Chesapeake & Ohio (C&O) and the Norfolk & Western (N&W) made their big bucks from gathering coal from mines in Virginia and West Virginia and hauling it either downhill to the Atlantic Ocean for export or westward to midwestern steel mills and power plants. The C&O and N&W both had the heavy-duty, double-tracked lines that were needed to handle coal traffic. Both operated a limited network of fine but money-losing passenger trains and neither had commuter services. Most importantly, however, these two railroads had the financial clout to enable them to survive and become the basis for restructuring eastern railroading. The rail system we have today, based on the CSX and NS, can be partially traced to the acquisitions made by the C&O and the N&W, and was fueled by those early coal profits.

As a sidebar of interest to the railfan, both the C&O and the N&W operated steam locomotives well past the time when other railroads had shifted to diesels. In 1955, the N&W still produced more than 99 percent of its transportation services—freight, passenger, and switching—with steam locomotives. That it still made a lot of money was testimony to the efficiency of its core coal business and to the high level of its coal rates.

MARKET CONSTRICTION AND MERGERS IN THE 1960S

The robust infrastructure that had permitted the northeastern railroads to move vast amounts of both cargo and passengers in the 1950s was now a huge economic liability. But paring the infrastructure required money for modern signals and new track connections, and that capital was increasingly hard to find. When the NYC automated Selkirk Yard, it had to take out tracks on the Hudson Division main line to obtain the rail needed for the yard. There were some brave attempts to change with the times. The New York Central's president Alfred E. Perlman modernized the NYC with the same tools Bill Brosnan was using at the Southern Railway (SR): automated yards, welded rail, traffic control, and a host of other efficiencies. But where business in the South was booming, all of the NYC's modernization could not compensate for the loss of freight traffic. Sometimes doing the right thing is not enough.

The 1960s were a grim time for railroads in the Northeast. Profits disappeared along with much of the traffic. In an effort to reduce costs, maintenance of both track and equipment was curtailed. That in turn led to slower speeds and a further loss of traffic, setting up a downward spiral. The lack of money showed, and the northeastern railroad scene looked increasingly shabby.

Mergers were one way to reduce overhead as well as remove redundant capacity. For example, the Delaware, Lackawanna & Western merged with the Erie in 1960, providing the Lackawanna with longer hauls and the Erie with some

A westbound Erie-Lackawanna freight train, the engines still in Erie colors, at Narrowsburg, New York, 1960. At the time, the Erie and the Lackawanna had just merged to reduce duplicate services and facilities. The savings were significant but could not outpace the rapid decline in revenues caused by a faltering northeastern economy and a vastly improved highway system.

An eastbound Erie-Lackawanna freight waits for a westbound passenger train at Delaware Water Gap, Pennsylvania, 1960. These six-axle Fairbanks-Morse units dressed in Lackawanna colors were a welcome relief in a railroad world that was growing increasingly shabby. The Erie-Lackawanna tried to keep up appearances until the very end.

13

A westbound Nickel Plate Road freight is ready to depart the Pittsburgh & West Virginia's Rook Yard for Bellevue, Ohio, 1958. The Pittsburgh & West Virginia teamed up with the Central of New Jersey, Reading; the Western Maryland; and the Nickel Plate Road to create a fast through service between the Atlantic Seaboard and the Midwest. Called the Alphabet Route, for obvious reasons, it provided a competitive alternative to both the Pennsylvania and the Baltimore & Ohio.

much-needed volume on its Chicago line (at the expense of former DL&W partners such as the Nickel Plate). The Norfolk & Western moved beyond its traditional coal base with its acquisition of the Nickel Plate and the PRR-owned Wabash, extending its empire from Tidewater, Virginia, to Kansas City, Missouri (still the longest single system reach of an eastern-based system under single ownership). Even then, coal played a role in the westward march: the new routes allowed the N&W to extend its existing coal business beyond the Columbus, Ohio, gateway into the heart of the Midwest.

The NYC's Al Perlman had long desired a merger with the Chesapeake & Ohio. It was a natural fit that would fill in gaps in both systems, and the C&O's coal profits would have provided much-needed financial stability to the NYC. In the late 1990s, after the split of Conrail by CSX and NS,

the NYC and the C&O essentially became part of CSX, the grandson of the C&O. But in the early sixties, the C&O pursued the B&O instead, and gained a controlling interest in the B&O in 1962. This put Perlman in a box. In 1968 he finally, and reluctantly, pursued a merger with the NYC's archrival, the Pennsylvania Railroad. The PRR was bigger and far less advanced technologically, and its passenger train losses were far greater. But some action seemed essential at the time, however misguided it now seems in retrospect. So the Penn Central was created. It turned out to be the equivalent of lashing two drowning men together with the hope that together they could survive—two drowning men who also did not like each other at all. It was a prescription for disaster. The failure of the Penn Central in 1970 created shock waves that forced a fundamental change in how railroads related to the government.

The Wabash Railroad's combined Blue Bird (to Chicago) and Cannonball (to Detroit) leaving St. Louis Union Station, 1962. The trains would split at Decatur, Illinois. Soon, the Wabash would be acquired by the Norfolk & Western as that carrier expanded westward.

A southbound Penn Central freight leaving Baltimore, Maryland, 1972. These electric engines were built for the Virginian Railway and were then purchased by the New Haven when the Norfolk & Western dropped electrification after it bought the Virginian. The New Haven was forced upon Penn Central as a condition of its merger, rather like throwing a drowning man an anchor.

A northbound Central of New Jersey freight train at Dunellen, New Jersey, 1960. The sorry state of CNJ maintenance was already evident at this relatively early date. Still, the railroad lingered as an independent carrier until its incorporation into Conrail.

Essentially, passenger train losses, a declining freight market, modal competition, excessive regulation, outdated work rules, and a lot of incompetent management decisions shoved the Penn Central over the edge. It was the largest US bankruptcy at the time and shook up investors, government officials, and rail customers. (See chapters 9 and 10 for more of this story.)

For both railroaders and railfans, the 1960s were a time of despair. Some railroads, such as the Erie-Lackawanna, tried to keep up appearances, while others, such as the Central of New Jersey, looked as ragged as their income statements. No one had any idea whether things would ever get better. It was an ugly and scary era.

GOVERNMENT INTERVENTION AND RESTRUCTURING

As the 1970s began, the Northeast railroad scene was coalescing into three broad groups:

- Solvent carriers. This group was dominated by the Chesapeake & Ohio/Baltimore & Ohio (C&O/B&O) and the now-expanded Norfolk & Western.
- A giant financial cripple. The core of the Penn Central's freight operations was only marginally profitable, and the passenger and branch-line services were such a drain that the entire enterprise was failing. The Penn Central was also encumbered by ownership of the hopeless New Haven, a financial burden forced onto the Penn Central by the Interstate Commerce Commission as a condition of merger.
- The smaller insolvents. This group included the Boston & Maine, the Erie-Lackawanna, the Central Railroad of New Jersey, and the Lehigh Valley. With the exception of the LV, most had substantial and very unprofitable commuter operations, and their freight traffic and revenues were in rapid decline.

Nixon was in the White House, and Republicans are not noted for wanting to expand the role of government. Their bias was to just let the railroads die and sell the assets at the courthouse steps. But as the northeastern rail crisis unfolded, there was pressure from some key Republican constituencies (think General Motors and U.S. Steel) to craft solutions to save the Penn Central. The smaller carriers were not deemed sufficiently important to require federal intervention. The task of finding a solution at minimum cost fell to the then-new Department of Transportation (DOT) and the Federal Railroad Administration.

Whether the railroads would be nationalized or not was a very real question. After all, the United States was the last major country other than Canada with a private-sector rail industry. And even in Canada, one of the two major companies was owned by the government. Even the best railroads' profits (measured by return on investment) were dismal, and many observers questioned whether private-sector railroading could survive. The DOT's initial hope was to contain the crisis by relieving the carriers of their intercity passenger train deficits; with those deficits gone, perhaps the Penn Central could avoid bankruptcy. The solution was Amtrak: a classic government compromise that satisfied none of the constituencies (see chapter 8). Amtrak did save a core intercity rail passenger service, but intercity trains were only part of the passenger problem. Amtrak did not address commuter service deficits, which for most sick railroads were even bigger losers.

Ultimately, and years later, most of the passenger train issues would be addressed. Relieving freight railroads of most of the financial burdens of passenger service was as important a part of the rail renaissance as the Staggers Act or improved labor productivity. But for the Penn Central, Amtrak was too little, too late: the railroad declared bankruptcy on June 21, 1970, almost a year before Amtrak started operations. Soon, thanks partly to the destruction caused by Hurricane Agnes, it was joined in bankruptcy by a host of smaller companies, including the Erie-Lackawanna, the Lehigh Valley, the Reading, the Central Railroad of New Jersey, and the Boston & Maine. All except the B&M opted to participate in the government-designed and government-funded rescue mission directed by the US Railway Association (USRA). The C&O/B&O and the N&W remained profitable and the railroad crisis did not engulf the entire Northeast. But Pennsylvania, New York, New Jersey, and most of New England were the domain of failed railroads that might soon be liquidated. Ohio, Indiana, Michigan, and even parts of Illinois were at risk as well.

Congress mandated a study—the Washington equivalent of kicking the can down the road. The DOT identified overcapacity as a core issue, and most of that redundant trackage was in poor condition and would have to be rebuilt with taxpayer dollars at a huge cost. In its *Rail Service in the Midwest and Northeast Region* report, the DOT suggested that about 25 percent of the region's railroad network, bankrupt and solvent carriers alike, was a candidate for abandonment. Further, the report said that there were too many railroads—that only major cities justified having two carriers. In a real sense, the report set the stage for two decades of mergers and line rationalization. Two competing railroads in a major market became the accepted standard for merging companies.

The report was a bombshell at the time and was partially responsible for the creation of another entity to deal with the crisis. The DOT, being a creature of the Nixon administration, was not trusted by Congress. In an effort to achieve a less harsh outcome, the USRA, which was created in January 1974, was charged with developing a binding solution (the Final System Plan, or FSP) to the bankrupt railroad problem. Finally, some six years after the Penn Central filed for bankruptcy, the Consolidated Rail Corporation, or Conrail, was born on April 1, 1976. (See chapter 10 for more on the creation of Conrail.)

The creation of Conrail did some good things. It drastically pruned the network, though more had to be done, and it merged sick railroads, thus cutting overhead costs. It shifted most passenger assets to public ownership, setting the stage for eliminating huge losses for commuter services. It made $2 billion in public rehabilitation funds—outright grants, not loans—available to start the rebuilding process. And it dodged outright nationalization of the freight operations and the freight infrastructure. Given the reluctance of the government to spend money for passenger trains or even highways, long-term dependence on government funding for freight services would have sounded the death knell for freight railroading.

But the FSP was a flawed effort and failed in several critical areas. It did not address some key structural issues, including the need for deregulation and the need for far greater labor productivity; although the USRA said these goals were important, it offered no plan for achieving them. The FSP also failed to achieve an effective competitive structure. The USRA did make a valiant effort to do so but the Chessie (C&O/B&O) pulled out of the proposed deal. Finally, the traffic and financial forecasts were hopelessly optimistic and the ultimate cost to the taxpayer was grossly understated. Much remained to be done and getting everything right would take another two

A westbound Conrail freight train passing MG Tower (MG for middle-of-the-grade) west of Altoona, Pennsylvania, 1984.

The Lehigh Valley engine terminal at Sayre, New York, 1976. The LV had just been swallowed up by Conrail when this picture was taken.

and a half decades, culminating in the split of Conrail between CSX and Norfolk Southern in June of 1999.

REGULATORY REFORM, REBUILDING, AND REACHING OUT

The fallout from the northeastern rail crisis marked the end of the traditional, vertically integrated structure that had existed since the dawn of railroading. Now service was divided along functional lines. Passenger services were the domain of Amtrak and commuter authorities and much of the light-density freight service became the specialty of short-line and regional carriers. None of these changes happened overnight; for example, it would be years before Amtrak would actually employ train and engine crews directly, and some commuter operations still use rail freight employees under contract to provide service. But financial failure led to widespread, fundamental changes in the way the railroad industry was organized and financed. And there were more important changes to come.

The Staggers Act (named for the chairman of the House Committee on Energy and Commerce) became law in 1980. It allowed railroads to quote contract rates (for example, giving customers lower rates in exchange for guaranteed traffic volumes) and otherwise align the commercial side of the business with what made sense from an operating and efficiency standpoint. Transportation deregulation had been a hot topic among economists for decades and finally the political process caught up with economic reality. Airlines were deregulated first, then trucking, and finally railroading. Initially some railroads did not want deregulation (the SR and the N&W among them), and the unions were opposed. But Conrail was racking up annual losses of hundreds of millions of dollars. Furthermore, a crisis was looming in much of the Midwest

west of Chicago. The government's options were to spend ever-increasing tax dollars funding the rail freight industry or to take a chance with deregulation.

Conrail, despite continued deficits, was making progress in rebuilding its network. The key to that progress came from two men from the Southern Railway: Stanley Crane and Jim Hagen. Crane tackled operating efficiency, while Hagen and his sidekick, Dick Steiner, used the newly passed Staggers Act to better align prices with the cost of the services provided. For example, CR lowered its costs by closing many inefficient junctions, much to the dismay of some solvent carriers. Conrail's improving financial condition led the DOT to seek a buyer for that company (the government held the CR stock). Norfolk Southern bid and won the approval of the DOT, but after over two years of effort it was unable to overcome the resistance of Conrail, CSX, and their political allies. In 1987, the DOT sold the government's Conrail stock in a public auction. (See chapter 11 for more about this protracted and disruptive battle.)

DOWNSIZING AND RESTRUCTURING

In the creation of Conrail, the USRA had excluded thousands of miles from the CR system. Many of those lines were acquired by states or by short-line carriers, and while many failed, some were successful. But the USRA did not cut enough, and Conrail followed up with another rationalization program. Meanwhile, CSX and NS, faced with dramatic changes in the marketplace following the deregulation of trucking, initiated downsizing programs of their own. They transferred lines to short-line carriers or simply abandoned them outright. In a sense, some of the pruning was long overdue, as both carriers had been slow to rationalize redundant main lines created by earlier mergers. For example, the Wabash and the Nickel Plate had parallel main lines throughout much of Ohio and Indiana; those lines were rationalized in the 1980s. (See chapter 11 for more on NS's downsizing efforts.)

By 1990, the northeastern region was fading away and morphing into the eastern region, anchored by CSX and NS. Conrail was left out of a railroad world that was consolidating in both the East and the West, and its survival was far from guaranteed. Still, it had a valuable franchise. Norfolk Southern had a weaker network than CSX and coveted the Conrail markets. It failed to acquire these when the DOT sold CR in a public offering. It tried to negotiate a friendly merger with CR and failed again. Next, NS joined with CSX in a plan to split CR, but CR was having none of that. Finally, in 1997, CSX reached an agreement with CR for a merger. CSX plus CR was a worst-case scenario for NS; it would be less than half the size of the proposed combination and would be quickly marginalized by the subsequent loss of revenue and profits.

Norfolk Southern responded by launching a hostile takeover bid for CR; it was a railroad battle reminiscent of the era of the Vanderbilts and the Goulds. In the end, CSX and NS reached a stalemate in the ever-escalating cost of the fight and agreed to split Conrail, with 58 percent (by estimated traffic volume) going to NS and the remainder to CSX. The result produced two balanced rail networks and reinstituted the effective rail competition that had died with the formation of the Penn Central in 1968. (See chapter 12 for more details.)

STABILITY AND SUCCESS

With the split of Conrail and the NS extension to New England (since reinforced with more investment in the line to the Boston area), the network in the eastern United States was set.

The Canadian Pacific did acquire the Delaware and Hudson (part of which it subsequently sold to NS years later), but that was a minor deal in the scheme of things.

By 2000, the once-mighty northeastern rail network had been assimilated into that of the two southeastern carriers, and northeastern railroading ceased to exist as such. Carriers could focus on improving their networks, removing choke points and adding clearances and terminals for a growing intermodal business. None of these improvements had quite the drama of a hostile takeover, but stability and investment was what the East needed now.

The ability of the eastern region to withstand adversity was tested in the Great Recession of 2007 to 2009. In October 2007, traffic simply fell off a cliff, declining as much as 25 percent for a few months for some carriers. It was the sort of traffic collapse that had sent railroads into bankruptcy in the 1960s, yet both CSX and NS remained profitable and continued to invest. (The infrastructure looks better than at any time in my lifetime.) The future is not altogether clear sailing, as markets (especially coal) continue to shift, but all in all it is a good story: government did the right thing; rail labor made some painful changes; and rail management focused on improved infrastructure and improved services (after a brief side trip into some nonrail ventures). But the transition has not been without its ironies. Eastern freight railroading is now controlled from the old Confederacy—Jacksonville, Florida, and Norfolk, Virginia. The PRR was once the largest owner of N&W stock; now the N&W's successor, Norfolk Southern, essentially owns what is left of the PRR. It's "the world turned upside down," if you will.

Things turned out a lot better than many of us involved in the process would have predicted. Nationalization was avoided and balanced competition restored. The importance of solving the northeastern problem in the entire story of the rail renaissance cannot be overstated. The core problems in the Northeast, including too many railroads, too much track, overregulation, and passenger (especially commuter train) deficits, were cancers that had a nationwide impact. The solutions first used in the Northeast were later applied to railroads everywhere and were the building blocks of the rail renaissance. And lest anyone think that substantive change is either rapid or easy, consider that these changes took over two decades to achieve.

A Chesapeake & Ohio/Baltimore & Ohio (soon to become known as the Chessie System) northbound freight leaves Potomac Yard, 1967. Colorful C&O and B&O paint schemes had been replaced with "basic blue" as the two railroads were integrated.

A southbound Richmond, Fredericksburg & Potomac freight train at Alexandria, Virginia, 1962. In the 1950s and 1960s, the Southeast had numerous small railroads. The RF&P was unique: it was only a little over one hundred miles in length, but it had double track and hosted a fleet of passenger and freight trains. Owned by the Atlantic Coast Line, the Seaboard Air Line, and the Southern, it provided a connection at Washington for the ACL and the SAL and northeastern railroads.

THE SOUTHEAST

Two southeastern railroads expanded to create networks that dominated not only the Southeast but the eastern United States.

VANTAGE POINT

I started my railroad career on a southeastern carrier, the Southern Railway (SR). I returned to the SR for a second tour when I was involved in the rail mergers and acquisitions. I was proactively seeking ways to expand the SR network while keeping an eye on the actions of our competitors. Mergers are always about moves and countermoves, seeking to get a leg up on the competition. Knowing the southeastern network and the southeastern players was part of my job description.

SIXTY YEARS OF CHANGE

In the 1950s, the Northeast was the home of the nation's premier (if already fading) railroads, and the West was where icons like the Santa Fe and the Union Pacific did their thing. The Southeast was something of a backwater.

Now fast-forward: The industrial base of the South exploded as the Northeast was contracting. With growth came new and expanded auto and chemical plants, more electric utility production, and more coal traffic to serve the utility market. As traffic increased, the network was upgraded with new sidings and traffic control and new or expanded yards. All of these improvements were being made at the same time that the northeastern railroads were downsizing their infrastructure. Today, two major Southeast-based rail systems control most of the railroad business east of the Mississippi. Let's drill down and see how these changes occurred. The southeastern story is about growth, consolidation, and invasion of the North.

THE VIEW FROM 1950

In 1950, steam locomotives still produced most of the southeastern freight ton-miles but steam was already fading. A mere five years later, steam was largely gone from most of the Southeast (the SR dropped its steam operations in 1953 to become the first major all-dieselized railroad). Otherwise, the southeastern rail scene looked much as it had for decades. The big players were the SR and the Atlantic Coast Line (ACL) and its family of aligned carriers. Below these majors was a second

Southern Railway F units passing Alexandria with a southbound freight, 1961. These first-generation diesels were already in the process of being replaced with newer power on many main-line freight services.

The Augusta Special arriving in Augusta, Georgia, 1957. The Southern Railway had an extensive passenger train network with service on virtually all of its main and secondary lines. The service was supported primarily by mail and express traffic.

tier of midsized carriers, and below them, yet another tier of regional or local operations.

Infrastructure was for the most part modest, reflecting moderate traffic volumes and a shortage of capital that dated back to the Civil War. Single track was the norm; some important lines did not even have signals. With some exceptions, alignment reflected the "man and mule" approach to construction—mechanized building equipment was not available. Branch lines especially followed the contours of the land with a minimum of cuts and fills and were a "hill and dale" affair.

To an outsider, the Southeast appeared balkanized until you looked behind the curtain and traced just who owned what. The reality was that the region was dominated by the SR and the ACL and their networks of affiliated companies. These two carriers would form the core of the future southeastern system; with subsequent mergers and acquisitions by both roads, they would ultimately control most freight railroading east of the Mississippi River. The SR operated a host of subsidiary lines such as the Cincinnati, New Orleans & Texas Pacific (CNOTP) and the Alabama Great Southern (AGS). Legally and for financial reporting purposes, these were separate entities, but the SR controlled these companies and operated them as a cohesive system. Its network formed a large *X* from Washington, DC, to New Orleans, and from Cincinnati to Jacksonville, crossing at Atlanta.

More than any other railroad at the time, the SR blanketed the Southeast, and its slogan—"Southern Serves the South"—was reality, not rhetoric. The SR touched all the major southeastern markets with the exception of Florida south of Jacksonville and Palatka. (For more on the SR during this era, see chapter 6.) But the Atlantic Coast Line was actually a far larger system than the SR; it had a financial interest in the Louisville & Nashville (L&N), the Georgia Railroad/

West Point Route (GA/AWP), the Charleston & Western Carolina and the Clinchfield (CRR). But those companies had their own management, their own corporate cultures, and their own paint schemes. Disjointed or not, in 1960 the ACL "system" was the second largest in the United States, after the Southern Pacific (at the time another collection of semi-independent properties).

The Atlantic Coast Line itself was true to its name; its main line ran through the coastal plain, but long secondary main lines found their way to Atlanta, Birmingham, and Montgomery. It blanketed the west coast of Florida, but relied on the Florida East Coast for access to Miami and other points on the east coast of Florida. In a sense, the ACL was the anti-Southern: as the SR pushed new technology, the ACL stayed with the tried-and-true. Its passenger service was excellent— the East and West Coast Champions were the premier trains and the seasonal Florida Special provided the fastest rail passenger service to Florida.

The second-largest component of the ACL's loosely formed empire was the Louisville & Nashville. It was primarily a merchandise railroad linking the midwestern gateways with Atlanta and New Orleans via Birmingham and Montgomery, but with huge coal operations in eastern Kentucky. The Georgia/West Point Route and the Clinchfield filled out the ACL network. Overall, the ACL and its affiliated companies' market coverage was superior to that of the SR, but its fragmented structure kept it from achieving its full market potential.

While the SR and ACL family of lines were the big dogs, the Southeast had a variety of other railroads, ranging in size from several hundred miles to thousands of miles in length. Some deserve mention in this story because some of their routes are important even to this day. The Seaboard Air Line

The Atlantic Coast Line's afternoon departure, train number 50, leaves Augusta, Georgia, 1957. At Florence, South Carolina, it connected with ACL main-line trains to the Northeast and to Florida. The train ran through the street for the first few blocks of its journey.

A track gang makes spot repairs at Augusta, 1957, as the inbound passenger train from Florence waits to proceed.

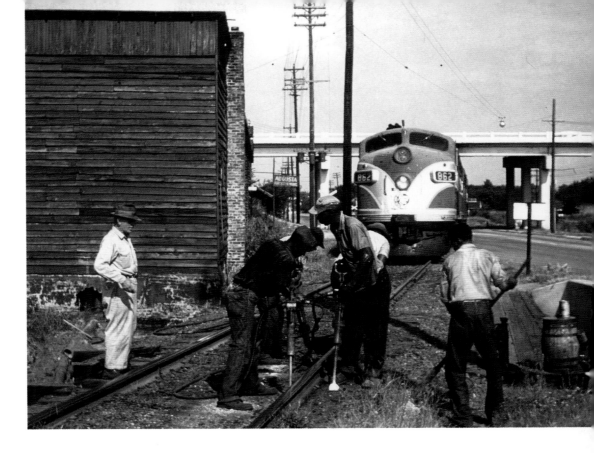

The southbound East Coast Champion at Folkston, Georgia, 1964. The distinctive ACL purple livery had given way to basic black. The purple, striking as it was, tended to fade.

The Louisville & Nashville's southbound Pan American pulls into Flomaton, Alabama, in 1961, en route to New Orleans. Austerity in paint schemes had arrived on the L&N as basic blue replaced cream and blue with red trim. The era of ugly railroading was underway.

The Georgia Railroad's day train to Atlanta a few miles from its origin, 1957. The Georgia Road, owned by the Atlantic Coast Line, connected with its parent at Augusta, Georgia. At the time, the ACL and its affiliated lines were the second-longest US rail system; the Southern Pacific ranked first.

Seaboard locomotives lined up in Richmond, Virginia, 1958. Using different paint schemes for passenger, freight, and switching power was a common practice at the time, but economics ultimately extinguished such variety.

The Seaboard's Silver Meteor crosses the Trout River north of Jacksonville, Florida, 1964. The Meteor was the leader of the Seaboard's Silver Fleet, which also included the Silver Star and the Silver Comet.

The Central of Georgia's Man o' War arriving in Atlanta, 1965.

A Florida East Coast local train southbound at Fort Lauderdale, Florida, 2003. The Florida East Coast is one of the few smaller railroads that has survived the consolidation movement that started in the late 1950s.

The southbound Seminole at Folkston, Georgia, 1964. The Seminole was the secondary train on the Illinois Central, Central of Georgia, and Atlantic Coast Line joint service linking Chicago and Florida. The City of Miami, an every-other-day service, was the premier train on the route.

(SAL), for instance, was the passenger rail alternative to the ACL in the Northeast-to-Florida market. ("Air line" did not refer to an airline; it was a term to indicate a short, well-engineered railroad, which in the case of the SAL was an outright lie.) Unlike the ACL, it served both coasts of Florida as well as the Florida Panhandle. It also reached Atlanta, Birmingham, and Montgomery on its own tracks. As the underdog, it was less stodgy than the ACL and more willing to embrace new technology (when I was a child in Florida during World War II, the SAL had diesels on its passenger trains; the ACL did not). The Silver Meteor, complete with a glass-topped Pullman lounge and a round-end observation, was the Seaboard's premier train.

Added to the mix of southeastern railroads were some small but important railroads, such as the Richmond, Fredericksburg & Potomac (RF&P), the Florida East Coast (FEC), and the Central of Georgia (CGA). Lower down the food chain, and mostly irrelevant even at the time, were such roads as the Georgia & Florida (G&F) and the original Norfolk Southern. All of these carriers except the FEC would be absorbed by larger railroads.

The northern border of the Southeast was the domain of the Norfolk & Western and the Chesapeake & Ohio, both early movers in expanding north. Holding down the Southeast's western border were the Illinois Central (IC) and the Gulf, Mobile & Ohio (GM&O), which was absorbed by the IC in 1972. The GM&O was a minor player except in the Chicago–St. Louis passenger market, thanks to its ownership of the Chicago and Alton. (See chapter 3 for more on the IC.) Thus, in the 1950s, the Southeast had everything from big railroads with great streamliners to lowly branch lines wandering through the weeds. But that would soon change.

The 1960s were as kind to southeastern railroading as they were hostile to northeastern railroading. The southern economy, buoyed by relatively low labor and energy costs and a business-friendly climate (just like today), took off. While trucks made major inroads in the Southeast, as they did in all regions, the growing economy softened the blow of truck competition. As traffic increased, there was money to improve tracks and other infrastructure; southeastern roads ended the decade with a better infrastructure than when the decade began (the converse was true in the Northeast). More business meant more revenue and more revenue meant more investment.

But if the competitive pressures were less severe than in the Northeast, they did depress rail profits. Improving efficiency was important, and with so many redundant routes, mergers were an attractive business strategy. The Southeast began to consolidate in a serious fashion with the SR's acquisition of the Central of Georgia in 1963. The CGA allowed the SR to "bulk up" in Georgia and Alabama, including giving it access to the important Savannah market. From 1960 to 1975, the SR acquired a number of smaller (and sometimes irrelevant) carriers, including the Interstate (a major coal-originating carrier), the Georgia & Florida, and the original Norfolk Southern. Several decades later, much of the mileage the SR acquired during its expansion phase would be either abandoned or transferred to short lines.

The ACL acquired the Seaboard in 1967. The merged company was called the Seaboard Coast Line (SCL), a somewhat redundant and uninspired name. And the company adopted the ACL black and gold, eliminating the more colorful SAL

A Central of Georgia local passenger train en route to Savannah, Georgia, at Millen, Georgia, 1957. The track was terrible but that did not stop the CGA from some fast running, especially by the Nancy Hanks.

A northbound Georgia & Florida freight train arriving in Augusta, Georgia, 1957. The G&F was swallowed up by the Southern Railway, and much of the railroad was subsequently abandoned.

Interstate Railroad power at rest in Andover, Virginia, 1964.
The Interstate originated a lot of coal traffic, a fact that
caught the attention of an expanding Southern Railway.

A northbound Louisville & Nashville freight roars through Lebanon Junction, Kentucky, 1976. At the time, the L&N track left much to be desired, so much so that I had my son wait around the corner of the brick station as a safety precaution.

A Seaboard Coast Line diesel south of Alexandria, Virginia, on Richmond, Fredericksburg & Potomac track, 1970. The once-colorful Atlantic Coast Line and Seaboard Air Line paint schemes had given way to basic black, the ACL scheme when it gave up on purple. By this time, most SCL power ran through to Washington, DC, on RF&P tracks. Today the whole notion of changing out power at Richmond to relay a train one hundred miles further north to Washington seems silly. But that was how it was done.

Clinchfield power sits next to Seaboard System power at Spartanburg, South Carolina, 1985. The gray color scheme was a pleasant upgrade from the basic black adopted initially by the Seaboard Coast Line. Unfortunately, the recent decline of coal traffic has forced much of the Clinchfield to be mothballed.

paint schemes. But the two companies were a good fit; much of the Seaboard traffic was shifted to the superior ACL line to Jacksonville, while the SAL was used for most traffic south of Jacksonville. Concurrently, the Louisville & Nashville had secured access to Chicago, first on the Chicago & Eastern Illinois in a joint deal with the Missouri Pacific, and then by acquiring the Monon. The Southern Railway, meanwhile, after failing to merge with the Missouri Pacific (see below), was still stuck south of the Ohio River and would be until it merged with the Norfolk & Western. The SR was hesitant to strike north lest it offend its historical connections, the New York Central and the Pennsylvania. They, of course, had problems of their own and were increasingly uninterested in short-haul connecting traffic.

Now the SCL began to consolidate its sprawling empire, integrating its holdings under the organization called the Family Lines, that would eventually merge into what would become the Seaboard System. The formerly semi-independent L&N, the GA/AWP, and the Clinchfield were now formally part of the parent organization. Over time, commercial and operating functions were consolidated. Still, the Seaboard Coast Line was slow to integrate the components of its new system, which allowed its smaller rival, the Southern Railway, to continue as the financially stronger carrier. Had the

Seaboard System power flashes by a grade crossing south of Charleston, South Carolina, 1984.

Seaboard focused on running a cohesive network, the SR would have been in trouble (and some of us at the SR stayed awake at night thinking about that very scenario).

Perhaps the most important southeastern merger, one with far-reaching consequences for the future alignment of the industry, was one that never happened. As Conrail was getting underway, the SR and the Missouri Pacific (MP) were discussing a merger. It would have been a merger made in heaven, linking two very efficient railroads in fast-growing regions of the country. The Missouri Pacific was the SR's largest interchange partner; moving petrochemicals from the Southwest to the Southeast was its primary goal, but the MP would also have given the SR its coveted access to Chicago. But it was not to be. The SR thought it could get a better deal by waiting. Even though no agreement was signed, the SR-MP merger talks had repercussions. Partially in response to those

A southbound Southern Railway freight train near Burke, Virginia, 1981. The SR missed the boat when it could not close a deal with the Missouri Pacific. It made a second effort, but the Union Pacific countered decisively and went on to orchestrate a merger of the UP, the MP, and the Western Pacific.

A southbound Missouri Pacific freight near Osawatomie, Kansas, 1984.

Southern Pacific trains on Cajon Pass, 1980. The SP's failure to merge with the SCL's Family Lines turned out to be a major misstep of strategic importance. The SP then made a significant effort to diversify but failed to maintain its once-great railroad franchise in the process. CSX made a similar mistake but recovered.

A southbound CSX freight train passing Halifax, North Carolina, 2008. The train is on the former Atlantic Coast Line main line (now known as the "A" Line), which became the primary route between the Northeast and Florida after the Seaboard Coast Line was formed.

A CSX eastbound grain train at White Sulfur Springs, West Virginia, 2012. When the dust settled from years of consolidations CSX was the largest railroad in the East, but Norfolk Southern had expanded as well, and the two systems now are well matched.

talks, the Southern Pacific (SP) followed with an overture to the SCL's Family Lines, a combination that would have linked the Southeast not only with the Southwest but with the West Coast as well. It would have been a dynamite combination. But as was the case with the SR-MP initiative, the chemistry between the respective managements did not mesh, and the SCL went in a different direction. Both prospective transactions represent an interesting "what if" question in the rail renaissance. Had the SR merged with the MP, or the SP merged with the SCL's Family Lines, the consolidation of the industry would have probably proceeded on an east–west axis, and we would now have transcontinental railroads.

The Seaboard Coast Line did not want to make a deal with the Southern Pacific, but as the 1970s were ending, Prime Osborne, CEO of the Seaboard, was looking for other consolidation options. As it turned out, the Chessie System, boxed into the low-growth northeastern markets and facing competition from a Conrail being rebuilt with public funding, was looking for more promising territory. In 1980, the Chessie and the Seaboard Coast Line announced their intention to form a holding company called CSX to control the two properties, setting in motion the first major breaching of traditional territorial boundaries. (There had been minor incursions before, such as the Louisville & Nashville's gaining access to Chicago by acquisition of the Chicago & Eastern Illinois.)

The SR did make another overture to the MP, but that door was blocked by the Union Pacific (see chapter 4). In a sense, the SR created a lose-lose situation for itself. Not only did it not merge with the MP, but it set up countermoves that would ultimately force it into a merger with the Norfolk & Western, something that its CEO, Stan Crane, did not want.

The Southern Railway was now going to face a huge competitor. It first sought relief through the regulatory process, seeking to gain access to CSX markets in western Florida and eastern Kentucky. Essentially this was a classic response when faced with increased competition: petition your regulator for

A southbound Norfolk Southern intermodal train near Front Royal, Virginia, 2009. This part of NS, a former Norfolk & Western line, is a critical link that joins the former Southern Railway with the former Pennsylvania Railroad at Hagerstown, Maryland.

An eastbound Norfolk Southern intermodal train passes a westbound intermodal train at Lilly, Pennsylvania, 2012. This chapter began with an image of a passenger train; passenger trains dominated this route in the 1950s. They are gone now, and intermodal is the big dog. The line has been a survivor and has remained a busy channel of commerce under the ownership of the Pennsylvania Railroad, the Penn Central, Conrail, and now Norfolk Southern. By and large, the best-engineered routes have been survivors.

A northbound Norfolk Southern automotive train near Lexington, Kentucky, 2008. This line is part of the famous Cincinnati, New Orleans & Texas Pacific, once the busiest line on the Southern Railway. It remains a busy railroad today.

salvation. But there was a new ICC in town. Under the newly passed Staggers Act, the ICC saw its role as protecting competition and not competitors. It did not take the ICC long to approve the CSX consolidation, essentially without conditions. The message to the SR and N&W was essentially, "You are perfectly capable of making your own deal." Which was exactly what they did: the SR and the N&W signed a consolidation agreement some months later and the Norfolk Southern was born in 1982. (See chapter 11 for more of this story.)

CSX proved to be more impressive in concept than in execution. Just as the Chesapeake & Ohio had moved slowly to integrate the Baltimore & Ohio, CSX retained vestiges of the Chessie and the Seaboard Coast Line. The integration of the corporate cultures, always a tricky part of any consolidation, took years—and that gave NS time to do its own merger. CSX lost its first-mover advantage with its dilatory execution. But NS was hardly home free. The new NS network was inferior to that of CSX in terms of market coverage.

With the formation of both CSX and NS, the power east of the Mississippi took a decided turn to the south, making the glory days of northeastern railroading but a distant memory. CSX established its headquarters in Richmond, and NS chose Norfolk over both Washington and Roanoke. In a few brief years the traditional boundaries between the Northeast and the Southeast had been breached. Conrail was left relatively isolated but still dominant in the Middle Atlantic region. That dominance, and NS's paranoia about CSX's greater market reach, triggered a fifteen-year battle between NS and CSX. Ultimately, CSX and NS split Conrail, and the northeastern and southern rail systems were effectively merged save for a few strays. (That story is told in chapter 12.)

The growth that had propelled the southeastern railroads moderated in the 1980s and both carriers looked to nonrail ventures for higher-growth markets. These efforts were not successful. CSX was far more aggressive than NS in trying to move beyond its rail base: it acquired a global shipping company, SeaLand (now part of Maersk), and a major resort operator, Rock Resorts. Norfolk Southern acquired North American Van Lines (NAVL), one of the largest trucking companies in North America (at that time, at least). And both companies proved that they lacked the management talent and depth to succeed outside of railroading. CSX failed to pay attention to its core business and the railroad suffered. For NS, NAVL was only a modest diversion, and the company stayed focused on the railroad; still, NAVL was a waste of time and money for NS.

Slower growth also forced both companies to reevaluate their rail networks. Both CSX and NS tended to view rationalization as something that poor railroads (such as the Penn Central) did. In the 1980s, both carriers learned that the problems of the Northeast could cross territorial boundaries. Both launched aggressive rationalization programs.

It was not just the feeder network that was trimmed; former main lines took a major hit as well. For example, the N&W had never sorted out the redundancies in the Midwest that had resulted from its acquisition of the Wabash and the Nickel Plate. The through traffic had been concentrated on the best lines soon after the merger but the N&W had not bothered to clean up the lines that were left. With the static business conditions of the 1980s, NS had to take action (see chapter 11 for more on this). CSX trimmed its main-line network as well—such

A southbound Conrail freight train near Odenton, Maryland, 1980.

icons as the former SAL main line south of Richmond and the SAL Atlanta–Birmingham line were abandoned.

Altogether, the 1980s were a depressing time. At one meeting, Paul Goodwin, then the CFO of CSX, characterized the former ACL main line between the Northeast and Florida as a "3P railroad—passenger, piggyback, and pulpwood." It was a term of derision because all three were marginally profitable at best. And another CSX vice president advocated for the railroad to transfer most of its Michigan lines to short-line carriers. Railroading in the East was in a twilight zone: many traditional markets were either static or in outright decline, and intermodal traffic, while growing rapidly, was not yet very profitable. Investments outside of railroading had not been a solution, so both CSX and NS turned to even more aggressive cost-cutting. It was not a happy time. Railroads were profitable, but where would the growth come from? For NS, the solution lay to the north.

REACHING NEW MARKETS

Norfolk Southern's inferior route structure weighed heavily on its strategic planning. Acquiring Conrail would provide it with access to some critical consumer goods markets. Making the first move, NS attempted to acquire all of Conrail when it was offered for sale by the government in 1984, but it was soundly defeated by a coalition of CR and CSX and finally gave up after two years. Still, NS kept chewing on the Conrail bone and cut a preliminary merger deal in 1994. That fell apart; NS did not want to pay what CR needed (shades of the SR-MP talks years earlier). In 1995, NS and CSX met in secret to plan how to split Conrail. The problem was that CR was not part of the discussions and was not about to sign off on its own demise.

CSX then took the initiative and made peace with Conrail. In October 1996 it announced a merger of equals. Its back to the wall, NS played the money card (its very robust balance sheet) and made a hostile bid for all of CR. It was a fight worthy of Hill and Harriman fighting over the Burlington at the turn of the twentieth century (or perhaps the Hatfields and the McCoys, given both carriers' roots in Appalachia). Norfolk Southern made an all-cash offer and CSX simply did not have the financial firepower for an escalating bidding war. CSX's CEO John Snow reached out to NS's CEO David Goode and proposed that NS and CSX split Conrail, with NS taking the larger portion.

After a few more iterations, a deal was cut. Norfolk Southern got 58 percent of CR (based on historical traffic levels). The former PRR east of Cleveland and the Reading went to NS, as did the former NYC west of Cleveland. CSX gained the former NYC routes east of Cleveland as well as the CR line to East St. Louis. It was hardly a done deal, however, and several years of work were ahead; splitting a major railroad between two competitors and then jumping a huge number of political and environmental hurdles delayed the actual split date until June 1999. Even then, there were serious service snafus.

It had taken thirty years but the industry structure in the eastern United States had been set. The outcome mimicked Alfred Perlman's proposal to merge the NYC and the C&O some three decades earlier. What goes around sometimes comes around. After fifteen years of conflict, the map was defined, and CSX and NS could now focus on the less dramatic but still essential tasks of improving both service and efficiency. (For more on this story see chapter 12.)

It is said that all fame is fleeting but as I write this, the southeastern story, which has now become the eastern story, ends on a happy note. The two carriers are well balanced in terms of market coverage, route structure, and financial and operating performance. This is good for competition because the better the competitors, the more they will have the means to improve service and efficiency. And the more balanced the systems, the less likely it is that there will be the kind of massive and disruptive changes that have been the norm for the last half of the twentieth century.

The future will not be without its challenges. Central Appalachian coal, which sustained many northeastern and southeastern railroads for decades, is in steep decline. But the decline of coal does not spell the end of eastern railroading. Norfolk Southern and CSX now have expansive networks, and new sources of traffic, such as crude oil by rail, can be cultivated as old sources decline. Conrail was pricey for both carriers, but no one at either carrier still thinks it was a bad idea. Change continues but I am now hopeful that the railroads will adjust. The bad old days of regulation and management lethargy are over, one hopes forever. The current railroad leaders in the East have been dealt a good, but not great, hand. How they play it will determine the future of eastern railroading.

A southbound CSX freight crosses Aquia Creek, an inlet off the Potomac River, 2013. This track had been owned by the Richmond, Fredericksburg & Potomac, the railroad featured in this chapter's first image. The track was busy in its former life and is even busier now, as fleets of CSX freight, Amtrak passenger trains, and Virginia Railway Express commuter trains vie for limited track capacity. Virginia is working with CSX to create a triple-track railroad between Alexandria and Richmond.

The southbound Morning Zephyr arrives in La Crosse, Wisconsin, 1964.
The Burlington was the premier midwestern railroad in the 1950s
and was a survivor as the midwestern network was rationalized.

THE MIDWEST

3

Chicago is the railroad hub of North America; today 25 percent of all rail traffic touches the city. But while there were once a half-dozen railroads headquartered there, now there are none. The midwestern railroads were merged or abandoned as "outsiders" sought access to Chicago. In the process, the once-overbuilt midwestern network was rationalized through transfers to short-line carriers or abandonment.

VANTAGE POINT

The Midwest was never one of my first loves; it struck me as too much like my home state of Texas. I like mountains and mountain railroading. But you cannot be a professional railroader, as I was for forty years, without spending a lot of time in the Midwest, especially Chicago. Breakfast in the diner heading into Chicago on the 20th Century Limited was always a treat; coming home eastbound was about sipping bourbon in a Creek followed by a steak dinner in the twin-unit diner as northern Indiana passed by the window.

Chicago loomed large in the creation of both Amtrak and Conrail; it was a major hub for Amtrak and the western anchor of the Conrail system. When I returned to the Southern

Railway for duties in merger planning, Chicago was always on the radar. Our main rail competitor, the Family Lines, had single-system service to Chicago. Getting to Chicago was always a goal for those of us in the merger business. The SR finally got there when it merged with the Norfolk & Western. After that consolidation, I spent even more time in the Midwest, often eliminating redundant lines from the new NS network. Then came the split of Conrail; Chicago anchored the busiest route on the expanded Norfolk Southern, appropriately called the Chicago line. It was the very same route I rode so many times on the 20th Century, and once again the route was part of *my* railroad.

SIXTY YEARS OF CHANGE

Railroads are cheap to construct and operate in the flatlands, because they have few physical impediments other than rivers. There were tracks to every village and hamlet, and many places had three or four or more railroads, all competing for what was often minimal traffic. As highways expanded, the Midwest was left with too many railroads serving too many places with too much track.

The Chicago skyline as seen from the departing Capitol Limited, 2009. This line is now part of Norfolk Southern; Amtrak's Chicago maintenance base is to the right.

The shakeout was brutal. Much of the gathering network was abandoned or turned over to short-line and regional carriers. The main-line network took a haircut as well. All of the major midwestern railroads were consumed by mergers, and Chicago lost its role as a railroad headquarters location. Now the decisions for midwestern freight railroading are made in Montreal, Calgary, Omaha, Fort Worth, Jacksonville, and Norfolk.

The midwestern story is one of massive retrenchment, bankruptcies, and "invasions" from the south, the west, and the north. But there has been good news as well. New sources of traffic, such as western coal and international intermodal movements, have restored profitability to a streamlined midwestern rail system. Perhaps it's too streamlined: Chicago is congested, as are several other key main-line routes.

THE VIEW FROM 1950

The Midwest was, and is, about Chicago. It had been the premier railroad destination since the late nineteenth century, and its starring role continues to this day. The important northeastern railroads—the Pennsylvania, the New York Central, and the Baltimore & Ohio—had reached Chicago in the nineteenth century. But in 1950, ties to the Southeast and the West were far less robust; the Gulf, Mobile & Ohio and the Illinois Central reached Chicago but were not major players in the Southeast. The big guns in the Southeast—the Atlantic Coast Line/Louisville & Nashville and the Southern System—went no further north than the Ohio River. In the West, only the Santa Fe and the Milwaukee Road had single-system service between the West Coast and Chicago. (And the Milwaukee's transcontinental line was never important in the scheme of things.)

The most successful midwestern carrier in the 1950s was the Burlington (the Chicago, Burlington & Quincy, or CB&Q, or simply the Q). It was jointly owned by the Great Northern and the Northern Pacific and provided both carriers with access to Chicago. But the Q was far more than just a connection for those carriers; it reached Omaha, Denver, and Billings, Montana, on its own, and subsidiaries stretched from Montana through Colorado to the Texas Gulf Coast. The Burlington was a premier passenger carrier in the same league as the Santa Fe. It hosted some of the greatest trains of the streamliner era, including the Denver Zephyr, the California Zephyr, the Twin Cities Zephyr, the Empire Builder, and the North Coast Limited. The Q ran fast and tried hard until the end.

The Q became a core part of the Burlington Northern, and then the Burlington Northern Santa Fe. Its main-line routes are a critical part of that sprawling system today. The other major Chicago-based railroads, however, did not fare nearly as well. Four other large carriers roughly mimicked the Burlington, reaching west and north from Chicago. The Rock Island (Chicago, Rock Island & Pacific, or CRI&P, or RI) headed west to the Quad Cities through Omaha to Colorado and had a north–south main line stretching from the Twin Cities to Houston via Kansas City. The Rock was a partner with the SP in the operation of the Golden State Route, providing joint line service between Chicago and California. But while the Rock went a lot of places and boasted an impressive map, it had too much railroad with too little traffic. It would be one of the first midwestern railroads to bite the dust.

The Milwaukee Road blanketed the upper Midwest and also reached the West Coast. Its Pacific Coast extension cost a fortune—more than $1 billion in current dollars. It was completed just before the once-robust Asian trade tanked and just

The train from Billings arrives in Denver, 1955. Though firmly anchored in the Midwest, the Burlington and its subsidiaries reached Billings, Denver, Dallas, and Houston.

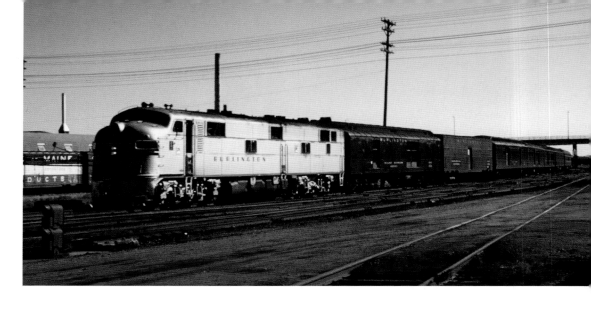

The Denver Zephyr is looking fresh and shiny as it waits to depart Denver for its overnight dash to Chicago, 1956. The train was "brand new out of the box" when this picture was taken.

The Rock Island's Rocky Mountain Rocket arrives in Denver, 1956.
The train split at Limon, Colorado; one section went to Colorado Springs
and the other to Denver. The Rock's expansive network simply could not
compete with that of the better-operated and better-financed Burlington.

The Milwaukee Road's Olympian Hiawatha rolls eastbound through Easton, Washington, 1960. The hugely expensive Pacific extension was a "line too far" and contributed to the demise of the railroad.

A North Western merchandise train en route to St. Louis, 1989. Like other midwestern railroads the CNW touched all the major markets but often with only a train or two per day. The interchange with the Union Pacific, the growth of the Powder River Basin, and a steely-eyed rationalization of the rest of its network allowed it to survive.

Soo Line trains pass south of Pig's Eye Yard in Minneapolis, 1981. The Soo Line paint scheme was the exception to the general rule that paint schemes got worse when first-generation power was repainted.

a few years before the Panama Canal opened. The Milwaukee was a scrappy innovator but, like the Rock, it had too much railroad and too little traffic to survive intact. It never really recovered from the cost of the Pacific Coast extension. The North Western (Chicago & North Western, or CNW) also blanketed the upper Midwest: one line straggled into the western Dakotas and another into eastern Wyoming. It had the best railroad in the overbuilt Chicago–Council Bluffs market (where it connected with the Union Pacific), but it too had far too much railroad to survive in the new world of truck competition.

The Soo Line (Minneapolis, St. Paul & Sault Ste. Marie) followed the same template as the other upper midwestern networks, linking Chicago to St. Paul and beyond to connections with the Canadian Pacific (CP), its parent road by majority stock ownership, at Portal, North Dakota, and Noyes, Minnesota. Its ties to the CP provided a base load of freight traffic. It did not run fast trains, it did not have streamlined equipment, and many of its lines did not have signals. But by staying lean it stayed in the black, and so it escaped unhappy financial travails. The Wabash, meanwhile, straddled the Midwest, linking Detroit with Kansas City; other lines reached Chicago and St. Louis from its hub at Decatur, Illinois. It also connected St. Louis directly with Kansas City. Its bread-and-butter traffic was Ford Motor Company automotive traffic from Detroit to West Coast markets. The Wabash was one of the first midwestern railroads to be gobbled up by an outsider, the Roanoke, Virginia–based Norfolk & Western.

The last major player in the midwestern drama marched to a different drummer. Whereas others left Chicago and headed

The City of St. Louis in Kansas City, 1956. The Wabash was one of the first major midwestern railroads to be merged out of existence. Many more would follow.

west and north into the cold and the dark, the Illinois Central (IC) headed straight south to Memphis and New Orleans. From this spine, secondary main lines reached to the east and the west to such points as Council Bluffs, Indianapolis, Birmingham, Meridian, and Baton Rouge. Coal, grain, and chemicals were its game. There were also a number of minor actors, including the Chicago Great Western, the Chicago & Eastern Illinois, the Minneapolis & St. Louis, the Monon, and the Illinois Terminal. Only the main-line routes of the Chicago & Eastern Illinois are relevant today.

CREATION OF THE BURLINGTON NORTHERN

One midwestern railroad was a survivor: the Burlington Northern (BN), which was larger than its owners, the Northern Pacific (NP) and the Great Northern (GN). When the BN was created, it had a place at the table thanks to its operating strength and management talent. The idea for the BN had been around for decades: James J. Hill, a Canadian known as the "Empire Builder," who conceived of and guided the building of the Great Northern, had proposed putting the GN, the

The southbound Illinois Central Southern Express at Carrollton Avenue Station, New Orleans, 1961. The IC, like the other midwestern railroads, was anchored in Chicago, but it was focused toward the south rather than north and west of the city.

A Burlington Northern intermodal train climbs up Crawford Hill, Nebraska, 1985. The Burlington Northern merger got the merger ball rolling in the West, forcing the Union Pacific to either expand or be marginalized.

NP, and the Q together early in the twentieth century, but Teddy Roosevelt and his trustbusters stopped the deal. Now, decades later, a new proposal surfaced. The three railroads filed a merger petition in 1966. That petition was denied by the ICC, but the parties reworked the deal and resubmitted the application. The merger was approved in 1970, the same year the Penn Central went bankrupt.

It was not a good time to talk about the merits of mergers. In light of the Penn Central debacle, mergers were no longer seen as the path to prosperity. Had the Burlington Northern merger failed, the entire rail consolidation movement would have been in jeopardy. Fortunately, the merger was a success—the plan was solid and the implementation unhurried and essentially trouble-free. The formation of the BN was a watershed event for midwestern railroading but a kiss of death for the other big granger railroads, whose survival depended on finding a well-heeled partner. Some succeeded; others did not. The creation of the BN pretty much set the stage for the current two-carrier industry structure in the West (see chapter 4).

"OUTSIDERS" COME AND CONQUER

Five major railroads were headquartered in Chicago: the North Western, the Milwaukee Road, the Illinois Central, the Burlington, and the Santa Fe, along with one minor railroad, the Chicago Great Western. Today, no freight railroads call Chicago home. In a sense, the importance of Chicago was the culprit: both southeastern and western carriers "invaded" the Midwest to reach Chicago. In the process they absorbed the traditional midwestern railroads.

A southwestern carrier, the Missouri Pacific (MP), made one of the first moves. In 1968 it acquired the small but strategic Chicago & Eastern Illinois (C&EI). The C&EI was shaped like a wishbone; starting in Chicago, it split near Danville, Illinois. One leg went to Evansville, Indiana, where it connected with the Louisville & Nashville, and the other went to Benton, Illinois, where it connected with an MP freight line on the east side of the Mississippi. (The C&EI also reached East St. Louis on trackage rights.) The MP cut a deal with the Louisville & Nashville to acquire and split the C&EI; the L&N took the Evansville leg, while the MP acquired the lines to East St. Louis and Thebes, Illinois. North of Danville (Woodland Junction), the two carriers operated the railroad jointly. This deal gave the MP single-system service between Chicago and Texas as well as a good bypass around the congested St. Louis area.

With these actions, the L&N gained access to Chicago, the first southeastern railroad to cross the Ohio. It was part of the Atlantic Coast Line family of lines, which meant that the largest southeastern network now had Chicago access. It would be well over a decade before its southeastern rival, the Southern, reached Chicago (when it merged with the Norfolk & Western).

Santa Fe had single-system service between Chicago and the West, and the BN merger closed the gap to the Pacific Northwest. The UP started its march east to Chicago when it negotiated an agreement to acquire the Rock Island. Subsequently the SP joined the party: the plan was for that carrier to buy the southern part of the railroad. (The SP and the RI already cooperated in a joint Chicago–California service over the Golden State route via Tucumcari, New Mexico.)

The proposed deal would have greatly strengthened the UP and the SP at the expense of others. The stakes were huge for the CNW. At Omaha/Council Bluffs, the Union Pacific interchanged trainloads of traffic with five railroads, and the

The inbound Louisville & Nashville morning arrival in St. Louis, 1962.
Originating in Evansville, this train carried through cars from both the
Georgian (from Atlanta) and the Hummingbird (from New Orleans and
Birmingham). Both the Southern and the L&N reached St. Louis but at this
time neither had direct access to the crown jewel of the Midwest, Chicago.

A loaded North Western coal train at East Antelope, Wyoming, 1985. The Union Pacific and the North Western had always been partners over the Omaha Gateway. They joined forces again to gain access to the Powder River Basin.

North Western got the bulk of that traffic. The CNW would be devastated by the deal, and there would be collateral damage to other railroads as well, including the Milwaukee Road, the Wabash (by then part of the N&W), and the Missouri Pacific.

With so much as stake, all hell broke loose in the regulatory arena. Opponents either wanted the deal turned down, or, if it was approved, they wanted a line here and a market there to compensate for real or perceived harm. Railroading in the sixties was a declining business; with the total pie shrinking, "beggar thy neighbor" was the only way to win. The proposed Rock Island merger was a bonanza for lawyers and consultants.

Ultimately, twelve carriers joined the fray, and the result was regulatory gridlock. After ten years the merger was approved, but by then the Rock was in such terrible condition that the UP walked away from the deal. The North Western was the winner; it retained the UP traffic. Later, when the then-doomed Rock Island was liquidated, the CNW was rid of a competitor and picked up a key RI route between the Twin Cities and Kansas City (the Spine Line, rich in grain originations) as well. Railroads like to complain about the burdens of regulation unless, of course, they are the beneficiaries.

Life got even better for the CNW. Powder River Basin (PRB) coal became the utility fuel of choice after the passage of the Clean Air Act of 1970. The CNW teamed up with the UP to create a new, competitive route into the PRB, much to the chagrin of the BN. The combined route used part of an almost defunct CNW branch line that ended in Lander, Wyoming. (In this instance, regulation had proven to be a good thing. Had it not been for regulation, the Lander line would

A southbound Rock Island freight train on the Spine Line in the 1970s.

have been abandoned years earlier. Today parts of it live on as a major coal route, complete with traffic control and concrete crossties. Occasionally, branch lines do rise from the dead.)

By this time, Ben Heineman, head of the North Western, had worked more creative magic. The CNW acquired weak competitors such as the Chicago Great Western and the Minneapolis & St. Louis, melded their best routes into the CNW network, and abandoned the rest. But the really big deal was the creation of Northwest Industries to pursue nonrail ventures. The railroad itself was sold to the employees in a leveraged buyout. That worked so well that a second employee buyout followed a few years later. The employees did own the company, but the bulk of the shares were held by members of senior management, who made a lot of money along the way.

All of this set the stage for the purchase of the CNW by the UP in 1995. With that, the UP got the Chicago access it had coveted for so long, plus substantial grain traffic and direct access to the PRB. But it had been a long process—more than three decades had passed since the UP's first overture to the Rock Island. (Recall that the BN merger had been proposed at the turn of the century. Railroading is not a nimble business.) While the CNW as an entity did not survive, it fared better than its main rivals, the Rock Island and the Milwaukee Road. The Milwaukee succumbed to territorial invasion, this time by the Canadians. The Canadian Pacific had enjoyed access to Chicago for decades through its majority ownership (later increased to total control) of the Soo Line. But the CP needed a better route to Chicago, and when the bankrupt Milwaukee was put up for sale by the trustee, the Soo/CP was awarded

A southbound Soo Line freight train near Red Wing, Minnesota, 2006, running on tracks for the former Milwaukee Road. The Soo had been controlled by the Canadian Pacific for decades, providing the CP with access to Chicago from western Canada.

A southbound Wisconsin Central train at Oshkosh, Wisconsin, crosses the Fox River, 1990. This line is now operated by the Canadian National.

the Milwaukee (defeating CNW) in 1985 (again, think "beggar thy neighbor," or a deadly serious game of musical chairs). That provided the CP with one of the premier, though by then shopworn, main lines in the Midwest.

Because the Milwaukee Road had the superior alignment, much of the former Soo Line system was transferred to Lake States Transportation. It was to be a "carrier within a carrier," designed to emulate the more nimble operations and lower labor costs being achieved by short-line and regional carriers. The unions were having none of that, and the Soo lost interest in making its offspring work. Lake States was sold to the Wisconsin Central (WC) and became a very successful regional railroad.

Ultimately the WC fell victim to the desire of the Canadian National (CN) to link the western part of its network to Chicago (the eastern access had been secured decades earlier by the CN's Grand Trunk Western subsidiary). It was acquired by the CN in 2001, thus providing the CN with an alternate route between eastern and western Canada via Chicago (see chapter 5).

When the music stopped, the CP gained Chicago access via the former Milwaukee Road, and its archrival, the Canadian National, gained access via the former Soo Line, which was formerly owned by the CP. Who would have guessed that outcome?

The biggest Canadian incursion involved the once-great Illinois Central. The IC, the "Main Line of Mid-America," had, and has, a superb route between Chicago and New Orleans/Baton Rouge (think chemical traffic), but, like its midwestern brethren, it was encumbered with thousands of miles of marginal trackage. After the Staggers Act was passed, the IC took a meat axe to that network: lines were sold to new regional or short-line carriers or abandoned outright. By 1990,

the IC had slimmed down to a viable north–south core. It then put a tough operating officer, Hunter Harrison, in charge and further efficiencies were achieved. This now-streamlined IC and its dynamic leader attracted the attention of the Canadian National; some say the CN bought the IC mainly to acquire Harrison.

With the absorption of the IC and the WC into the CN, the Midwest story, as such, came to an end. Just as the northeastern story became the eastern story, the midwestern story became the western story and the Canadian story. The tracks and yards and traffic remain, but the decision-making now resides elsewhere.

BANKRUPTCIES AND ABANDONMENTS

Not all changes to midwestern railroading were coming from the outside. By the 1960s, most midwestern railroads were in dire financial straits due to overcapacity. There were too many main-line routes: six railroads vied for traffic between Council Bluffs and Chicago, and there were three main-line routes between Chicago and the Twin Cities. That said, most of the railroads involved were reluctant to make the first move lest they lose a competitive advantage to others. (Of course, someone has to exit the market, but it should be the other guy, not me.)

The even bigger problem was the branch-line network. It had been built on the cheap to originate grain in an era before the paved road. The lines were built to marginal standards (light rail weight and light load limits on bridges). When the hundred-ton grain car was widely introduced in the 1970s, much of the midwestern feeder network was rendered obsolete and, ultimately, inoperable. Railroads bought hundred-ton cars because the ICC cost formulas indicated costs would go down. This was absolutely wrong, as it turned out, because the formulas did not take into account the fact that the railroad had to be rebuilt to handle the cars. The only possible solutions were to find money for rehabilitation or abandon the lines. But private-sector money was not an option for most; the Rock Island filed for bankruptcy in 1975, and the Milwaukee followed right behind it in 1977. The North Western avoided bankruptcy but it was touch and go. The railroads were forced to look to the government for funding.

There was some support in Congress, at least among midwestern politicians, for a Conrail-type solution: the federal government would design and then fund the rehabilitation of the network. That idea failed to gain traction for two reasons. First, unlike in much of the Northeast, there were healthy carriers such as the Burlington Northern, the Santa Fe, and the Soo in the major markets. Second, Conrail got off to a rocky start and was losing hundreds of millions of dollars a year just as the midwestern crisis hit. President Carter, though a Democrat, was a fiscal conservative and had no stomach for another railroad bailout.

Ultimately, political pressure did force the feds to take some action. But it was a Band-Aid approach; there was no grand plan like the USRA solution in the Northeast. Rather, the DOT's Federal Railroad Administration (FRA) doled out loans and grants on a case-by-case basis. The redundant mainline problem was addressed by creating "corridors of excess capacity," a concept first raised in the DOT's so-called Orange Line Report in 1974. Public investments would be focused on the lines that either handled or would handle twenty million gross ton-miles per mile, thus encouraging joint use. Despite immense political pressure, the FRA did the right thing and the money largely went to worthy projects. The branch-line network also received some public money, with Iowa being especially aggressive in rehabilitating portions of that state's grain-gathering network.

This piecemeal approach at the federal and state levels was a success. Portions of the network that were used and useful were saved. As the major carriers exited many markets, short-line and regional carriers stepped in with lower-cost solutions usually anchored by lower-cost labor agreements. Still, thousands of miles were abandoned outright. In recent years, government-mandated use of ethanol has created a source of new traffic (at least for now, and subject to the whims of Congress) for the now-rationalized granger network.

ONCE IT WAS A MIGHTY FINE ROAD

This story would not be complete without an additional word about the Rock Island. After the proposed acquisition of the Rock by the UP and the SP was terminated, the Rock lingered in bankruptcy, growing ever weaker and more run-down. Creditors battled with shippers, rail labor, and politicians over the fate of the railroad but without any resolution. The Rock's future was sealed when the clerks' union led a strike that essentially shut down the railroad (though management did try to run some trains). The unions were betting that the federal government would come in and save the company, as it had done in the Northeast. Rail labor guessed wrong and was shocked when a Democratic president (Carter) simply let the company be liquidated. Other railroads stepped into the breach and operated segments of the Rock on a temporary basis. Over time, many of those temporary arrangements became permanent—for example, the SP stepped in and operated the Tucumcari line, and the Katy bought the line south

A Rock Island freight at Joliet, Illinois, 1964. The first signs
of deferred maintenance were beginning to show.

from Herington, Kansas, to handle export grain. In the end, much of the RI remained in service, but the railroad itself was dead.

But that liquidation turned out to have an unanticipated benefit. When President Reagan came into office, Conrail was still bleeding cash. The Republicans essentially said that they would liquidate Conrail unless it was put on a paying basis. With the memory of the Rock Island fresh in everyone's mind, rail labor and commuter authorities came to the bargaining table and made meaningful concessions. In a few years, Conrail returned to profitability. So perhaps the Rock did not die in vain.

A NEAR-DEATH EXPERIENCE AND RECOVERY

The Midwest has morphed into the East, the West, and Canada. It was a painful process and one that took four decades to play out. Along the way thousands of jobs were lost and thousands of miles of track were torn up. But some very bad things, such as nationalization or total liquidation, were avoided. Now the midwestern network, so ragged for so many years, has been rebuilt. It is a much better outcome than appeared possible in the dark days of the 1970s and 1980s.

In all of this turmoil, Chicago remains the most important railroad junction in the nation. The headquarters are gone but the tracks and terminals remain—and they're busier than ever, so much so that rail congestion at Chicago is the number-one capacity challenge for the railroad industry, one that has yet to be resolved as of this writing. But overall the midwestern story has been a good one: the important routes have been rebuilt, and the region is the domain of profitable railroads, albeit ones that are headquartered elsewhere.

The combined Burlington–Rock Island Zephyr Rocket arrives in
St. Louis after an overnight trip from the Twin Cities, 1962.

A westbound Santa Fe intermodal train heads for the summit of Cajon Pass, California, 1990.

THE WEST

4

The West was the star of the railroad renaissance. Rail technology works best for heavy-volume, long-haul movements, and the market was kind to western railroads with the development of low-sulfur coal and international intermodal traffic. Adding to growing volume was the merger of the network into two strong systems, which produced huge efficiencies.

VANTAGE POINT

I was born in Texas, and lived there on and off until I went to college. By birth and temperament, I have strong roots in the West and I have returned there time and time again to observe western railroading. Along the way, I have both ridden and photographed virtually all of the main lines in the West and many of the secondary lines.

Professionally, I never worked for a western carrier. That said, my work at the DOT, the Association of American Railroads, and Amtrak meant that I had to know a lot about western railroading. As the rail merger guru at Norfolk Southern, I analyzed all of the major western railroads (some of them multiple times) as NS sought to find the right merger partner. Along the way, I got to interact with many of the key players in the western railroad drama.

SIXTY YEARS OF CHANGE

The West escaped the crisis that engulfed northeastern railroading. Starting in World War II, and well before the coal and intermodal booms to come, western markets were growing rapidly, especially in Texas and California. Long hauls, often several thousand miles, provided some protection from truck competition, although those same long hauls made the passenger side of the business vulnerable to air transportation.

Over the last six decades, four factors have dominated the western story:

- The Clean Air Act of 1970 mandated reduced sulfur outputs from power plants and created a whole new market for long-haul western coal.
- The shift of some manufacturing to Asia was a boon for western railroads. Like coal, it was high-volume, long-haul traffic ideal for rail technology.
- The western railroads, which were almost as fragmented as those in the Northeast and the Southeast, ultimately coalesced into two major systems: the Union Pacific and the Burlington Northern Santa Fe.

- In a real David-and-Goliath story, the Kansas City Southern came from nowhere to become the dominant railroad in the growing trade between Mexico and the United States.

THE VIEW FROM 1950

The big guns in the West in the mid-fifties were the Santa Fe (Atchison, Topeka & Santa Fe, or AT&SF) and the Southern Pacific (SP). The Santa Fe stretched from Chicago to California and Texas, and provided single-system service between Chicago and those growing markets. "Santa Fe All the Way" was more than a mere slogan; it gave the Santa Fe marketing and service advantages over competitors. Santa Fe had a superbly engineered main line between Chicago and California, which was either double-tracked or had alternate routes virtually the entire distance.

But if the Santa Fe had an excellent transcontinental main-line network, its gathering network was inferior to that of the Southern Pacific, both on the Gulf Coast and on the West Coast, and the Missouri Pacific also had a superior network in the Texas Gulf Coast. That was a handicap when carload traffic dominated the rail marketplace. Finally, Santa Fe did not have a direct link to southeastern carriers, nor did it reach St. Louis. It was a good but imperfect network.

The Santa Fe was justifiably famous for its passenger service. The Super Chief, Chief, San Francisco Chief, and Texas Chief blanketed the Santa Fe network, supplemented by such secondary trains as the Grand Canyon and the Fast Mail. The Super Chief was one of the most famous trains in the world (along with the 20th Century Limited); it was used by Hollywood stars before airplanes gutted the first-class rail passenger market.

The Southern Pacific was the longest railroad in the country when its subsidiaries are included—the Texas & New Orleans, the Cotton Belt, and others. It linked New Orleans and Portland, Oregon, in a long arc via Houston, El Paso, Los Angeles, and Oakland. The Cotton Belt (the St. Louis–Southwestern, or SSW) gave it a route to East St. Louis, and from there, connections to all of the important northeastern carriers. It connected directly with southeastern carriers at New Orleans and Memphis. The SP line east from Oakland to Ogden, Utah (the "Overland Route"), part of the first transcontinental railroad, connected with the Union Pacific at Ogden. It was the best of the transcontinental routes between the Bay Area and the Midwest.

The Southern Pacific and its subsidiaries were run as an integrated system; while the Texas & New Orleans had offices in Houston and the Cotton Belt in Tyler, Texas, the key decisions were made at 65 Market Street in San Francisco. The SP had it all: it was big, it was the dominant railroad in California, and it blanketed most of the fast-growing West. David P. Morgan, then the editor of *Trains* magazine, dubbed the SP "the new Standard Railroad of the World," replacing the Pennsylvania Railroad (this title was self-assigned by the PRR but was widely accepted). In 1959, the SP generated more revenue ton-miles than any other railroad, reflecting its growth as well as the decline of the former champ, the PRR. But it was far from perfect. Its key transcontinental route was circuitous and did not reach Chicago, nor did it have any coal business. These deficiencies would come to haunt it later.

The Southern Pacific operated an extensive passenger network in the postwar era, but soured on the business in the early 1950s. D. J. Russell, the SP's chairman, was outspoken in his contempt for passenger trains; he was among the first to understand the hopeless economics of the long-haul train, for

A westbound Santa Fe intermodal train at Olathe, Kansas, 1984. The Santa Fe was an early intermodal pioneer, and its fast, largely double-tracked route between Chicago and Los Angeles gave it a powerful advantage over its rail competitors, the Union Pacific and the Southern Pacific.

The westbound Santa Fe Chief pauses at Joliet, Illinois, 1965. The Santa Fe operated what was arguably the finest rail passenger service in North America.

The Texas Chief poised to leave Houston en route to Chicago, 1959. In the background the Rock Island's Twin Star Rocket will soon depart for the Twin Cities via Dallas and Kansas City.

An eastbound Southern Pacific freight near San Antonio, Texas, 1956. The SP had extensive services in Texas but never exploited the Texas market as well as the Missouri Pacific did.

A westbound Southern Pacific freight train just west of Truckee, California, 1960. The SP crossing of the Sierra Nevada Mountains was the western link of the first transcontinental railroad. The SP and the UP jointly provided service on this route, but the SP preferred its longer route to the East via Texas.

The westbound Sunset Limited just east of San Antonio, Texas, 1954. The Sunset was one of the last streamliners placed in service by the SP, which soon became a vociferous critic of the passenger train.

The westbound Overland Limited west of Truckee, California, behind Alco locomotives, 1960. The SP was replacing the striking orange, red, and black paint scheme with a simpler gray and red livery.

which he was vilified then and now. When it was a believer, the SP ran some of the finest passenger trains in the nation, including the Coast Daylight, the Shasta Daylight, the City of San Francisco, and the Sunset Limited.

Below these two carriers were a number of important though less dominant railroads: the Union Pacific (the UP was in the second tier at the time for reasons I will explore), the Missouri Pacific, the Frisco (the St. Louis–San Francisco, or SLSF), the Great Northern, and the Northern Pacific. Below them was yet a third tier of carriers, including the Katy, the Rio Grande, and the Western Pacific.

The Union Pacific had the advantage of being the first transcontinental railroad and it locked up the best route early, following the gentle contours of the Platte River Valley to central Wyoming. There it crossed the Rockies at a relatively modest elevation west of Cheyenne (Sherman Hill). That crossing was further enhanced with the building of the lower-grade Borie Cutoff. But as good as its core route was, the UP network, like those of its competitors, was imperfect. Its eastern termini were Omaha, Nebraska, and Kansas City, Missouri. From those points, it depended on other railroads to connect to the East. Its access to the West was far from ideal; competitors had better routes to both Los Angeles and the Pacific Northwest. Finally, its access to the Bay Area depended on an often hostile SP, which promoted its own, longer-haul routes. The UP would spend the next three decades correcting these defects. It was a major passenger carrier but not quite in the league of the Santa Fe. Still, its City fleet included some of the finest trains in the country at a time when fine trains were the norm.

The Missouri Pacific (MP) was a key player in the western story. With its Texas & Pacific subsidiary, it stretched south from the St. Louis area to Texas and Louisiana and west through Missouri and Kansas to Colorado. The MP

A westbound Union Pacific freight train on the Borie Cutoff (west of Cheyenne, Wyoming) one very cold winter day, 1980. The UP had a superb railroad between Omaha, Nebraska, and Ogden, Utah, but did not reach either Chicago or Oakland on its own tracks.

The Union Pacific's City of St. Louis and City of Portland ready to depart Denver, 1962.

Two eastbound Union Pacific freights just west of Cheyenne, Wyoming, 1960. A 4,500 hp gas turbine is overtaking an 8,500 hp gas turbine. In an effort to obtain maximum horsepower in a single locomotive, the UP embraced gas turbine locomotives for a brief period in the late 1950s.

system was anchored by Dallas, Houston, Laredo, New Orleans, and El Paso. Its routes along the Texas and Louisiana chemical coast gave it superb access to the growing and hugely profitable petrochemical business. But it did not reach either Chicago or the Pacific coast.

In the fifties the MP operated an extensive passenger train system; its network of Eagle passenger trains served all of the important markets on the railroad. The MP tried hard to promote passenger service but failed, just like its peers.

The Frisco was a southwestern version of the Wabash. It bridged the Mississippi River barrier between the Southeast and the West by connecting Birmingham with Kansas City, Missouri, via Memphis. Its St. Louis–Texas line crossed its Kansas City–Birmingham line at Springfield, Missouri (not unlike the Wabash, whose main lines crossed at Decatur,

Illinois). It was a bridge route for the Santa Fe, providing that carrier with access to both St. Louis and the Southeast. It did not operate any passenger service of note—its premier train, the Meteor, was adequate but hardly in the same class as a Super Chief or a California Zephyr. The Frisco as an entity did not survive, but some of its main routes remain as important parts of today's Burlington Northern Santa Fe (BNSF). Railroads are where they go, and a good route structure often outlasts the corporations that owned those routes.

There were two important railroads along the northern tier. The Great Northern (GN) was built for efficiency at a time when the quality of infrastructure took a backseat to cost and speed of construction. ("Build it quickly and cheaply, fix it later," was the theme.) The GN's legendary leader, Jim Hill, insisted on high standards: the GN was the best-engineered

The Missouri Pacific's Texas Eagle leaving San Antonio for St. Louis, 1955. The train carried a through sleeper to New York via the PRR and a through Slumbercoach to Baltimore via the B&O.

The Aztec Eagle at San Antonio after its arrival from Mexico City, 1955. Note the pristine condition of the E unit.

Frisco train number 107, the Sunnyland, departing Kansas City, 1956. The journey to Birmingham would be a slow one, as this train made all stops.

The Great Northern's Empire Builder and the train to Vancouver, British Columbia, sit side by side at King Street Station, 1960. The Empire Builder still operates under the Amtrak banner.

railroad to the Pacific Northwest. Starting in St. Paul, the railroad stayed on the prairies and did not encounter any serious physical impediments other than rivers until western Montana.

Together with the Northern Pacific (NP), the GN owned the Burlington and the Spokane, Portland & Seattle (SP&S). These two carriers gave the GN and the NP access to Chicago to the east and Portland to the west. The GN and the NP also operated two of the finest passenger trains in the United States, the Empire Builder and the North Coast Limited.

The Northern Pacific was the first northern transcontinental railroad. It pushed west from St. Paul, Minnesota, and followed the twists and turns of the Yellowstone River in southern Montana. That alignment produced a scenic

railroad, but with the scenery came operational challenges, so the NP never matched the efficiency of the GN. The NP was a good railroad but not a great one—pretty much Basic Railroading 101. Like the GN, and in deference to a sparse online population, the NP's passenger services were modest. But the railroad did boast one of the handsomest streamliners of the era, the North Coast Limited.

As was the case in the other regions, the big players in the fifties were supported by a group of lesser lights, including the Rio Grande, the Western Pacific (WP), the Katy (Missouri-Kansas-Texas), the Frisco, and the Kansas City Southern (KCS). These smaller companies were swallowed up by the major carriers, with one exception: the Kansas City Southern, whose fascinating story will be discussed later in this chapter.

A westbound Northern Pacific freight leaves Easton, Washington, after waiting for the eastbound North Coast Limited to pass, 1960.

The North Coast Limited leaving
King Street Station, Seattle, 1960.

The Rio Grande and the WP provided competition for the UP/SP Overland Route and teamed up with the Burlington to operate the California Zephyr, one of the stars of the streamliner era. The Rio Grande was one of my favorites: the scenery was awesome, it had some neat passenger trains, and it even ran narrow-gauge trains into the 1960s. It had to hustle to stay in business, however, since the UP had a far better-engineered route. The "Grande" was nimble and produced one of the finest railroaders of the era, Alfred Perlman, who later became CEO of the troubled New York Central, and after the Penn Central debacle went on to save the Western Pacific.

Today, the Rio Grande is part of the Union Pacific and the through freight it once hosted now moves on the UP main line through Wyoming. But the former Denver & Rio Grande Western still hosts Amtrak's San Francisco Zephyr and numerous coal trains—and the scenery is still stunning, other than through Glenwood Canyon where Interstate 70 has spoiled the view. The Katy also deserves a mention. Besides being my favorite hometown (San Antonio) railroad, it managed to survive the dark days of the seventies thanks to some outstanding leadership. It ultimately became part of the Union Pacific but most of its main routes survive today.

Some midwestern railroads—the Burlington, the Rock Island, the Chicago & North Western, and the Milwaukee—reached into the West across the plains, but only the Milwaukee made it to the West Coast.

An eastbound Rio Grande merchandise train at Pine Cliff, Colorado, 1956.

One of the most famous trains of all time was the California Zephyr, the slower but more scenic alternative to the Overland Route's City of San Francisco, seen here in 1959. The Burlington, the Rio Grande, and the Western Pacific operated the train jointly, each providing cars for the endeavor.

The engines of the California Zephyr are fueled at Grand Junction, Colorado, 1959. To the right, a switch engine is dropping the two extra coaches that came from Denver; the load was lighter west of Grand Junction and the train consist was adjusted accordingly.

The Katy's Bluebonnet leaves New Braunfels, Texas,
1955, near the end of its run to San Antonio.

An empty Burlington Northern coal train just east of Alliance, Nebraska, 1985. As coal traffic exploded, routes serving the Powder River Basin received huge investments—in more track, heavier rail, and better signaling. But expanding capacity is yesterday's story because of the rapid decline in coal traffic in the PRB and elsewhere.

An empty Burlington Northern coal train descends Crawford Hill, Nebraska, 1986. One does not associate Nebraska with mountain railroading but this grade in the northwest corner of the state is a serious impediment to the movement of loaded coal trains. Stand up on the hill and you can see the trains coming for miles.

HERE COMES THE COAL

Government fiat created the greatest boom in railroad traffic since World War II. The Clean Air Act of 1970 and subsequent amendments mandated a substantial reduction in sulfur emissions from power plants. The utilities had a choice: install costly scrubbers or use low-sulfur coal. Many chose to shift to low-sulfur coal, and that decision created a whole new transportation market. Not all government regulatory actions have been harmful to railroads.

The most abundant supply of low-sulfur coal was in the Powder River Basin of Montana and Wyoming. The coal seams were thick, and many were close to the surface. This made low-cost strip mining possible, which meant the coal could be produced far more cheaply than coal from deep mines in Appalachia and elsewhere. But the coal wasn't perfect—its heat content was far less than that of Appalachian, Illinois Basin, Utah, and Colorado coal. And the Powder River Basin was a long way from most power plants. It was a market made to order for rail technology: a heavy-loading commodity moving long distances. But exploiting the potential was a huge challenge. The Powder River Basin was remote and thinly populated.

The PRB lay right on the Billings–Omaha line of the Burlington Northern (it was a former Burlington route). The BN line was, and always had been, a secondary main line, totally inadequate for heavy-loading cars and high-volume traffic. To move the coal, a few miles of new line had to be built. More significantly, many existing routes needed to be rebuilt from the ground up, with heavy rail, signals, and yards (which

A CNW train leaves the Powder River Basin, 1985.

Two Union Pacific coal trains pass on Logan Hill, Wyoming, 2009. These tracks are part of the joint line owned 50-50 by the Burlington Northern Santa Fe and the Union Pacific.

meant a great deal of work for routes like Wyoming to Texas and Wyoming to St. Paul or Omaha). More critically, the railroad would need people to operate the trains and maintain the track and equipment, no easy task in this sparsely populated part of the West. In addition, thousands of locomotives and cars were needed, since long-haul services, even those using efficient unit trains, require a lot of equipment.

Essentially, the BN had to create a whole new railroad. The cost would be huge. It was not an easy decision: while PRB coal looked like a good bet, the future market was far from assured. Lou Menk, then the CEO of the Burlington Northern, deserves credit for convincing the BN's board to bet the future of the railroad on PRB coal. The decision ranks right up there with the guts it took to build the first transcontinental railroads.

The BN wanted to keep the PRB coal market to itself, but that was not to be. A Chicago and North Western branch line to Lander, Wyoming, touched the south end of the basin; the line was built as part of a dream to expand the CNW to the Pacific. Using the regulatory process, and over the objections of the BN, the CNW gained the right to reach the south end of the PRB. The next challenge was to find the money needed. The CNW was a poor railroad and turned to the well-heeled Union Pacific for funding. Totally new rail lines were built, old rail lines were rebuilt, and rail competition came to the PRB. Rather than rebuild the CNW all the way west to its core at Council Bluffs, a connection was built to an existing UP line at South Morrill, Nebraska. Soon trains with combined UP and CNW power were plying the coalfields. Competition between the BNSF and the UP has been intense ever since.

The amount of tonnage moved has been monumental. Railroad ton-miles exploded: nationwide ton-miles went from 919 billion in 1980 to 1.713 trillion by 2009. Most of that growth was in the West, and most of the western growth was PRB coal. Consider this: in 1984, soon after the first PRB coal was moved, the BN's single-track line handled nineteen million tons. Now, a double-tracked and triple-tracked railroad— even four tracks on Logan Hill—handles more than three hundred million tons of coal a year (though volumes are now declining as natural gas is replacing coal in many markets).

All in all, bringing PRB coal to market was one of the great accomplishments in the entire history of railroading. The coal trains still grind up Logan Hill and will for a few more years to come.

A TSUNAMI OF NEW INTERMODAL TRAFFIC

Historically, intermodal traffic was the great shining city on the hill. There were all of those trucks on the highway, and if just some of them could be diverted to rail, life would be good. The first serious intermodal operation, the Pennsylvania Railroad's TrucTrain service, was inaugurated in 1954. (I wrote my Wharton thesis on this service in 1960, and declared intermodal to be the future of railroading.) In the 1960s and 1970s, intermodal was a high-growth business, one of the few growth markets in an otherwise declining industry. But if the growth rates were impressive, profits were not. It took a change in the marketplace (imports from Asia) and a change in technology (the double-stack car) to bring intermodal to its true potential. It was western railroading that nurtured these changes.

There were some very good intermodal operators in the 1960s, including the New York Central and the Santa Fe. But for other railroads, intermodal was a sideshow. The marketing folks wanted an intermodal product, but the operating people were indifferent and sometimes downright hostile. For them, intermodal was a new version of the passenger train,

An eastbound Santa Fe intermodal stack train east of Bealeville, California. The train is climbing the Tehachapi Mountains and will soon traverse the famous Tehachapi Loop.

requiring a lot of operating discipline—a lot of work for not much money.

The world changed when Asian imports began arriving, predominantly at West Coast ports. Ships disgorged huge volumes of containers at one time, and it was easy to build big trains for long-haul movements to the Midwest and beyond. As was the case with western coal, it was the kind of high-volume, long-haul traffic perfectly suited for rail technology.

All those containers on flatcars made for very long trains, which are difficult to operate: the longer the train, the longer it takes to navigate through speed restrictions such as curves, junctions, and towns. Enter the stack car, a creation of the Southern Pacific in cooperation with SeaLand (then a US water carrier, later absorbed by Maersk). The design was not a stretch; ships were already stacking containers both below and above decks. Initially, the stack car was a solution looking for a problem—when imports were a minor source of traffic,

why redo the entire network so you could operate stack cars? Think of all those bridges and tunnels that would have to be modified to accommodate a stack car! Fortunately for the SP, it had few clearance issues on its line from Los Angeles to the East.

Other railroads and other routes, especially in the East, needed a lot of improvements, but as international volumes grew, most routes reached a traffic density in which shifting to double-stack cars saved enough in operating costs to justify investment in clearance projects. As business grew, so did the stack train network. But investment costs were substantial and it was not an overnight revolution. As was the case with western coal (and concurrent with the investment needed to handle that traffic), billions of dollars would ultimately be spent to improve clearances, add more track capacity, build new terminals and expand old ones, and work on the cars themselves. Some thirty years after the first double-stack train crossed the

An eastbound Santa Fe intermodal train leaves Belen, New Mexico, 1993. Note the J. B. Hunt containers behind the locomotives.

A westbound Santa Fe intermodal train climbs Tehachapi just a short distance from the famous loop. Although Mike Haverty's greatest success as the Santa Fe's CEO was the contract with J. B. Hunt that provided a jump-start for domestic intermodal, the railfan community will remember him mostly for bringing back the Santa Fe's classic War Bonnet livery.

An eastbound Montana Rail Link train heads into Helena, Montana, 2004. This former main line of the Northern Pacific was spun off to a regional carrier but still functions as an integral part of the BNSF network for through freight traffic.

nation, the job is not quite done. A few routes, notably the CSX line between the Carolinas and Virginia to the Midwest, are still being upgraded to handle double-stack trains.

The double-stack car changed the future of railroading. More than any other factor, it was the technology that fueled the rail renaissance. But it took still another transformational event to achieve the full potential of intermodal shipping. If international shippers were sold on containerization, domestic shippers were not. A bold alliance between the premier intermodal carrier, Santa Fe, and the biggest truckload carrier, J. B. Hunt, was what made domestic intermodal a reality. Riding west from Chicago in a business car, Hunt and Santa Fe president Mike Haverty cut a deal to put Hunt's long-haul traffic on

the railroad. With that deal, domestic intermodal transportation came of age. Other truck lines and other railroads got on the bandwagon, and the rest, as they say, is history.

A virtuous cycle was created: as traffic increased, more terminals were built or expanded, and trains were added. As service improved, more traffic was diverted from the highway to the railroad, and with more traffic, service got even better. Now intermodal is the largest rail commodity by volume.

Given the rapid growth in traffic, the western rail network, at least the part west of the granger states, evolved far differently than networks in the Northeast and Southeast. Once rail lines reached the Rockies, construction costs were high and there was never as much overbuilding as occurred in other parts of the nation. All of the transcontinental rail lines are still in service today, with the exception of the Milwaukee Road's lines in Montana and points west and the former Rio Grande route over Tennessee Pass. The former never should have been built in the first place (it was too expensive), and the latter was rendered redundant when the UP acquired the SP and rerouted merchandise traffic to its superior route through Cheyenne, Wyoming. That said, there were still opportunities for rationalization. The major effort was that of the Burlington Northern, which leased part of the former NP main line to the Montana Rail Link in an effort to escape then-high labor costs. The MRL has been a successful enterprise partly because of the substantial growth in traffic. It is always easy to second-guess decisions, but I wonder if the BN would have done better just retaining this segment of main-line railroad. (I am sensitive to second-guessing because many of my decisions have been questioned over the years and some of them, frankly, were wrong.)

CREATING TWO BALANCED SYSTEMS

The West today is dominated by two major carriers—the Burlington Northern Santa Fe (renamed BNSF Railway in 2005) and the Union Pacific—and one outlier, the feisty Kansas City Southern. In the 1950s, it might have been expected that the Santa Fe and the Southern Pacific would be the anchors for today's rail structure. But it did not turn out that way.

The explanation lies in the ascendency of the Northern Lines (Great Northern, Northern Pacific, and the Burlington) with the formation of the Burlington Northern in the 1970s; the failure of the SP to leverage its once-dominant position; and the expansion of the Union Pacific. None of this was preordained, and the state of things today is the product of very smart decisions by some, and equally dumb choices by others.

I discussed the rise of the Burlington Northern in chapter 3. But once the Northern Line merger was done, its CEO, Louis Menk, bought his alma mater, the Frisco. It was a relatively minor addition but it did strengthen the BN in the Southwest where the BN had only a small presence—a single line from Colorado to the Texas Gulf Coast, via Fort Worth and Dallas.

The sprawling BN, stretching from Chicago to Seattle to the Gulf Coast at Houston, already had the attention of the "Lords of Omaha" (the sometimes arrogant Union Pacific management). The UP looked pretty puny when arrayed against a map of the BN. (In a UP conference room during this era, I saw a map of the BN on the wall—a not-so-subtle reality check for the UP folks.) But happily for the UP, its CEO was the very capable John C. Kenefick, formerly a protégé of Al Perlman at the New York Central. In 1978, the UP was at a crossroads; the UP board was more enamored with the energy business than with railroads. The SR was once again making a bid for the Missouri Pacific, and were it to succeed, one of the UP's best options would be off the table. Using the SR threat, Kenefick convinced a skeptical UP board that the railroad would die a slow death unless it expanded.

In one bold move, the UP cut a deal for both the Missouri Pacific and the Western Pacific. The merry mapmakers (and I was one) thought that the MP was a better fit with the Santa Fe and that the WP really ought to be tied to the Rio Grande and the Burlington. But money is what matters, not some theory of the perfect network. The UP had the necessary bucks and ambition and thus became the other big gorilla in the West. Kenefick's action put the SP and the Santa Fe on the defensive.

But the western story still had a lot of chapters left to play out. Clearly the system was unbalanced, but would the BN align with the SP or the Santa Fe? And where would the UP go next? Perhaps a true transcontinental merger would be created by aligning the SP or the Santa Fe with CSX, NS, or Conrail. (In fact, NS did take a hard look at both the SP and the Santa Fe.)

The Southern Pacific had chances to expand its network, but although it usually got the strategy right, it could not close the deal. Merge with the the Seaboard Coast Line's Family Lines? Sure, a brilliant move—but the SP's Benjamin Biaggini could not convince Prime Osborne of the Family Lines to go along. Create a better route from Los Angeles to St. Louis by using the Texas and Pacific east of El Paso? Good move, but the SP could not get that deal done, either. Buy the lower half of the Rock Island? That initiative got bogged down for ten years at the Interstate Commerce Commission. Concentrate on the markets where the SP had a clear advantage, such as traffic between the West and the Southeast? That would have been smart, but the SP seemed to have another vision. Based on the West Coast, it was focused on being the alternative to the Santa Fe between the West Coast and the Midwest. The Missouri Pacific, with no access to the West Coast, built a powerful franchise in the Gulf Coast while the SP let its Gulf Coast franchise languish.

Finally, in 1983, the SP reached out to its archrival and signed a merger agreement with the Santa Fe. That proposal was turned down by the ICC. The culprit was a memo by John Schmidt, then the Santa Fe's CEO. Looking at the map it was clear that the combination (SFSP) would dominate traffic to and from California. An internal memo by Schmidt, obtained through legal discovery, outlined how the SFSP could eliminate a competitor. (Schmidt, a lawyer, should have known better than to put his thoughts in writing.) Further, the companies started to paint locomotives (with a really, really bad paint scheme) in anticipation of the merger's approval. That did not sit well with the ICC, which was jealous of its prerogatives and resented the presumption that it would "rubber-stamp" the proposed merger.

Bottom line: the SP had plenty of opportunities but could not execute a deal (acquisition of the Tucumcari line was too little, too late). As its fortunes weakened, the SP fell prey to Phil Anschutz, who made his fortune in oil and gas. Anschutz already owned the small Rio Grande and now took on the much larger SP, retaining the Southern Pacific name. It was a case of a little railroad buying a much larger property, a move not unlike US Airways acquiring the much larger American Airlines and retaining the American brand. Anschutz moved to find value in the SP, focusing principally on selling substantial parts of its California network to public agencies. It was a liquidation strategy and ultimately the SP would have to find a well-heeled merger partner. Meanwhile the SP got weaker and weaker.

The Santa Fe started from a position of strength, but its efforts to expand came to naught. It looked at the Missouri Pacific—which would have been a dynamite merger and a great fit—but did not pursue that. Then it got involved in the ill-fated SFSP proposed consolidation, but when that failed, the SF had no backup strategy. (Until then, the ICC had been routinely approving rail mergers.) But the SF was still a solid franchise; it still had the premier route and the strongest intermodal franchise in the country, a position that was strengthened by its deal with J. B. Hunt.

Rob Krebs was number two at SFSP, and when that deal died, he took over as CEO of the Santa Fe alone. There was no room for both Krebs and Haverty at the Santa Fe, so Haverty

Two BNSF stack trains pass near Mesita, New Mexico, 2012. This former Santa Fe main line is the premier intermodal route in the world.

An empty eastbound BNSF coal train at Arvada, Wyoming, just west of Gillette, 2009. Here the tracks follow the Powder River.

A westbound Santa Fe intermodal train just east of Mojave, California, all decked out in the "Kodachrome" paint scheme chosen for the Santa Fe Southern Pacific. The Interstate Commerce Commission was not amused that the two railroads started repainting motive power and building connections assuming that the commission would approve the proposed merger.

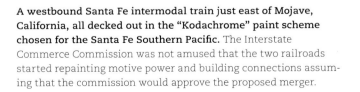

moved on and landed at the Kansas City Southern. Krebs was the driving force behind making the Santa Fe's transcontinental line (known as the Transcon), already a star, into something even better. The domestic intermodal boom started by Haverty would have overwhelmed the Transcon without the improvements that Krebs pushed through.

During all of this, the BN and the Santa Fe proposed to merge. (The BN had looked at the SP, but the deferred maintenance was too much for the BN to swallow.) The combination would have put the UP at a disadvantage, so it also made a bid for the Santa Fe. The BN countered the UP's bid and emerged the winner in the resulting bidding war. At least the UP action kept the BN from acquiring the SF on the cheap.

Blocked from one deal, the UP acquired the Chicago and North Western in 1995. Both railroads were already closely aligned. They had cooperated over the Omaha Gateway for decades and were partners in a joint service to the Powder River Basin. In a sense, UP-CNW simply formalized an existing alignment. It should have been an easy merger to implement, but the UP takeover of the CNW did not go well: service deteriorated because an arrogant UP simply did not listen to the folks running the CNW. The UP had always thought it was a cut above other railroads and often decided to do things "the UP way," ignoring any thought that it might just be wrong. This attitude was a harbinger of what was to come when it absorbed the SP. Hubris has gotten a number of railroad mergers off to a bad start.

With the Santa Fe now in the Burlington camp, the UP targeted the last large western railroad remaining: the Southern Pacific. (Both had been part of the Harriman empire before Teddy Roosevelt's trustbusters did their thing at the turn of the twentieth century—the first transcontinental railroad was made up of the UP and the SP.) But a UP-SP merger presented

a host of problems along the Gulf Coast. The two dominant railroads in that region had been the MP and the SP; putting both of them in one company was bound to create a backlash from the powerful chemical industry, a group long fearful of railroads having too much market power.

Or at least I thought so at the time. But after a speech to the Chemical Manufacturers' Association, I talked with many of the chemical logistics executives. They did not like the proposed merger but seemed unwilling to put much of an effort into the battle. This could have been an important piece of information for Conrail; it wanted to acquire the SP Gulf Coast franchise, but to accomplish that it needed the strong support of the chemical shippers.

The UP executed a brilliant strategy to counter opposition. First, it promoted the theme that the SP was a sick railroad that would likely become a western version of the Penn Central unless acquired by the UP. No regulator wanted another railroad crisis on their watch, and the SP was on course to implode. The UP and the BNSF then worked out a complicated package of line sales and trackage rights to solve the competitive issues. The UP's top planner, John Rebensdorf, deserves a round of applause for both this concept and its execution. The merger gained Surface Transportation Board (STB) approval, and with that the basic railroad structure seemed to be in place—or not, as we shall see.

The UP takeover of the SP in 1996 did not go well. The UP did not fully understand just how fragile the SP was. Changes in operations were made before the necessary infrastructure changes had been completed. The UP closed a key SP yard (Strang Yard, near Houston) and the network essentially melted down, starting with the lines in Texas and Louisiana but ultimately spreading elsewhere. Trains were parked all over the system waiting for locomotives and crews. Ultimately the

An eastbound Southern Pacific freight heading along the Arkansas River, bound for the Royal Gorge, 1990. This line over Tennessee Pass was the original main line of the Rio Grande, but after the SP was acquired by the UP this line was taken out of service.

An eastbound Union Pacific has climbed through Weber Canyon just east of Salt Lake City, Utah, 2009. This route is part of the first transcontinental railroad and when the UP acquired the SP, the route was finally united under one owner, a goal for over a century.

UP found enough resources to solve the problem, but 1996 and 1997 were ugly, ugly years for western railroading.

Mike Mohan, former vice president for operations at the SP and by then a consultant to NS in its effort to acquire part of Conrail, stormed into my office in Norfolk, pounded on my desk, and declared, "It's over."

"What is over?" I asked.

"They closed Strang Yard and the system will congeal."

How right he was! The SP had been held together with baling wire for years, relying on old hands in its Operating Department (think Mohan and Rollin Bredenberg) who knew just where you could tweak the system and where you could not. The UP did not have that knowledge and was unwilling to listen to the SP people, whom they saw as losers. Norfolk Southern would make the same mistake with its part of Conrail. Hubris is rarely a good thing.

As it turned out, the BNSF was not done; Rob Krebs had a vision of a transcontinental merger. In 1996, the BNSF approached NS. There were very hush-hush talks in Pittsburgh and NS took the proposal very seriously. But in the end, NS feared that a BNSF-NS merger would create a countermove by CSX-Conrail-UP. In such an outcome, BNSF-NS would have been the far weaker rail system. Norfolk Southern said no to the BNSF and continued with its goal of acquiring Conrail, setting up a dramatic fight with CSX for control of the East (see chapter 12).

CSX and NS eventually came to terms, and Conrail was split. In December 1999, just six months after the split, the BNSF and the Canadian National proposed to form North American Rail, a coast-to-coast reaching from Halifax to San Diego. The other four major players—CSX, NS, the UP, and the Canadian Pacific—rose up in outrage. In part citing the recent problems with implementing mergers (which could be laid at the doorsteps of the UP, CSX, and NS, a fact duly noted by BNSF-CN), these carriers argued that this was a deal too far. Ultimately, the STB, which had been blindsided by the proposal, ordered a fifteen-month moratorium on any major merger. The BNSF and the CN, after challenging the STB order in court and losing, called the whole thing off. Part of the failure was due to Krebs's failure to read the STB order and get NS on board. (He had called David Goode, the NS CEO, and told him to be patient, implying that NS would be included once the bigger deal was done.)

With that burst of activity, the merger scene quieted down. The next did not involve another railroad; rather, Berkshire Hathaway acquired all of the BNSF. After four decades of confusion, bankruptcies, liquidation (the Rock Island), and government takeover of the passenger business, the railroad industry had recovered and was now a desirable investment for one of the most astute financiers of our time. Warren Buffett's bet on the railroad industry created a halo effect for all railroads and a very good ending to our story. The rail renaissance had truly arrived.

THE RISE OF THE KANSAS CITY SOUTHERN

The most improbable of the western restructuring stories is that of the Kansas City Southern. The KCS had a limited route structure: Kansas City to the Gulf at New Orleans and Beaumont, with not much in between. Oddsmakers, including me, saw it being acquired by one of the other major carriers. But Mike Haverty proved, once again, that he was likely the cleverest railroad executive of his time—or at least the best poker player.

The "big six" all had broad market coverage and strong balance sheets, and the KCS would have been a welcome addition

It is rush hour at Bond, Colorado, 2004, as coal trains and a merchandise train vie for the use of a single-track main line. At Bond, the branch line to Craig, Colorado, diverges to reach coal mines near Craig. This former main line of the Rio Grande remains a busy coal railroad, though most of the merchandise traffic has been shifted to the lower-grade UP main line through Cheyenne, Wyoming. With the dramatic decline of coal, this main line of the former Denver & Rio Grande Western is now suffering.

for any of them. (I know for a fact that NS, the CN, and the CP all took a hard look at the KCS.) It seemed to be only a matter of time before someone made a move on the KCS. But it did not happen. Everyone knew that such a move would set off a war. At dinner one night in Fort Worth, the BNSF's CEO, Matt Rose, told me, "Don't cross the river," referring to the Mississippi. The KCS was too small to survive and too big to be ignored by the majors. What Haverty did was to sneak in between the big guys and create a freestanding system. To survive, the KCS had to be bigger.

The first move involved the MidSouth, a former Illinois Central line between Meridian, Mississippi (where it connected with NS), and Shreveport, the hub of the KCS system. The MidSouth looked good on the map but in fact it was a "bridge route to nowhere" unless the BNSF or the UP in the West and NS in the East could be convinced to short-haul themselves. Years later, the UP and NS decided to do exactly that: they created a great intermodal service route between the West Coast and the Southeast using the KCS line. Norfolk Southern poured millions into the infrastructure, creating a short route between Los Angeles and the Southeast that bypassed congestion at both Memphis and New Orleans.

The KCS also picked up the Gateway Western, another former IC line, which gave it a route to St. Louis. But both the Gateway Western and the MidSouth deals were overshadowed by the KCS's next move. In 1996, it bet the farm on Mexico. When that country decided to privatize its creaky freight rail network, the UP thought that winning the franchise for the Laredo-to-Mexico main line would be a slam dunk. After all, the Missouri Pacific had been the preferred connection to the Laredo gateway for decades. (Through passenger cars from Mexico City rolled through San Antonio on the Aztec Eagle when I was in high school there.)

But the KCS took on a load of debt and bid the price so high that even the UP had second thoughts. Although the KCS won the bidding, it still had a problem: the KCS did not actually reach Laredo. Its next moves were truly creative. It rebuilt portions of an abandoned SP line south of Houston. Using a Federal Railroad Administration loan, it bought and rebuilt the small Texas-Mexico Railroad to connect Corpus Christi and Laredo. It then connected these pieces with trackage rights until it had a line from its Mexican subsidiary (which is now KCS de Mexico) to its core system at Beaumont. On the map it looks like the wanderings of a drunk trying to find his way home—but it works.

The importance of KCS de Mexico to the KCS franchise cannot be overstated. It used its ability to originate and terminate traffic in Mexico to feed traffic to the rest of the KCS system. Many in the railroad business, including me, never thought Haverty could pull it off. Even the trackage rights it obtained north of Kansas City suddenly made sense, once it created an anchor in Mexico (Mexico imports a lot of US grain). The disparate pieces work, thanks to the strength of the Mexico franchise.

COPING WITH GROWTH ONCE AGAIN

The West, with its coal and long-haul intermodal traffic, was the engine of growth for the rail renaissance. Intermodal remains a solid bet for the future, but coal is under huge pressure. It looked as though hydraulic fracking, which has made the United States a powerful player in oil and gas production, would bring huge increases in rail traffic, focused on the rail lines connecting North Dakota to markets on both the East and the West Coast. But as this is written, oil prices have collapsed and some predict that in the future, production of US

The Kansas City Southern's executive train rests between assignments at Shreveport, Louisiana, 2007. The paint scheme goes back to the KCS's steamliner era and has been applied to newer freight power as well.

The Kansas City Southern day train to New Orleans is ready to depart Kansas City, 1955. The KCS was one of the few railroads around in the 1950s that would survive into the twenty-first century.

Three BNSF intermodal trains wait to head east near Fargo, North Dakota, 2014. A huge surge in crude oil and grain traffic led to severe congestion on the former Great Northern main line. A major investment in double track was underway in 2014 and 2015, but with the collapse of oil prices much of this investment will no longer be needed.

oil will grow slowly if at all. Meanwhile, the BNSF has been on a spending spree on the former Great Northern main line. Whether some of this will ultimately be a stranded investment is unknown, but it does underscore how technology and a worldwide economy can make railroad investment a somewhat risky proposition.

But the whole story of crude-by-rail underscores the financial strength of the industry. The BNSF has made a large bet on the future of crude-by-rail, but even if the growth of hydraulic fracking moderates, the railroad will survive quite nicely on other sources of traffic. We have come a long way from the capital-starved era when the BN literally bet the railroad on the future of Powder River coal. With a fast-changing global economy, risk taking is part of the game; fortunately railroads now have the balance sheets and the networks needed to take those risks and a management attitude willing to bet big on the future. Stranded assets, sure. But no stranded companies needing a government bailout. It is a far cry from the risk-averse, hunker-down mentality that existed when I joined the industry.

BNSF trains passing in Kingman Canyon, Arizona, 2011. This
is one of the more scenic locations on the Transcon.

An eastbound Canadian Pacific intermodal stack train at Three Valley Gap, British Columbia, 2005. The CP's crossing of the Selkirk Range is one of the great mountain railroads in the world.

CANADA

How a sleepy government-owned railroad achieved the best operating ratio in North America, and the once-majestic Canadian Pacific was sliced and diced as it sought to catch its rival.

VANTAGE POINT

Canadian railroading seemed remote and exotic when I was growing up in Texas. Perhaps it was the idea of running trains in the snow, something that was not part of the South Texas scene. Perhaps it was simply because Canada was a "foreign" country at a time when I had never been out of the United States other than on minor incursions into Mexico.

Certainly David Morgan's articles in *Trains* magazine, with photographs by Phil Hastings, had an influence. Morgan's accounts of riding up the St. Lawrence behind steam in winter remain one of my most vivid images of steam and snow. I wonder how many people Morgan lured into railroading with his priceless prose. After that, all it took was a single morning watching trains at Montreal in 1961 to make me a lifelong fan of Canadian railroading. I have returned time and time again, especially to the Maritimes and to western Canada. Along

the way I have ridden virtually all of the main-line network on passenger trains, executive trains, freight trains, locomotives—even a snowplow. Now, riding Via Rail's Canadian in winter is an annual event for me. Professionally, I worked with the Canadian Pacific on several joint ventures, and in my rail merger job at Norfolk Southern I took a hard look at both the Canadian National and the Canadian Pacific as potential merger partners.

SIXTY YEARS OF CHANGE

The Canadian railway story is easier to tell than that of the United States. There were two major railways in 1950 and there are two major railways today. Though the Canadian railroads have generally been a few years behind their US counterparts (at least until recently), Canadian railroad history has followed a similar pattern. Canadian railroads shed passenger trains, eliminated a lot of the light-density lines, experienced deregulation, embraced the two-man crew and technology, and expanded their market reach by acquiring other railroads, mostly in the United States. The most remarkable shift in

Canadian Pacific commuter trains at Windsor Station, Montreal, Quebec, 1961. This was my first view of Canadian railroading and I was hooked for life.

Left, **the Atlantic Limited arriving at Montreal's Windsor Station after an overnight journey from St. John's, New Brunswick, 1961.** Some years later, the CP withdrew its operations from the Maritime Provinces; some lines were transferred to regional operators and others were abandoned outright.

Below left, **the Canadian Pacific shield mounted on the cab of restored Hudson number 2816, 2007.** In 1950 when our story begins, the 2816 was hauling fast passenger trains and the CP was not just a railroad: it operated an airline, a steamship company, hotels, and telecommunications services. It did, in fact, provide transportation service around the world. Shields similar to this one adorned the cabs of CP passenger engines in the steam era.

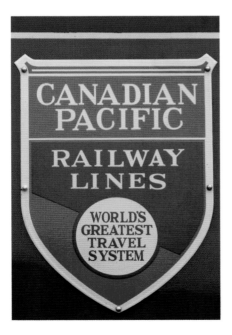

Canadian railroading is that the premier Canadian railway in 1950, the Canadian Pacific, is now playing catch-up to the often-ridiculed Canadian National.

THE VIEW FROM 1950

In 1950, the Canadian Pacific was one of the premier transportation companies in the world. It boldly claimed to be the "World's Greatest Travel System." The CP operated hotels, an airline, steamships to both Europe and Asia, and a sprawling transcontinental railroad, something the United States does not have to this day. The railroad was elegant. Along with the Hudson Bay Company, it was the enterprise that built Canada. The CP even made its way into the United States in parts of New England, and its majority interest in the Soo Line gave it access to the Twin Cities and Chicago.

The westbound CP Canadian along the Bow River west of Banff, Alberta, 1965. The Canadian was the next-to-last streamliner built; soon after it was placed in service the CP became disenchanted with passenger service. Via Rail's Canadian now uses the equipment, though the route has been shifted from the CP to the Canadian National.

A northbound Canadian Pacific freight north of Wells River, Vermont, 1962. The CP reached south of Newport, Vermont, to connect with the Maine Central, the Boston & Maine, and the St. Johnsbury & Lamoille County Railroad. Locomotives built by Montreal Locomotive Works, the Canadian subsidiary of American Locomotive, were doing the heavy lifting.

It had extensive passenger operations; its premier train was the Canadian, the next-to-last Budd dome streamliner built. Supplementing that train was an expansive network of local services, many operated with rail diesel cars.

The Canadian National was huge by any standard—with twenty-four thousand route-miles it was substantially longer than the CP or any US railroad at the time. If the CP was sprawling, then the CN was sprawling on steroids. The CN stretched from Newfoundland (a narrow-gauge system, no less) all the way to Vancouver and Prince Rupert, British Columbia. Like the CP's, its lines extended into the United States to Portland, Maine; New London, Connecticut; Duluth, Minnesota; and, most importantly, Detroit and Chicago. All of these routes were owned by the CN but most were managed locally. The Canadian National operated an extensive passenger train network, but its best trains, the Continental and the Super Continental, were not as good as the CP's Canadian. However, there were CN trains everywhere, including Newfoundland and Prince Edward Island. Where a pure passenger train could not be justified, there was often mixed train service: a freight train carrying one or more passenger cars.

The CN operated a high-density corridor (at least for Canada) between Quebec-Montreal-Toronto and Sarnia. That route is now the centerpiece of Via Rail's franchise and it continues to be improved in terms of both capacity and service frequency. In fact, the line is one of the few places in North America where 100 mph passenger trains commingle with a high-density freight line.

Like the CP, the CN was a diversified company that operated ferries, coastwise steamships, hotels, a telegraph service, and an airline. Most of these services were supplemental to its rail operations. Such diversification was common

A southbound Central of Vermont freight train near White River Junction, Vermont, 1963. Owned by the Canadian National, the CV linked St. Albans, Vermont, and New London, Connecticut. While the CN has long since shed ownership, the line is still in service and hosts a daily Amtrak service.

A Canadian National corridor train for Toronto leaves Montreal's Central Station behind Montreal Locomotive Works power, 1961. The engines sport the old CN paint scheme and the passenger cars are in the new livery of off-white and black.

A CN train inbound to Central Station behind Fairbanks-Morse power, 1960. The locomotives sport the new paint scheme, which is still in use by the CN. After the Union Pacific, the CN sports the longest-lived paint scheme of any major railroad.

An eastbound Via Rail corridor train near Belleville, Ontario, as seen from a westbound intermodal train, 2006. Via Rail now operates a good corridor service linking Quebec, Montreal, Ottawa, Toronto, and Sarnia. Via still operates some long-haul trains but they are an endangered species.

on many North American railroads in the era when railroads dominated transportation, and in many cases these services lingered on long after the rail monopoly was gone. (The New Haven and the Southern Pacific, for example, owned interurban lines.) Also, the CN was a crown, or government-owned, corporation. When several major railroads failed in the late 1910s and early 1920s (notably the Grand Trunk Pacific and the Canadian Northern), the government acquired them and operated them under the CN name. In the 1950s, CN was still owned by the government—and would be for decades to come.

The CN was better-engineered than the CP: there was double track on the Montreal–Toronto corridor, and the CN crossed the Rockies at Yellowhead Pass, the lowest railway crossing of the Rockies in North America. (The CP made a deliberate decision to take a more rugged route closer to the US border; it wanted to block US railroads from incursions into Canadian markets.) In the 1950s and beyond, the CN would be best described as top-heavy and bureaucratic. Its trains wore a green-and-yellow livery that was pedestrian in contrast to the CP's more elegant gray and maroon.

In the 1950s and 1960s, there were also several important regional railroads, including the British Columbia Railroad (BCOL) and the Ontario Northland. The British Columbia merits a few more words. The southern end of the railroad (from North Vancouver to the Fraser River Canyon just north of Lillooet) ranks as one of the most spectacular rail routes in the world. But that magnificent scenery creates huge operating headaches. Since the CN bought the railroad in 2004, much of the traffic has taken a shorter, less arduous route east, using the CN's Prince Rupert line east of Prince George, British Columbia.

A westbound CN freight just east of Jasper, Alberta, 1965. The lead unit is in the old paint scheme.

A southbound British Columbia Railway train south of Lillooet, British Columbia, 1970. The BCOL was owned by the province of British Columbia until it was sold to the Canadian National. Now most of its traffic takes a turn east at Prince George and uses the CN line to reach eastern markets.

A westbound Canadian Pacific freight train at McAdam, New Brunswick, 1968. This line is now operated by a regional carrier, since the CP has exited all markets east of Montreal.

DOWNSIZING

Both Canadian railroads operated extensive feeder line networks. These lines blanketed the Prairie Provinces where construction was cheap and grain was the game, with elevators every ten miles or so. It was a gathering system based on farmers being able to bring their grain to a local elevator located a short distance from their farm. From there, the traffic moved over branch lines in light-loading boxcars for the rail haul. It

was inefficient railroading at its worst: costs were high and rates were low. (The infamous Crow's Nest Pass rates capped what the railroads could charge.) The resulting deficits were substantial and mounting. In railroading, you ignore infrastructure costs at your own peril, but that has been a common mistake over the decades.

The introduction of larger cars and the gradual elimination of the Crow's Nest Pass rates led to a massive change in grain transportation. Highways assumed the dominant role

The eastbound Continental at Jasper, Alberta, 1970. The CN was pro–passenger train for a brief period in the late 1960s. It proved that riders could be attracted with aggressive pricing and advertising, but profits did not follow.

The westbound Continental just east of Jasper, 1970. The full-length dome car was acquired from the Milwaukee Road. To grow its business the CN acquired cars from US carriers that were exiting the passenger business.

An eastbound Via Rail Canadian at Winnipeg, 1990. When Via Rail assumed control of passenger services, it still ran a daily service on both the CN route (the Continental) and the CP route (the Canadian). Subsequently, the Canadian was shifted to the CN and service was reduced to triweekly (biweekly in the winter).

The Canadian on the CP route near Lake Louise, 1990. This consist in the dead of winter was typical of off-season operations. Although the Canadian no longer operates on the scenic CP route, there is summer service provided by a heavily used tourist train, the Rocky Mountaineer.

A westbound CP intermodal train descends the grade from the Spiral Tunnels into Field, British Columbia, 2009. This crossing of the Rockies is dramatic but the Selkirks, farther west, are a greater challenge because of extremely heavy snowfall. It is hard, hard railroading. The CN's crossing is far more efficient but not as scenic.

for the gathering function, and the railroads introduced the hundred-ton car to improve rail efficiency. As was the case in the midwestern United States, many of the prairie branch lines could not accommodate the heavy cars, and much of that network was subsequently abandoned.

Other low-volume lines in areas such as the Maritimes suffered a similar downsizing. The Canadian Pacific was especially aggressive in its retreat west; Montreal became the eastern terminus of the CP as it exited St. John, New Brunswick, and Quebec City. The CN's rail networks on Newfoundland and Prince Edward Island were also abandoned.

FOCUSING ON RAIL FREIGHT

There are two major reasons to shed a line of business: it is unprofitable and shows no prospect of ever being profitable, or it no longer fits a company's strategic business plan. The Canadian Pacific became disenchanted with its money-losing passenger trains by the early 1960s and systematically pruned its network. In 1978 its remaining trains were transferred to Via Rail Canada, the Canadian version of Amtrak. (Amtrak preceded Via Rail by seven years.) While the CP was cutting passenger trains, the CN was increasing its passenger services. In the 1960s it revamped its passenger marketing, bought new corridor trains (with new equipment such as TurboTrains and Tempos), and expanded its long-haul services using equipment made surplus by US railroads. Coupled with aggressive pricing, those changes led to an increase in ridership, but profitability proved elusive. Finally, after a valiant effort, the CN threw in the towel and also joined Via Rail in 1978. Today, virtually all Canadian intercity passenger trains operate over CN tracks or tracks owned by government entities.

FOCUSING ON THE RAILROAD

As noted above, back when railways were growing, diversification into related lines of business was common. Hotels fed traffic to passenger trains, and ferries and coastwise ships extended the market reach of the rail network. But as profits declined, the two Canadian railroads began to shift nonrail activities to separate profit centers, and ultimately shed them altogether. The CN sold its hotels to the CP, its ferry operations became CN Maritime, telecommunications subsidiaries were merged with those of the CP, and so on.

In 1968 the Canadian Pacific, in a major revamping, separated its nonrailroad assets into CP Air, CP Ships, CP Hotels, and Fording Coal. All were run as separate entities and pursued business strategies unique to their individual markets. CP Hotels, for example, acquired the US-based Fairmont chain and retained that name. All of this corporate reengineering ultimately led to divestiture; in 2001, the holding company spun off these companies to shareholders, leaving a "pure" railroad. It was a dramatic change for a company that once billed itself as the "World's Greatest Travel System."

The CP refocused its rail operations as well, moving its headquarters to Calgary to better manage a slimmed-down railroad geared toward natural resource traffic (coal, grain, and potash) and intermodal traffic. But the CP seemed to be ambivalent about the direction of its railroad business, and contraction was followed by expansion.

PRIVATIZING THE CN

For all US railroads, the 1980s were a time for downsizing the workforce, especially the executive ranks. The Canadian

National came late to that effort, but when the decision was made to privatize the CN, Paul Tellier, its CEO and a former top civil servant, tackled the railroad's bloated head count. Thousands of jobs were eliminated. When asked how he felt about eliminating fifteen thousand jobs, Tellier responded that he was proud to have saved twenty-five thousand jobs. Not only was the workforce reduced, but the line rationalization efforts, already underway, were accelerated.

But Tellier is only part of the CN turnaround story. When the CN acquired the Illinois Central in 1998, the IC's CEO, Hunter Harrison, became the chief operating officer of the CN (some say the CN bought the IC just to get Harrison). His forte was efficient operations, executed—and that is the right word—at a fast and furious pace. Managers who could not make the transition were soon gone. Hump yards were closed, locomotive utilization was vastly improved, remote-controlled yard switchers were deployed, and the network was trimmed by sharing track with the Canadian Pacific. For example, in one of the longest joint operations in North America, the CP and the CN essentially merged their main lines west of Kamloops, British Columbia, all the way to the Vancouver area. Westbound trains use the CN line and eastbound trains the CP line. A double-track railroad was created; no longer would trains have to wait in sidings to meet a train going in the opposite direction. These and other changes led those inside the company to declare that they were either "the hunter or the hunted," so relentless was Harrison's focus on eliminating inefficiency. Under the regime of Tellier and Harrison (who ascended to the CEO position in 2003), the CN became the most efficient railroad in North America, measured by the ratio of operating expenses to revenue, or OR. (While there are other ways to measure efficiency, the OR is the most recognized measure.) The privatization of the CN was a textbook case on how to successfully move a stodgy government-owned entity into the private sector.

In the meantime, the CP was making progress in streamlining its system. In fact, it went too far, withdrawing from much of its carload franchise. At the same time, it made a huge strategic bet on the future of bulk traffic in western Canada by building a second tunnel through the Selkirk Mountains. The Mount MacDonald Tunnel is the longest rail tunnel in the Americas; building it in the middle of a national park was an incredible feat, given environmental concerns.

The CP's overhead costs were reduced and operating efficiency improved, but at a more leisurely pace than at the CN. In the end, the CP fell behind its rival in efficiency, profitability, and market reach. It was a dramatic change in positions; for decades the CP management had considered the CP far superior to its government-owned rival.

EXPANDING THE NETWORK

The Canadian story, like that of the US railroads, was a mixture of contraction and expansion as old markets were shed and new markets developed. The need to expand was never as great in Canada as in the United States because both carriers went to all the important markets in Canada, and both had access to the key US market of Chicago. (Neither risked being totally marginalized by the action of a competitor, as was the case for CSX when Norfolk Southern moved to take all of Conrail, or for NS when CSX proposed to do the same). Still, there were opportunities to upgrade each network. The CP acquired the bankrupt Milwaukee Road in 1985, thereby

Above, **An eastbound CN train in the Fraser River Canyon near Spences Bridge, 2008.** The canyon is an operating nightmare because of slides. The CN and the CP used to operate separate lines but now run directionally—west on the CN and east on the CP.

Facing, **Changing crews at Lillooet, British Columbia, 1970.** The British Columbia Railway is now part of the Canadian National, and freight traffic has been largely rerouted through Prince George, British Columbia. Now scenes such as this no longer occur, thanks to the use of two-person crews.

MY LIFE WITH TRAINS

improving its Chicago access from western Canada as well as gaining access to Kansas City.

In 1991 it acquired the Delaware & Hudson, one of the weakest of the northeastern US rail franchises. The D&H looked good on a map, reaching such markets as New York and Philadelphia, but it had only very limited access to industry in those markets. Always dependent on overhead traffic (it called itself the "Bridge Route" for a reason), it resumed that historical role in 1999 when Norfolk Southern acquired over half of Conrail: NS used the CP (the D&H) to access New England, just as the Pennsylvania Railroad had done decades before. Norfolk Southern finished this "back to the future" transition by acquiring the southern half of the former Delaware & Hudson from the CP in 2015. In essence, the CP shed its low-volume, underperforming network in eastern Canada, and then turned right around and acquired a low-volume, underperforming network in the northeastern United States, which it has now largely divested. Go figure!

The CP's acquisitions also included the Dakota, Minnesota & Eastern (DM&E) and the Iowa, Chicago & Eastern (ICE), in 2000. The price it paid exceeded any realistic value for these properties, however, and the western portion of the DM&E has now been divested yet again to another newly formed regional carrier, in a railroad version of musical chairs. Throughout this period, the CP seemed to lack a cohesive vision for its network.

By contrast, the CN's expansion program has been very focused. It strengthened its access to Chicago from Ontario by replacing the old tunnel at Sarnia, Ontario, with a new tunnel that could accommodate domestic double-stack equipment. (The CP parallel route through Detroit could accommodate only the smaller international double-stack containers.) And it expanded in Canada, with the acquisition of

the British Columbia Railway in 2004. But its most aggressive actions have pushed it south into the United States. The CN had historically reached into US markets, reaching Chicago via Sarnia with its Grand Trunk Western, and New London, Connecticut, with its Central of Vermont subsidiary. Its next move, the acquisition of the Illinois Central in 1998, expanded it all the way to the Gulf of Mexico. The slimmed-down IC was rich in chemical, coal, and grain traffic. The former IC lines to Des Moines and Waterloo were added to the mix as well. The expanded CN was now shaped like a *Y*, serving major ports on the Atlantic (Halifax), the Pacific (Prince Rupert, Vancouver), and the Gulf (New Orleans, Mobile).

The next challenge for the CN was to connect the western part of its railroad with the IC. In 2001, the CN acquired the Wisconsin Central, a regional railroad created when the CP had spun off lines of its Soo subsidiary some years earlier. The last gaps were closed with the 2011 acquisition of the Duluth, Missabe & Iron Range (DM&IR) and, a year later, the Elgin, Joliet & Eastern (EJ&E). Now the CN controlled the entire route between the CN in western Canada and the former IC line. Like many operating people, Hunter Harrison wanted his own railroad so he could avoid depending on the kindness of strangers.

TWEAKING THE CN, REMAKING THE CP

By any measure, the CN has an efficient route structure, a diverse traffic base, and a highly efficient operation. Today, it is building on that base, adding capacity to a network that reaches capacity whenever the weather turns ugly (which is most winters). It is also reaching out to the government and to customers in a more open manner—an area where Harrison paid less attention than he should have.

The CP has a more difficult road ahead. It is undergoing an extreme makeover led by Harrison, who, after retiring from the CN, could not resist the chance to work his magic one more time. Hump yards have been closed, hundreds of loco-motive units have been stored, and thousands of employees have been cut from the roster. It is a repeat of his performance at the CN. Investors, believing that lightning can strike twice, have bid CP stock up accordingly. But the outcome is hardly a slam dunk, as the CP is inherently a weaker system and one without nearly as much fat as the CN had. Further, it needs investment in some of its long-neglected core routes, such as the line from Winnipeg to St. Paul. The new management team knows this and is addressing the capacity issues. The CP has also resolved its uncertainty about the Delaware & Hudson—it will keep the line from Montreal to Albany that provides a route for crude-by-rail moving to river transload operations at Albany. It sold the railroad south of Albany to Norfolk Southern, the majority user of this part of the former D&H. It is a good move for both NS and the CP.

Running a railroad in today's uncertain economy is like a game of whack-a-mole.

There is simply no stability in major markets. Spend millions to handle a growing crude-by-rail business, and wham! The oil market collapses, leaving a lot of stranded assets. Gear up for more Asian imports—just as that market cools off. But the Canadian roads are now efficient and have both the balance sheets and the management skills to adjust.

A Canadian Pacific local freight south of Golden, British Columbia, 2008.
This is the line that serves the coalfields, though there is some merchandise business, as is seen here. The SD-40s had been the CP's core mainline power for decades until the AC locomotives arrived on the scene.

PART II. RAILROADER

The Tennessean behind E units cruises through Burke, Virginia, 1960.

LOOK AHEAD, LOOK SOUTH

My first job as a railroader was on the dynamic Southern Railway, led by the brilliant but autocratic Bill Brosnan. The SR was decades ahead of its rail competitors in marketing and operations.

REPORTING FOR DUTY

"Good morning, Mr. McClellan. Welcome to the Southern Railway." The guard, Mickey Hayhurst, greeted me as I walked in the door. It was November 1, 1963, and my very first day as a railroader.

Getting here had been difficult. Though I had graduated near the top of my undergraduate class at Wharton, railroads were focused on hiring people with engineering or finance backgrounds; my transportation economics degree was a bit too abstract for their perceived needs. Letters to the Chesapeake & Ohio and the Norfolk & Western brought instant and negative responses. Sensing a problem, I cobbled together a trip around the country, stopping at railroad headquarters in St. Louis, Denver, and San Francisco, hoping a face-to-face meeting with potential employers might improve my chances. Of course, it was also a chance to take a transcontinental train trip with my wife.

While on the California Zephyr west of Grand Junction, Colorado, I got a telegram out of the blue, demanding (and that was the right word) that I call Mr. Hamilton of the Southern Railway as soon as possible. I had never met Bob Hamilton, the SR's new assistant vice president of marketing and an industrial engineer from General Motors and the New York Central. I had previously interviewed with the Southern's John Ingram, its new director of costing, who reported to Hamilton. Ingram asked a lot of questions, but when I left, my feeling was that the SR was looking for experienced hands, not a novice just out of the Navy. So the telegram was a complete surprise.

After a night in a tiny, tiny room at the YMCA, Joanne and I went down to the waterfront to discuss our future. We both loved San Francisco, but I had a gut feeling that Hamilton was going to offer me a job. So it just might come down to living in the East or in the West, a major fork in the road. I made the call to Hamilton, whose offer was too good to refuse. I canceled an interview with the Southern Pacific that same afternoon and, despite my western roots, spent the rest of my railroad career in the East.

View from the second dome of the westbound California Zephyr near Bond, Colorado, 1962. A few hours later, west of Grand Junction, I got a telegram that led to my being hired by the Southern.

The Southern's general offices were located at 15th and K Streets, in Washington, DC, only a few blocks from the White House. The elegant headquarters building still had elevator operators, elderly black women with white gloves. It reeked of tradition. That I was greeted by name was another SR tradition; it sweated the little things like no other railroad.

I rode the private elevator to the executive floors and reported for duty in the newly created Market Research Department. I was officially a railroader, fulfilling a lifelong ambition. Market Research was part of a new marketing department, an effort by SR president Bill Brosnan to bring innovation to the commercial side of the SR. Headed by Bob Hamilton, it was one of the few marketing departments in the entire railroad industry. His two key managers were John Ingram (later to be

the head of the Federal Railroad Administration and CEO of the Rock Island), who headed the costing department, and Harvard-educated PhD Paul Banner, who headed Market Research. Jim Hagen, a man who would loom large in the history of railroading as well as my career, would soon join them. These men became my early mentors. I could not have been luckier; all were dedicated to the notion that railroads were going to have to change if they were to survive. Our paths would continue to cross many, many times.

Change was the name of the game. The Southern came out of World War II as a marginal property. It had no modern steam locomotives on its roster; its main-line operations relied on power designed during World War I, when railroads were under government control. Though inefficient, some were

A northbound mail and express train at Alexandria, Virginia, 1964. It was mail and express traffic that sustained the SR's extensive passenger network.

among the handsomest engines ever built. (The only survivor is in the Smithsonian's National Museum of American History.) No other large railroad's steam fleet was as antiquated.

The SR's infrastructure was circa the 1920s, with hundred-pound rail on many main lines and much lighter rail on its sprawling network of branch lines. It was, from a cultural standpoint, a genteel company—but think Virginia, not the Deep South. Never an innovator, it had a diverse traffic base, but much of its business was rooted in agriculture, paper, and paper products.

Its passenger operations were extensive but hardly cutting-edge. It operated only four streamliners: the Royal Palm

Signals at Burke, Virginia, 1965. The double-track main line from Washington to Atlanta was replaced with traffic control and long passing tracks with a crossover in the middle, a higher-capacity and more flexible configuration than double track with directional operations only.

(Cincinnati–Jacksonville, with connections to the Midwest and Florida), the Crescent (Washington–Atlanta–New Orleans, on the West Point Route and the Louisville & Nashville beyond Atlanta), the Southerner (Washington–New Orleans via Birmingham), and the Tennessean (Washington–Memphis via Bristol and Knoxville). The rest of the network relied mostly on heavyweight equipment, though many of the cars had been modernized. All but one of its sleeping cars were streamlined, however. Mail and express were also a huge part of the passenger franchise. On many routes, passenger trains outnumbered freight trains; for example, between Washington and Lynchburg (where some trains diverged to the Norfolk & Western, rejoining the SR tracks at Bristol, Tennessee),

there were nine passenger round trips (one was mail and express only), compared to just three through freight round trips a day.

This once-sleepy railroad was undergoing massive change when I arrived. Brosnan was now in charge. Earlier, as operating vice president under the progressive Harry DeButts, Brosnan had led one of the most extreme makeovers ever seen in the railroad business. First, the SR dieselized. Most railroads were doing the same thing, but the SR beat the crowd as the first large railroad to eliminate its ancient, inefficient steam fleet, with enormous gains in productivity. (Its future merger partner, the Norfolk & Western, would be the last to do so.)

Left, **An SR intermodal crane, 1965.** The Southern was a leader in containerization; it was a lift-on, lift-off system, and the SR had to build its own cranes because there was no commercial builder of intermodal cranes. Double stacking of containers came decades later.

Facing, **The Carolina Special descends Saluda Grade, 1964.** Saluda is the steepest main-line grade in North America, at 4.7 percent. During my first tour at the SR, I managed to ride all of the passenger routes except for Chattanooga to Memphis (a segment of the railroad I still have not ridden).

The infrastructure was being modernized as well—lines that had been double tracked with light rail became single track (but with long segments of double track to assure a fluid operation) with traffic control, and were laid with 132-pound welded rail. The maintenance-of-way function was mechanized, with much of its equipment designed and built by the SR itself. In the actual running of trains, the SR used modern, automated classification yards and long, long trains (often with remote, distributed power) in the quest for efficiency. Both are common today, but that was not the case in the early sixties. The SR not only possessed cutting-edge technology, but applied that technology on a massive scale.

There was innovation on the commercial side as well. The SR introduced unit coal trains with aluminum cars, the very first true unit train run in North America. Its most celebrated commercial effort was "Big John," an aluminum-covered hopper car that could transport one hundred tons of grain. With Big John, the SR could slash grain rates and go head-to-head with the river system that penetrated much of the Southeast. The lower rates proposed by the SR were opposed by barge lines, grain shippers, and other railroads. Why would the grain companies oppose lower rail rates? Well, grain prices included transportation to the destination; the grain companies added in the higher rail rate to determine the delivered price of the grain. Grain companies often used lower-cost barge transport for shipping and pocketed the difference. Other railroads felt that their short-haul grain traffic (including movements from the river to the customer) would be in jeopardy. It sounds

crazy today, but that was how regulation worked: it was hard to raise *or* lower rates without challenges from vested interests. Only a determined and patient management could buck the system. Innovation took guts—and years of litigation and two trips to the Supreme Court—before the SR was allowed to publish the lower rates.

Containerization is now the standard method of handling intermodal traffic. But in 1962, intermodal itself was relatively new, and the technology was primitive. Most railroads were simply trying to replicate their carload network using trailers with circus-style loading (the trailers were backed onto a string of flatcars using a ramp at one end of the string), a practice that combined poor efficiency with poor service. The SR opted for containers—and since no one was building lift-on, lift-off cranes, the SR built its own. But this initiative came to naught: other railroads stayed with trailers, and because in those days so much intermodal traffic moved in interline service, SR had to go with the flow. Today, of course, containers are the dominant means of handling intermodal traffic.

LIFE AS A MARKETING TRAINEE

On most railroads, the commercial function was lodged in the traffic department, rather than in a marketing department like the SR's. Competition was limited, since railroads had antitrust immunity to make rates jointly. They met regularly at rate bureaus to set rates, which then had to pass regulatory muster if challenged. So the commercial focus was on convincing customers to route on your railroad for the longest possible distance: effectively, the Santa Fe's slogan—"Santa Fe All the Way"—was its core commercial strategy. For the Santa Fe and most other railroads, selling was the name of the game, and customer relations were extensive and deep.

At the Southern, the Market Research Department, using research and direct customer interviews, was charged with understanding individual customers' needs and then developing equipment and services to meet those needs. It sounds simple, but it was a radical concept at the time—very few railroads had any marketing efforts underway. The commercial function still focused on wooing customers with lavish meals and golf and other perks. As it turned out, I was the SR's first-ever marketing trainee, an accident of timing rather than a result of any competence or qualifications on my part. While I had taken a few marketing courses at Wharton, I was a novice. The SR was not going to turn me loose without some training, so for the next year I touched most of the bases at the SR, from pricing to operations to equipment to computers.

It was a real adventure. I was being paid very good money to learn all I could about the railroad, which involved extensive travel by rail, almost all in sleeping cars and almost all on an expense account. For a railfan, being told to ride as many trains as possible was not exactly hard duty.

The fun was in delving into the operating side of the business. Of course, in those days, hanging out an open vestibule window was an accepted practice. Or I might just ride the locomotives. While I did not have an engine pass, it was fairly easy to go to the superintendent's office and get the necessary permit. A perfect trip would be to ride the Crescent's engines the two-plus hours between Atlanta and Spartanburg, South Carolina, and then go back to the dining car for a steak dinner.

SWITCHING CARS IS HARD WORK

Not long after I was hired, I was sent to Atlanta for a switching study. I learned that working sixteen-hour days six days a week was difficult even for a twenty-four-year-old. But that

Illinois Central and Seaboard power wait for their next assignments at Jacksonville, Florida, 1963.

was how Brosnan was pushing productivity: keep the people count low, but make them work incredible hours (minimizing the number of employees reduced the costs of insurance and railroad retirement). But before going on duty, I had to buy a hat. Officers wore hats; it was part of the drill. The one I bought was too small, so I looked pretty dorky when I reported to my switching crew, and I took a lot of joshing. Another time I was in Jacksonville, heading north to home. Thinking I was some cool railroad official, I marched into the station

bar, ordered a beer, and was promptly carded. So much for being an important railroad official. But I swallowed my pride and I did get some pictures of engines waiting for their next assignments.

While doing the switching study, I learned that the Southern's efficiency was driven primarily by aggressive front-line supervision. It seemed that every time we paused from our switching duties, a trainmaster would show up and ask, "Y'all having some problems?" Well, not really—and off we would

Southern office cars bring up the rear of the Southern Crescent at Alexandria, 1977. As a trainee I rode an executive special to Almond, North Carolina, for a three-week "retreat" for management, where I got to see Bill Brosnan in action.

go again. Aggressive supervision was very much Brosnan's style; he seemed to believe that his operating crews were just goofing off.

I still have memories of those three weeks, some good and some bad. But I sure learned a lot about how hard it is to be a railroader, and the experience made me more sensitive to the people issues involved in running a railroad. It was perhaps the best lesson I learned from my time in the training program.

BOOT CAMP, SOUTHERN STYLE

It was always "Mr. Brosnan." I never heard anyone call him by any other name—he was not that kind of man. Save for an occasional encounter in the executive elevator (I was on ten, he was on eleven), I never really had a one-on-one conversation with him. But I did observe him in action during a three-week stint at the SR "camp" at Almond, North Carolina. These annual fall meetings were legendary. Essentially, every management employee on the railroad came down for a three-day session of training and motivational encounters. Getting there was fun: imagine leaving Washington in the evening on a special train of fifteen or so office cars, then eating breakfast while climbing the mountain to Ridgecrest, capped by a ride down the scenic Murphy Branch. (Years later I would oversee the sale of most of that line to a short-line carrier.) Once in Almond, though, life was not as much fun. The day would start with a chow line in the mountain cold, and for the rest of the day there were lectures on important subjects from technology to work processes—useful, if tiresome by the end of the day.

Train number 153 waits ready to depart Alexandria, Virginia, 1963. Number 153 was the premier freight train on the SR.

But in the evening, things got a bit weird. First we had a happy hour and sang hymns. We were allocated two drinks each, and the SR police roamed the crowd to make sure we were not drinking more than that—and to make sure that we were singing loudly. After dinner came the entertainment, Brosnan style. A series of skits, performed by Brosnan's office staff, would essentially ridicule many of the people in the room for mistakes they had made—or were believed to have made. It could be brutal. Having spent a summer training with the Marines as part of my NROTC training, I was no stranger to hazing, but these skits were over the top. Sometimes it was not just ridicule; at one session, Brosnan fired a man right in front of hundreds of his peers, by title, not name: "Mr. Atlanta Terminal Superintendent, you are fired." (Shades of Donald Trump!) The SR police then escorted the stunned man out of

the tent. Being fired is a bad thing (I've been there), but being fired in front of your coworkers seemed unnecessarily cruel. Brosnan slipped down a notch in my book once I saw him in action.

As a trainee, I had to endure three solid weeks of this, and by the third session or so, the evening entertainment was simply boring. So along with a couple of sales trainees, one of whom had a car, I would crawl down the embankment to the river, then sneak past the SR police and get up to the highway. (I knew all that crawling around I had learned with the Marines that summer would be useful in civilian life!) There was absolutely no point to this endeavor except the fun of escaping. We would go into Bryson City, a town that closed up after dark, drive around (this was when most of North Carolina was dry), and then return to camp for our ride to whatever motel

Looking back from the head end of number 153 near Culpepper, Virginia, 1965. There were six GP-30s up front and another one two-thirds of the way back, tied to the lead units with a radio car. The train normally had over two hundred cars. A lot of the technology that was routine on the SR in the 1960s did not show up for years, or even decades, on other roads.

we were staying at. I have no idea what the punishment would have been had we been caught but I suspect we would have been fired. Discipline was part of the culture—you messed with Mr. Brosnan at your own peril.

RIDING NUMBER 153

Train 153 was the SR's premier train—passenger or freight. One of my favorite pastimes was to get a cab permit and ride the train between Alexandria and Monroe, Virginia. Only 160 miles from Alexandria, Monroe was the crew change point and the end of the Washington Division. The train was often two hundred cars long, with six GP-30 locomotives up front and normally one back in the consist along with a radio car.

It was an early example of using distributed power, now the norm (at least in the West) but unique in the early 1960s.

The SR had a lot of folks onboard: the regular train crew of five (three up front and two on the rear), all of whom got off at Monroe, plus a trainmaster, a road foreman, and a mechanical officer. That tells you a lot about railroading in the 1960s: even the SR had inefficiencies everywhere.

Train 153 had a schedule that demanded a 40 mph average speed to Atlanta, so to keep the train moving, the crew change at Monroe was done on the fly. The train never stopped: the new engine crew swung on at 5 mph and took control, then the old crew swung off and the long train accelerated. The rear-end crew had been driven to the north end of the yard, and when the caboose was at the right spot, the train slowed

The view from the cab of number 153 as it passes the northbound Birmingham Special near Orange, Virginia, 1964. Number 153 essentially had rights over anything else on the railroad.

The Gulf, Mobile & Ohio's Midnight Special backs into St. Louis after its overnight run from Chicago, 1962. I had passes on all southeastern railroads as well as the New York Central and made full use of them to explore most of the Southeast and beyond.

The Frisco's Sunnyland leaves St. Louis bound for Memphis, 1962. After riding the Midnight Special from Chicago, I rode this train to Memphis and then returned to Chicago on the Illinois Central.

for the transfer. The caboose was called a "cab" on the SR, so when the crew change at the end of the train was complete, the radio call of "cabs on" was the signal to notch up the throttle and go. Number 153 met a number of northbound passenger trains that dutifully waited for it to pass. The SR knew where the money was made.

Number 153 was due in Atlanta around midnight. There, some cars would be set off for other trains and other cars added to the consist. The core consist would also get a mechanical inspection. The tension was palpable before the train arrived; supervisors showed up along with mechanical department staff, and woe to the operating officer who delayed the train.

Fear of Mr. Brosnan's wrath permeated the operating division, but railroading today could use more of this tough love—just consider the success Hunter Harrison has had as CEO of the IC, the CN, and the CP.

A POCKETFUL OF PASSES

As a trainee, I was required to travel a lot, almost always by train. For this railfan, there was the perk of all perks: passes for free transportation (including free roomette space) on all southeastern railroads as well as the New York Central (the SR's historic partner north of Cincinnati, for such trains as

Above, The southbound Silver Meteor crosses the Trout River just north of Jacksonville, Florida, 1964.

Right, The Carolina Specials pass near Marion, North Carolina, 1964.

Left, The Georgia Railroad's number 2, the day train to Augusta, sits in a siding near Social Circle, Georgia, waiting for a westbound freight to pass, 1965. It was clear that freight trains had priority and equally clear that track maintenance was not on the Georgia Road's to-do list.

The Chesapeake & Ohio's Fast Flying
Virginian crosses the New River
near Hinton, West Virginia, 1965.

the Royal Palm). Those passes covered a lot of territory, from Kansas City (on the Frisco) to Chicago (on the IC and the GM&O) to Miami (on the ACL/FEC and the SAL) to Cincinnati (on the N&W and the C&O). Think of that: Miami to Chicago to New York to Kansas City—it was a railfan's dream and I took advantage of the benefit.

The best department for travel was Customer Service Engineering, another part of the marketing department. The SR was creating a variety of exotic new freight cars to meet specific customer needs. The customer service people worked with shippers to determine just what those needs might be, and when a new design was placed in service, they went out to educate customers on how to load and unload the equipment.

The customer service staff spent much of their time traveling around the entire eastern United States. Each week, I would review the upcoming week's assignments and pick trips

that seemed interesting and that would allow me to cover as much of the rail network as possible. One typical trip: overnight to Atlanta on the Crescent, then overnight to Brunswick, Georgia (which just happened to have the last heavyweight Pullman in scheduled service), and concluding with an overnight trip back to Washington on the Silver Meteor. Or a trip to Atlanta might involve a route via the Atlantic Coast Line and the Georgia Road, or a trip to Cincinnati might use an SR-C&O combination or an N&W-SR routing.

OF BRICK AND OYSTER SHELLS

After training, I went to the Market Research Department, headed by Paul Banner (later the chief commercial officer at the Rock Island). A Harvard-trained economist, he had come to the SR from heading the research arm of the southwestern railroads' pricing bureau. Banner was a man who believed that information, properly organized and analyzed, would lead to truth. Now that might sound fairly obvious, but we're talking about 1960s railroading here. By necessity, the business was dominated by operating departments, and operating officers are inclined to make decisions and move on. Action, not analysis, was typically the goal, although I would learn that a balance of the two really worked best. Intuition and experience count when you are dispatching trains or picking up wrecks.

While I was in this job, Banner hired Jim Hagen from the Missouri Pacific. Hagen went on to serve as head of the policy office at the FRA, president of the USRA, chief marketing officer at both Conrail and CSX, and, finally, CEO of Conrail. Our careers intertwined over some thirty years. In the early days at the SR, he was my mentor, basically cleaning up messes that I created.

The new market research effort focused on drilling down and finding out what was really driving customer decisions. The answer was often *not* what the customer said it was. For example, one of my assignments was to work with a customer who shipped oyster shells from Mobile, Alabama, to much of the Southeast. He wanted lower rates to expand (he said) his markets, and he promised more long-haul oyster shell business. But a trip to the US Department of Agriculture revealed that oyster shells, used in chicken feed, have the same chemical ingredients as cheap, locally available limestone. The shipper's game was to convince farmers that oyster shells were better than limestone, but my conclusion was that oyster shells were going to lose out to limestone and lower rates were not going to save our oyster shell business. The SR should get all the short-term revenue it could, because there was no long term.

A request for reduced brick rates presented a more complex problem. In the 1960s, brick was still important to the SR (and would be for years to come). The traffic moved in small lots, often over very short distances. The brick producers wanted a flat 25 percent reduction in rates. The fundamental issue was whether lower rates would lead to such an increase in volume that overall revenues and profits would increase. In this instance traffic would have to increase 50 percent to overcome the lower freight rates desired by the customers.

Hamilton and Banner charged me with analyzing the request and coming up with recommendations. After running the numbers and talking to most of the important manufacturers, I concluded that such a huge reduction in rates was not going to do much to stem the continuing shift to trucks. For shorter-haul movements, trucks were often cheaper on a door-to-door basis; they could go directly to a job site without transloading. I proposed that the SR reduce its long-haul brick rates to points such as Washington and Cincinnati, which would allow southeastern brick producers (which had lower production costs) to truck from SR transloading points to markets in Ohio and Maryland. The brick producers were not happy, but the rates went in as proposed. Some long-haul traffic was gained in the short term, but overall the movement of brick by rail continued to decline.

I learned an invaluable lesson in negotiating style. Hamilton and I were in Atlanta to meet with the brick shippers, and Hamilton outlined our proposal. The lead negotiator for the shippers said that our proposal was totally unacceptable. Hamilton said nothing. Rather, he got out his airline timetable, studied it, packed up his papers, and headed for the door. I was essentially clueless and remained seated. As he passed me, Hamilton asked if I was coming with him, at which point my mind reengaged and I got up as well. The shippers pleaded with Hamilton to return, and after a dramatic pause, he did just that. A deal was cut along the lines that the SR had proposed. Taking a walk can be a good thing if negotiations are going badly.

What I learned from the brick study and other studies I did was that just believing that the railroad was a better option did not make it so. If customers wanted something that rail technology could not provide, it was better to move on and find other markets. Letting some uneconomic markets go was a better course of action than tilting at windmills. In the coming decades, as the shift from rail continued, I would get to apply that principle more times than I care to recall. A lot of railroad folks are still tilting at windmills today.

THE AGGREGATE WARS

The southeastern railroads were losing most of their short-haul aggregate business to trucks; given the economics, trucks were the more efficient mode except for special circumstances. (Now, however, there are many effective, profitable movements of aggregates in multiple-car or trainload services.) But that did not satisfy Mr. Brosnan—he charged Banner and Hagen with coming up with rates that would defeat trucking across the board. Banner proposed a rate scale that Brosnan rejected. (Banner showed me the graph where Brosnan had simply cut the proposed rates in half.) When the proposed rates were made public, the reaction, much of it from other railroads, was fierce. Under existing ICC costing formulas, the rates were unprofitable by a wide, wide margin.

But the ICC cost formula contained a loophole: if one car was used instead of two, then the rates made money. The SR did not want to buy (nor should it have) new high-capacity cars for a low-utilization service. The solution was to take old small hopper cars, replace the coupler with a drawbar, and give the two new cars the same number. It was an economic sham, of course; the "new" cars were virtually the same as the old cars, save for a drawbar and a common braking system. But the ICC cost formulas said it was one car, which was a huge savings—at least on paper.

That ruse still did not solve the problem. The low rates could not support new train starts, so the aggregate traffic had to be moved in existing trains, including passenger trains. The SR set out to prove that there was surplus train capacity throughout its network. To support that contention, Market Research went out to the field to copy train sheets and determine just how many more tons our trains could haul without adding power. I spent many a day and night poring over train sheets at various division headquarters. But it was an opportunity to ride some new mileage, and nothing is more fun or educational than spending time in a dispatcher's office.

Because these were short-haul movements, generally within the boundaries of a single state, the legal battle was fought before state railroad regulators. I went to a number of hearings, amazed that something as mundane as aggregate rates could engender so much passion. In the end, the SR won some cases and lost others, and the shift from rail to truck was not diminished much at all.

At the time I thought it was a silly, irrelevant waste of time and energy, and I still do today. But it gives some insight into just how oppressive regulation was: were lower rates on aggregate traffic so much a threat to commerce as to require such oversight? It was also indicative of Brosnan's personality: when he had an idea, good or bad, he was willing to devote a lot of resources to winning. The SR had a slogan: "It can't be done," with a slash through the 't in "can't." That pretty much summarized the spirit of the SR under Brosnan. Another favorite slogan was "YCSFSOYA"—"You can't sell freight sitting on your ass!"

GOODBYE TO THE SOUTHERN
(FOR A WHILE AT LEAST)

At the SR, I worked with some of the smartest people I have ever known. Still, the pace seemed slow, and in January 1966, when I was offered an opportunity to work in the New York Central's marketing department, I took it. It was a major move, from a good job with good potential at a growing company in a growing region to an uncertain future. But I was still tempted by big-time northeastern railroading (already dying, as I would find out shortly). Over the objections of my wife, who had lived in New York City and did not ever want to go back, I accepted the job.

It was another fork in the road, one that would give me important knowledge of northeastern railroading that would be invaluable in the future, though I did not know it at the time. But in all honesty, the professional challenge was not nearly as important a factor to me as the lure of a "white pass." That pass would let me ride the 20th Century Limited and every other train on the railroad—passenger, mail, express, and freight—and to ride in locomotives and cabooses as well. (And since a merger with the Pennsylvania Railroad was pending, I had a pass on that railroad as well—good on the Broadway but not on locomotives.) The railfan gene overcame the sensible choice to stay with the SR.

My departure from the SR was tense, to say the least. Banner simply wrote me a note saying, "Sorry to see you go," but Hamilton, seeing that I was determined to leave, got fairly hostile and actually threw an ashtray across the table in my direction. (I never knew if his aim was poor or if he meant to miss.)

In hindsight, I can see why he was angry. He had brought me to the SR sight unseen, had given me good training and an excellent career path (though not one that excited me), and thought it churlish of me to then leave. And he was right.

THE SR EXPERIENCE

Though awash in southern gentility—headquarters was very much a Virginia-gentlemen culture with a lot of Virginia Military Institute overtones thrown in for good measure—the SR was anything but laid-back. It was on the cutting edge of railroading, and it took me years of involvement with other railroads to understand just how good it was.

I have not worked for, nor observed, a better-disciplined railroad than the SR under Brosnan. He was autocratic and intimidated many of his officers. His attitude was very much "Ready, fire, aim," at a time when the industry tended to be run by conservative people who were slow to embrace change. Brosnan had plenty of faults, which seemed to multiply toward the end of his tenure at the SR. He would issue absolute orders, such as "no more overtime," and the railroad would promptly seize up. (One trip on the Southerner ran through the engine terminal tracks because both main tracks were filled with idled freight trains.) Some good people left—Stan Crane to the PRR and Jim Gessner to the MP (Crane later returned, but Gessner did not). At the end of his career Brosnan was too harsh and too arbitrary an executive and was no longer effective. The SR board understood this, and essentially forced him out in 1967. Brosnan's replacement, Graham Claytor, though focused on performance and change, had a style that greatly reduced the fear factor among SR executives.

Many SR alumni made a mark on railroading beyond the SR. Stan Crane and Jim Hagen deserve a lot of the credit for

Graham Claytor followed Bill Brosnan as the SR's president. He was responsible for bringing steam back to the SR, and here he is seen on one of the SR's steam excursions, 1975. The Southern produced some of the finest executives of the rail renaissance, including Brosnan, Claytor, Stanley Crane, and Jim Hagen.

Conrail's recovery. John Ingram was the FRA administrator during the Penn Central crisis and played a pivotal role in the drama. Graham Claytor ended his career as the best CEO Amtrak ever had.

As it turned out, I was not finished with the Southern. Years later, after tours at the New York Central and the Penn Central, and then with the government and Amtrak, I would return to the SR—not in the marketing department, but in planning, where rail mergers would occupy most of my time.

Flying green flags, the first section of the Southerner passes Burke, Virginia, 1964. The Southern was aggressive in promoting special movements to the Washington market, especially for school groups.

The 20th Century Limited westbound at Oscawana, New York, 1967.

ROAD OF THE CENTURY

My days at the New York Central, and how it tried to innovate but could not overcome fundamental changes in its core markets. The Penn Central merger, with its clash of cultures and mountains of debt, was doomed from the beginning.

STARTING AT THE NEW YORK CENTRAL

The New York Central's Industry Planning Department, a rarity in the railroad business at the time, was all that I had hoped it would be when I began work there in February 1966. The NYC was a far less structured environment than the SR, where a few top people tended to make all of the big decisions. There was a "band of brothers"—or perhaps "masters of the universe"—feel about the entire marketing department at the NYC. We were young and aggressive and smart, or surely thought that we were. We were out to change railroading, starting with the NYC. Working with Market Research, the Industry Planning group focused on innovation: finding new markets and new ways to run the railroad at a profit. And the NYC's talent was not confined to the new marketing group. Alfred Perlman had assembled what he thought were the best and the brightest to transform a declining northeastern

railroad. Although they did not succeed at the NYC, most went on to leadership positions both in the industry and in government.

In terms of technology, the NYC looked a lot like a flat-land version of the Southern Railway. Automated hump yards and centralized traffic control were the standard. The NYC had embraced containerization; its version was a side-loading system called Flexi-Van. The Central was a major hauler of finished automobiles handled in multilevel cars, another recent innovation. Like the SR's Bill Brosnan, Perlman was totally committed to change and surrounded himself with people who shared his vision. Also like Brosnan, he knew that the passenger train was doomed and he set out to do something about it, much to my chagrin as a railfan.

The NYC was a "hot" railroad, running a lot of trains at high speeds—exciting stuff for one used to wandering around the Blue Ridge at 40 mph. But all the bright people and all the high-speed glitz tended to mask an unpleasant reality: markets for rail freight service in the Northeast were imploding as the Interstate Highway System expanded. Technology notwithstanding, the cost structure was simply too high. New York Central trains still carried a four-man crew that changed out

Merchandise freight train eastbound at Oscawana, New York, 1967. The overhead bridge at Oscawana was a swell place for watching trains. Now freight trains are few and far between; commuter trains and Amtrak services are the big dogs.

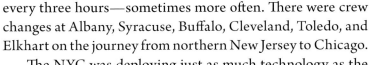

Left, **Track east of Syracuse, 1967.** Deferred maintenance was evident and would get worse until the coming of Conrail a decade later.

Below left, **Wreck at Poughkeepsie, New York, 1968.** As the physical plant deteriorated, wrecks were an increasingly common occurrence.

every three hours—sometimes more often. There were crew changes at Albany, Syracuse, Buffalo, Cleveland, Toledo, and Elkhart on the journey from northern New Jersey to Chicago.

The NYC was deploying just as much technology as the SR, but it had two fatal handicaps. First, the Northeast was contracting and the Southeast was expanding. While trucks took traffic from rail in both regions, there was no inherent growth in the Northeast to offset the loss of market share. Second, the SR was a far more disciplined railroad than the NYC: the SR had a very high ratio of supervisory personnel to agreement people and the NYC did not. Railroading is a sprawling "outdoor sport," and the right level of supervision and discipline was critical to keeping things running efficiently. (Information systems can keep better tabs on things now, but good first-line supervision remains essential.)

And the NYC was falling apart. Rail and tie renewals were well below the rates needed to keep the railroad properly maintained, and the motive power suffered from deferred maintenance. There was mud in the ballast, even on the highest-density main lines. For a railroad geared toward a high-speed, truck-competitive marketplace, the physical constraints were very real and very damaging. I learned that if you have a choice between crossties and smart, creative marketing folks, choose crossties. In short, the NYC was a company in deep, deep financial and physical trouble. It is hard to execute creative new services if the infrastructure is not up to the task.

At that time, international containerization was still in the future. New York, the premier East Coast port, was hopelessly primitive by today's standards. Rail freight came into yards in New Jersey where the cars were sometimes floated to other points in the harbor. The more common practice was lighterage, in which freight was unloaded in vast sheds, moved onto docks, reloaded onto covered barges called lighters, towed to a steamship pier, unloaded, and then reloaded onto a ship using cargo nets. It was a horribly complicated and costly process, and the costs far exceeded the revenues. For the NYC it was an *On the Waterfront* kind of operation—inefficient, with a definite criminal element.

One of my first jobs, under the direction of Phil Ohl, who headed the international freight industry planning effort, was to stem the losses. I made part of the presentation to Perlman and the executive committee. (This was a big deal for me—after living in the shadow of John Ingram and Bob Hamilton, I was making a presentation to the elite of the NYC management.) The economics, I told them, were grim. The direct costs of the lighterage operation (wages, benefits, and the payment for damage and stolen goods—a big problem in New York) absorbed about 90 percent of the NYC's total revenue from the traffic. That left precious little to actually move the cargo from, say, Ohio to Weehawken. The recommendation was to simply drop the lighterage service, tie up the equipment, and when customers called, just say we could not accommodate them. The management team agreed. In retrospect, it was probably illegal, but with the company drowning in losses, the niceties of the regulatory process took a backseat. I did not see it as an illegal act. We had to do it to survive.

The NYC lighterage problem was symptomatic of the times: rapid change was needed, and the regulatory mechanisms were a huge anchor dragging the company down. But I recall sitting in Weehawken looking out on rows of idled lighters while Bill Frechette, the superintendent of marine operations, took calls, saying he was sorry but all of his equipment was tied up and he would get to the customer when he could. I was pretty proud of the fact that my analysis had led to the right decision for the NYC. In a sense, it was a northeastern version of the Brosnan strategy of "ready, fire, aim."

Later in my career, I would work steadfastly to eliminate those things that did not make economic sense: passenger trains, branch lines, or redundant main lines. This was the first of many downsizing efforts in which I would be involved, but I tended to see all of them as "rightsizing" efforts, focused not on what was being lost but on what could be saved. Today, we can see how a failure to face reality can bring an entire company down (think Kodak, for example).

But it was all for naught, because when the NYC later merged with the Pennsylvania Railroad, the PRR's international freight people were proud of the increase in lighterage traffic they had enjoyed. Their gains just about exactly matched what the NYC had deliberately shed. We were back to square one, and it was an indication of why this was not going to be a union made in heaven.

International freight was not just about downsizing. Containerization was coming to the steamship industry, led by a trucker, Malcolm McLean. Using converted tankers, he created a coastwise container service between New York and Houston. One day, at a luncheon with some of the leaders of the steamship business at a posh restaurant overlooking the Hudson River, we all watched one of the first ships depart. "It will never work," declared one of the senior shipping executives. Railroads were not the only business resisting change.

Right, **A commuter train bound for Poughkeepsie arrives in Croton-Harmon behind a P Motor, 1967.** These electric engines were the mainstay of the electric locomotive fleet. They were built for the operations at Cleveland Union Terminal and came east when electric operations in Cleveland were abandoned. Note the mail train on the right, inbound for Manhattan.

Below right, **A commuter train bound for Poughkeepsie blasts through Oscawana, New York, 1966.**

THE HUDSON DIVISION

I have ridden trains all over the world now, but the Hudson Division, from New York to Albany, remains one of my favorite routes. I think I fell in love with the NYC when I saw Alfred Hitchcock's 1959 movie *North by Northwest*. The images of the 20th Century running along the Hudson were simply stunning. From Croton, one of the loveliest places I have ever lived, commuting was a breeze—a brief walk to the station, a one-stop, forty-five-minute ride to Manhattan, and a five-minute walk to the office. In all seasons, the trip was a joy.

An added advantage was that I could ride the locomotives anytime I wanted. My normal train came from Poughkeepsie; at Harmon the diesel units were replaced with an electric locomotive, and I would simply go to the engine and enjoy the ride. The 20th Century Limited, with its 6:00 PM departure, was an elegant evening commute. My buddy Dave DeBoer and I were frequent passengers in its observation car, enjoying a gin and tonic or a Jack Daniel's and water. If we were riding the engines, we would get off on the fly, always trying to disembark at a higher and higher speed—dumb and dumber!

The railroad might have been going to hell, but there were compensations.

Left, **View from the cab of a P Motor heading to New York, 1966.** I would often ride the locomotives when I was commuting.

Below left, **View from the cab of an eastbound passenger train, 1967.** There was no better entertainment on a summer evening than riding locomotives on the Hudson Division. Then and now, it is one of the great train rides in North America.

RIDING THE CENTURY

In October 1967, the 20th Century Limited—the Central's most famous train, and one of the world's most famous passenger trains—made its last trip, along with a number of other named trains on the NYC. The long-haul intercity service was consolidated into one east–west service, and a new short-haul service with coaches and snack service began serving the New York–Albany–Buffalo route. Dubbed Empire Service, it was a dramatic effort to reduce the Central's mounting losses from passenger operations.

The end of the Century was one of the milestones in American railroading. If a luxury train could not make it on a fast schedule (it averaged 60 mph, a blistering pace compared to current Amtrak timings on this route) between two of the largest cities on the continent, what hope was there for the rest of the passenger network? In my gut, I knew really bad times were coming—I just did not appreciate how bad they would be or how fast things would unravel.

It was bittersweet. Growing up in Texas and loving trains, I had always longed to see big-time railroading. The Pennsylvania and the New York Central were the pinnacle of railroading—multiple tracks, lots of trains—and no train loomed larger in my imagination than the Century.

Soon after I arrived at the NYC I took my first trip on the Century. It was a huge letdown. The red carpet at Grand Central was only a memory, but worse still, the train itself was showing many signs of deferred maintenance. A lot of things simply did not work very well. On that first trip I was surprised to wake up to the bright lights of the Syracuse passenger station because my window shade had crept up during the night; I learned how to jam it shut with a paper cup. Postwar sleeping cars generally came with private rooms, complete with their own toilet, which would rattle all night long if you did not secure the hopper out of the toilet with a hand towel.

But there were some elements of the old glory. The dining car was first-rate. The crews were all veterans who took pride in their work, even if the railroad that ran the train no longer cared. (A lot of very good, very dedicated railroaders were hurt in the process of adjusting to change—not just economically but emotionally as well.) And the observation car, with its big windows, was the perfect location to have a drink and watch the scenery. I have fond memories of staying up late and watching the parade of eastbound freights pass in the darkness. It was terrific, high-speed, big-time railroading.

Above, **The 20th Century's Hickory Creek observation car has been saved and restored to its former glory.** Here we see it in Washington Union Station at the end of a Northeast Corridor train, 2012.

Left, **The westbound Century at Oscawana, 1967.** Hickory Creek brings up the markers; the consist had been swollen thanks to an airline strike.

Often I would ride to Albany and have dinner along that leg of the trip, then go up front and ride the locomotives to Syracuse. On one trip, there had been a derailment, and I awoke in Ohio, not Indiana, plodding along on the Nickel Plate line to bypass the wreck site. At 8:00 AM in Cleveland, I went forward to ride the locomotives into Chicago. But I missed the Chicago meeting I was supposed to attend, so I turned back and rode the Century home—another hard day at the office.

The most interesting trip was during the winter of 1966–67. A light snow was falling at Elkhart, Indiana, but the storm grew in intensity with every mile we traveled toward Chicago. We limped into Englewood Station, in South Chicago, and could go no further. The passengers disembarked; we were all essentially trapped at the station. The still-raging storm ultimately dumped thirty-six inches of snow on Chicago and, coupled with high winds, crippled the city. You could not walk, and there was no public transportation. Most passengers were stoic, but some were scared and some were angry. It remains one of the worst storms in the history of Chicago. O'Hare Airport was closed for three days.

Only one agent was on duty at Englewood, so, as a company man, I volunteered to help him out. It proved to be a long, long day. Trains could not make it downtown. Trains heading east were trapped in the coach yard and never showed up. Finally the Rock Island managed to run a commuter train, and those stranded at Englewood were loaded onboard and taken downtown.

The word from the coach yard was that trains were being readied for departure and would be dispatched to Englewood, which would become their Chicago stop. In late afternoon, as darkness fell and the drifting snow still kept the roads and sidewalks closed, a Rock Island train made it out from La-Salle Street. All the people booked for NYC departures that day—the morning train to Detroit as well as the Century and the Wolverine—were crammed onto the Rock Island train, and they all got off at Englewood. The single clerk and I were overwhelmed.

Hours passed. All we were told was that the trains would be there as soon as the switches could be cleared, but a fierce wind and a shortage of crews pushed things later and later. There was little information, and the stranded passengers, now numbering more than eight hundred, became increasingly restless, even hostile, trapped in the station if they were lucky, and out on the cold, windswept platform if they weren't.

Finally a train appeared. It was now past 6:00 at night; the train was the 8:00 AM departure for Detroit. A large mass of people boarded, and the crowd began to put away their pitchforks. I began to think the clerk and I might actually survive. Another train appeared, this one for Toledo and Cleveland, and another large group left. Finally the 20th Century Limited arrived. The train had not been turned, so the observation car was running backward, next to the engines.

Onboard, those of us in the know headed straight to the diner in case the train had not been provisioned in Chicago. After dinner I went to the observation car, had a couple of drinks, and listened to the chant of the E units. At Toledo, we pulled alongside the earlier eastbound departure, only a few feet away, with no platform in between. All its passengers (many standing) had their coats on; obviously the heat was failing. The scene was something out of *Dr. Zhivago*. And there we were, sitting in the Hickory Creek having drinks, all warm and toasty and relaxed—and praying that we would be fueled quickly and depart before those on the other track took up arms against us.

When the end of the Century came, I could not make a final trip. I opted to ride the locomotives on the Chicagoan to

A westbound Mail 13 train passing though Ann Arbor, Michigan, 1967, on its last trip after nearly a century of operation. Note the Railway Express containers on the train; that company was making one last attempt to modernize.

Syracuse, and come back on the last eastbound trip of number 26. But the Chicagoan was late, and I could only watch as the Century was serviced at Syracuse and then pulled out for New York. I took a mail train back to Albany, where I picked up one of the first Empire Service trains.

My friend Dave DeBoer had a better plan: he caught the Century at Harmon and had a final breakfast onboard during the short ride to Grand Central. Decades later, he still reminds me that he got it right.

MAIL 13 AND OTHER NYC CAB RIDES

I spent a lot of time wandering around the operations offices. One day I learned that Mail Train 13, a New York–Chicago schedule via the Canada Southern and the Michigan Central,

would be making its last trip a week later. It was a chance to ride from Syracuse almost all the way to Chicago in daylight, something I had not yet done.

I rode the Chicagoan to Syracuse, got off in the middle of the night, and then got on Mail 13 in the early morning hours. The train had two E units and one GP-40 and a long train of Flexi-Van and baggage cars. It was hardly a flawless journey. The engines should have been fueled on the main-line fueling rack at Syracuse, but that did not happen, due to the failing operating discipline on the NYC. A cumbersome fueling move had to be made at Niagara Falls, and then there were further delays. (Late trains get later.) Several hours late, we finally limped into Englewood Station in South Side, Chicago, where I managed to go down to the street and get a cab without incident. Lucky me—it was a really bad part of town, and it was

A T-Motor westbound into Croton-Harmon, 1968. These engines were used to switch Grand Central Terminal and it was rare to find one outside of the terminal area. We used a T-Motor to switch Grand Central one hot July night during a railroad strike.

after midnight. The engine crew thought I was crazy to leave the security of the locomotives.

STRIKE DUTY IN GRAND CENTRAL TERMINAL

In July 1967 there was a brief strike—my chance to get out on the railroad. I went to see the superintendent and volunteered for duty.

"What can you do?"

"Switch cars."

Later that night I went off to the bowels of Grand Central Station. Fortunately our crew, the only one operating in the vast terminal, consisted of real railroaders who knew what they were doing—and me. Our job was to switch up cars for the main-line departure in the morning. It was now close to midnight, and stifling underground. We had a trusty T-motor electric engine as our power. There were six of us: an engineer, a tower operator, a conductor, and three brakemen. Each move had to be set up in advance; the tower operator would be dropped off to go into the appropriate tower and align the switches. We would proceed to a track, pick up the required cars, pull back, and move them to the appropriate track for the outbound train.

Coupling cars in a terminal with a third rail and a high-level platform is hard, and I'm a bit claustrophobic to boot. I would squat over the third rail, my head against the edge of the platform, as the train came toward me. By necessity, my body was going to be between the cars. As all of that steel came my way, I was not really *convinced* there was room between the cars. There was, of course—folks had been doing this for decades—but it still looked pretty scary. When the coupling was made, I would crawl further under the car to connect the heating and cooling steam lines, then crawl back out and hoist myself onto the platform. Imagine being the only engine in Grand Central moving from track to track, with no one else in the huge underground station complex. It was surreal.

We were done by 4:00 AM and the intercity trains were ready to roll. The strike ended about the time we finished. After a hot shower and a couple hours of sleep, I was good to go for the workday. My clothes were filthy, but I wore them as a badge of honor—when folks asked how I got so dirty, I proudly told them about my adventure. Virtually no one was impressed. Our very pretty young secretary suggested that I go home and shower. So much for impressing people with my night of switching cars.

SETTING THE TRANSCONTINENTAL SPEED RECORD

When the NYC dropped lighterage service, the international freight group had to find new projects. If containerization was to be the future, the NYC would lead the charge—with its Flexi-Van system, it was the big gun in railroad containerization. The Santa Fe had contacted us and was interested in comparing the operating efficiency of containers versus trailers. A few of us believed containers would be lighter and have better aerodynamics, hence lower fuel consumption. No one questions that thesis today, but at the time it was out-of-the-box thinking.

A young creative thinker named Dave Gunn, later of transit and Amtrak fame, was exploring the issue at the Santa Fe.

We made contact and soon worked out a plan to run two test trains, one with eighty trailers on flatcars and one with eighty Flexi-Van containers, for an apples-to-apples comparison. The tests were organized over a weekend in October 1966. West of Chicago, the Santa Fe's main line was authorized for 90 mph speeds. The Flexi-Van cars were those used in mail service on the NYC and routinely ran at 80 mph. The loaded NYC train arrived in Chicago on Friday night. The train was to be prepped on Saturday and the tests run Sunday on the Santa Fe. Then the loaded cars were to be returned by midnight to the NYC's Ashland Avenue Terminal.

The first problem was that the Santa Fe mechanical people found numerous safety problems with the cars, including the fact that the brake shoes did not meet specifications—some were worn down to the brake shoe hangers. Consideration was given to simply canceling the test, but in the end the Santa Fe replaced about half of the brake shoes and authorized the tests.

We all arrived Sunday morning at Corwith Yard in Chicago for the test. The Santa Fe used five U-25C locomotives, GE power that was normally used on the Texas Chief. The power coupled up and off we went, heading for Coal City, Illinois. The tests would be run between Coal City and Verona at speeds starting (as I recall) at 50 mph and working up to 90 mph in 10 mph increments. The dynamometer car would record the power (tractive effort) required at each speed, and those results would then be compared to the results of the trailer consist operated earlier.

We learned that speed kills: the five units simply could not get the train operating faster than 80 mph. But the tests did prove that containers required less power than trailers.

By this time, Gunn and his team had their sights on bigger things. The NYC Market Research team (Dave DeBoer, et al.) had done some analysis of the transcontinental truck

An eastbound Santa Fe passenger train near Coal City, Illinois, 1967. This picture was taken from the engines on a high-speed test of Flexi-Van equipment conducted on the Santa Fe.

market. Even in the sixties, truckers had almost 20 percent of the market. For example, about twenty trailer loads of garments headed to the West Coast each night from New York. Surely the railroads could compete for that long-haul business. I put together a presentation arguing that we ought to explore that market.

Like the lighterage presentation I had made earlier, this was another really big deal—bigger, actually, because the stakes were higher and the project far more controversial. There I was, standing in front of Mr. Perlman and the entire management team, arguing for a new initiative. We didn't have PowerPoint in those days; a simple flip chart had to suffice. I was pretty darn scared—I had left the Southern partially because I did not get any exposure to the very top management. Now I had more exposure than I wanted.

What I was asking for was the operation of another test train, this time from coast to coast. But it was a recession year and the NYC had suffered a greater loss of traffic than any of its peers. Perlman was not in a good mood. Sitting up front, only a few feet away, he suddenly burst out, "Goddamn marketing department, we are last, and what are you doing about it?" (I did *not* say, "Well, sir, I am trying to get through the presentation.") He interrupted several more times with the same theme. Where my leaders were at the time, I have no idea—but the test train was approved.

Of course, I pushed the envelope. I suggested that, among other things, we cut the number of crew districts in half for this train because of the proposed fast schedule. Those remarks got me an audience with John Kenefick, the vice president for operations. Like a lot of NYC leaders, he was both young and very smart. (He later went on to resurrect a stodgy Union Pacific, playing a pivotal role in turning that railroad into the powerhouse that it is today.) Kenefick lectured me

about all the trouble I was causing. It was a pretty good chewing out, but in the end he said, "I'll bet you're one of those railfan types." Guilty as charged. At that point he opened one of the drawers in his desk and displayed numerous copies of *Trains* magazine. With a wink, I was dismissed.

We did run the test train. It was the fastest train ever to run across the nation, passenger or freight, before or since.

On a hot June night we set out from Manhattan's West Side with forty containers of mail behind four GP-40 locomotives. The goal was to reach Chicago in sixteen hours, the same schedule as that of the 20th Century Limited—a 60 mph average. The schedule was certainly doable, and I had met with senior operating officers to set the stage. Selkirk Yard was being rebuilt, and the train needed to run on the passenger route. The GP-40s were geared for 78 mph and the Flexi-Van equipment was good for 90 mph. So I argued that we ought to run at the maximum speed of the locomotives. Off we went, roaring up the Hudson Division through the darkened suburbs north of New York City at 60 mph, the maximum speed on that segment of the railroad. It was exhilarating! While we had a rider coach, most of us preferred to ride in the trailing unit in order to be closer to the action.

Soon the concept met the reality of NYC operations. The trailing unit had no drinking water onboard, nor did it have a deck plate to the unit ahead. One by one, we made our way forward at 60 mph in the dark. I can still remember dropping down the steps, swinging onto the running boards, crossing over to the next unit, and repeating the process.

Safety first? Not really.

Things went downhill from there. We were routed through Selkirk, where our speed was held to 10 mph because of the construction. The food that was supposed to be put on at Syracuse did not make it. On some divisions we ran at authorized

SFV-1 stopped at Gibson, Indiana, 1967. The train was being held by the Indiana Harbor Belt tower operator; as unofficial "train commander" I went forward and negotiated clearance through the interlocking.

Flexi-Van speeds—70 mph—but on others we ran at 78 mph, as fast as the locomotives would go. We fell further and further behind the proposed schedule. At Gibson, Indiana, we got a red signal. I climbed down and went up to the tower, where the Indiana Harbor Belt operator simply did not know we were coming and did not know that this was a priority train. I negotiated our way out of that one and we finally made McCook, Illinois, for the interchange with the Santa Fe. John Reed, the president of the Santa Fe, was there to greet us, along with a multitude of operating and mechanical personnel. Looking at the beat-up rider coach, Reed asked if we had taken it off the 20th Century Limited. That remark hurt but it was justified; our train was pretty ragged-looking, and we were a couple of hours late.

But the Santa Fe came to the rescue. The mechanical forces replaced about half the brake shoes, and four big GE U-28 six-axle units backed onto the train. They were normally assigned

to the Texas Chief and could run 90 mph, the speed limit on much of the Santa Fe's transcontinental line. We boarded the business car, a rolling office for railroad executives that contained a dining room in the center, a lounge at the rear, and several bedrooms. Reed picked up the radiophone and called the dispatcher. "I do not want to see anything but green signals all the way to Hobart Yard [in Los Angeles]," he said. And that was the way it was—the Kansas City Terminal Company did hit us with an approach signal (which required that we slow down through Kansas City), but otherwise it was high green all the way.

In automatic train stop territory, we ran passenger train speed, 90 mph. Otherwise the limit was 79 mph. We had a fine dinner in the office car and then slept for a very brief time. I awoke early just west of Amarillo, Texas. (The train was using the main freight route of the Santa Fe to avoid the steep grades of the Raton Pass crossing). By mid-morning we were

in Belen, New Mexico, where the train was serviced. One man actually ran with the fuel hose; that was the kind of railroad the Santa Fe was. Leaving Belen, we joined with the passenger main line and ran at 90 mph all the way to the steep grade leading down to the LA Basin.

I rode the locomotives all the way into Hobart Yard except for meals and a brief sleep. Going back and forth from the second unit to the office car involved walking along the catwalks at 90 mph—now that was a real thrill. Crossing between units was exciting as well, but at least the Santa Fe had deck plates in place.

Through New Mexico and Arizona, old US Highway 66 parallels the railroad. At our speed, we were blowing by the truckers, all of whom were doing 70 mph. I have always wondered what they thought of our performance.

We did have one near mishap: the engineer was not familiar with the throttle on the GE engines (it was different from

the throttles used on most engines on this part of the railroad), and the train was going far too fast for a 50 mph curve up ahead. It took an emergency brake application to get us back to an acceptable speed for the curve.

Dusk came as we changed crews in Needles, and then we were off across the California desert. It was dark as we started our descent down the 3.5 percent grade of Cajon Pass, and I still remember the look on the face of the marketing man with me. Ira Heisler had never seen big-time mountain railroading before and was just a little bit nervous on the descent—it really does look like you are falling off the edge of the world, especially at night.

We arrived at Hobart Yard just after midnight, local time. The total journey had taken fifty-four hours and twenty minutes, for an average speed of 59 mph. We had proven that the sixty-hour schedule proposed for the transcontinental service was doable with some time to spare. The test train was going to be proof that the railroads could perform.

As it turned out, our arrival in Los Angeles was on my birthday. The trip was a wonderful present. The return trip was anticlimactic but still pretty neat. We rode east on the Chief the next morning, and it does not get any better in this life than riding the office car on a first-class passenger train.

While I was out riding trains, Dave DeBoer, in the NYC's Market Research group, was finding specific customers for this proposed premium service, which would be a niche market but enough to sustain a train per day. Surprisingly, the proposed fast service was not received favorably in many quarters. First, the freight forwarders—consolidators who handled less-than-carload (LCL) traffic in competition with the less-than-truckload (LTL) services provided by truckers—were still important rail customers. Their business model was based on low rail boxcar rates, and the forwarders saw this

higher-priced premium rail service as a threat to the low rail rates they relied on.

The Southern Pacific also felt threatened. The SP struggled to compete with the Santa Fe for traffic to and from the Northeast, and its Blue Streak Merchandise (BSM) train was, at the time, the fastest freight schedule in the country. The BSM operated from St. Louis, its connection with eastern carriers, to Los Angeles; it averaged 50 mph. But the route was four hundred miles longer than the Santa Fe's Chicago–LA route. Running the wheels off the train made it competitive, but the fifty-hour schedule between East St. Louis (where the St. Louis–Southwestern connected with eastern carriers) and Los Angeles was pushing the envelope. It could not ever match the proposed schedule of forty hours from an eastern connecting railroad. For reasons explained below, NYC pulled out, but the Santa Fe kept the faith and ran an expedited intermodal train from Chicago to Los Angeles. Dubbed the Super C, it was never a commercial success.

Along with Jim Sullivan, the NYC's vice president of marketing, and Henry Hohorst, head of the Industry Planning Department, I was summoned to San Francisco. The meeting went badly. I was part of the problem, directly challenging Benjamin Biaggini (then the number two at the SP and soon to be number one). "I am from South Texas and I know your railroad," I told him, "and it cannot provide this type of high-speed service." I viewed Biaggini as an ill-informed bully, and my visceral responses were hardly helpful to our cause.

The SP played hardball, and so did the freight forwarders. They threatened to divert traffic from the NYC, and that was too much for an already weakened company. I was called to the office of Wayne Hoffman, NYC executive vice president (later he was president of the Flying Tigers, an air freight company). I'm tall, but Hoffman was taller—and a combat

An eastbound Southern Pacific freight train waits for a westbound train near San Antonio, Texas, 1956. The SP ran the fastest freight train in the nation, the Blue Streak Merchandise, over infrastructure like this. The SP wanted the NYC to work with it on a high-speed service, but I declared that their railroad was not up to the task.

The inaugural run of the Santa Fe's Super C train, 1968. When the NYC pulled out of transcontinental operation, the Santa Fe went forward with an expedited service between Chicago and Los Angeles. But the train never generated the traffic volumes hoped for.

infantry veteran. He told me the project was terminated. I protested. It finally got so testy that big Wayne stood up from his desk. Even I had the sense to know that it was time to leave.

I thought senior management folks were a bunch of wimps for giving in to the freight forwarders and to the Southern Pacific. But later in my career, when I was part of senior management myself, I realized that Perlman and Hoffman had a lot of considerations to balance. Taking a shot on an unproven market at the risk of losing existing markets would probably not have been a prudent decision. That is often the dilemma: the more a company needs to break out and take a risk, the more a deteriorating financial position pulls it toward being averse to risk. A lot of railroads found themselves in exactly that position in this era.

The transcontinental train trip was the high point of my railroad career for decades. After that, the challenge shifted from finding new markets for the future to simple survival, as railroading entered a long period of bad times.

THE PENN CENTRAL

The loss of most of the NYC's long-haul passenger trains was depressing. It was even more depressing against the backdrop of the pending merger of the New York Central and the Pennsylvania Railroad. That merger, which had been delayed for years, was something that many of us at the NYC fervently wished would never happen. NYC executives, starting at the top, had little respect for the PRR. Personally, I thought that the PRR was hopelessly out of date while we at the NYC were at the forefront of new, market-focused railroading.

Even Perlman, the leader of the NYC and one of the finest railroaders I have ever worked with, was hardly a fan of the merger. At one luncheon we happened to be sitting at the same table, and he said some very uncomplimentary things about the PRR management, namely, that most of them were incompetent. Another time he called the PRR a "wooden-axle railroad."

So when the merger became a reality, there was little joy at 466 Lexington Avenue. We felt it was a bad merger that was not going to work. We had few illusions that the kind of aggressive marketing effort that existed at the NYC would survive, and we were right. Almost to underscore our negative thoughts about the merger, both the new solid black paint scheme and the new logo, which looked like white worms mating, were simply awful. With the creation of the Penn Central, northeastern railroading took a hard turn downward, both financially and aesthetically.

Our marketing vice president, Jim Sullivan—as fine an executive as I have ever worked for—asked us to stay the course. He said that once his key staff left, he would have no leverage in negotiating with his counterparts at the PRR. Almost to a person, we did stay for months. I remember much of the spring and summer of 1968 as a time of idleness. There were one or two initiatives, but we seemed to be treading water. We would dutifully ride down to Philadelphia to meet with our PRR counterparts, but nothing seemed to come of most of those meetings. I think most of us went into the meetings thinking ill of the PRR people. To a large extent it was generational: most of our counterparts were a decade older, and our youthful arrogance blinded us to the possibilities for cooperation. The PRR personnel might have been old-fashioned, but they probably could have taught us a thing or two.

Some months after the merger, Jim Sullivan released us from our promise to stay. Then the exodus began. In a sense

And here comes the Penn Central. An eastbound Empire Corridor train passes North Croton, New York, 1968. Penn Central engines were dressed in basic black, with one of the worst logos ever designed. The merger got off to a rocky start and went downhill from there.

A car float approaches the Brooklyn Bridge, 1968. The Penn Central was dominated by PRR commercial officers and there was little interest in innovative marketing initiatives. I spent a lot of this time being a railfan, or in this case, a boat fan. Riding a tug around New York Harbor was a fine way to spend a workday.

it was childish, but we were young, we were passionate, and we had made the PRR people into the enemy. Further, it was clear to most of us that the merger was not going well. There were all sorts of operating fiascos. I had little experience with mergers at that time, but I had gone through the SR takeover of the Central of Georgia, and as minor a transaction as it was, there were still all sorts of problems. The Penn Central was on a far larger scale and numerous screw-ups further weakened an already weak company. Lacking both perspective and patience, I tended to see the worst in most decisions. Now I see that most mergers have problems at the beginning, though the Norfolk & Western–Southern merger was an exception.

Gloom fed upon gloom, exacerbated by the continued departures. DeBoer and I hung out together and spent a lot of time bitching about everything over games of bridge supplemented with a lot of bourbon. We both made some modest efforts to find other work.

Being a railfan helped ease the pain. Because there was not that much going on at the office, I spent a lot of time out on the railroad, or out on the water. My job gave me unlimited access to the NYC tugboats that plied New York Harbor. So I would often wander off to Weehawken to "inspect operations" and spend the day riding the boats.

I also roamed farther afield. From my perspective, one good part of the merger was that my engine pass was now good on the PRR, giving me a whole new railroad to explore in locomotives. So I would ride the GG-1 locomotives, one of my all-time favorite engines, on numerous trips back and forth

Right, The eastbound Colonial south of Trenton, New Jersey, as seen from the cab of a GG-1, 1968.

Below right, **Portrait of a GG-1 engineer, 1968.** There were periodic meetings in Philadelphia, the Penn Central's new headquarters. The meetings never accomplished much but the going back and forth was a good excuse to use my locomotive pass and ride the head end. Nothing quite like a GG-1 running at high speed!

to "world headquarters" at Philadelphia. There were other things to explore as well, such as the Erie-Lackawanna main line west of Port Jervis, the New Haven line around New Haven, and the PRR main line to Pittsburgh. The railroad world was imploding and I wanted to see as much of it as I could. I still roamed around the Hudson Division, too, hoping to find all-NYC consists—a futile effort, as more and more PRR motive power made it into locomotive consists. At least the PRR passenger power was quite handsome in its Tuscan red with a bold yellow stripe. But when the NYC or PRR power was repainted with the Penn Central's black scheme and the white "mating worms" logo, I began to lose interest in taking pictures.

The Penn Central merger was a sad and depressing end to both the NYC and its passenger legacy. It turned out to be a bad merger, badly executed; correcting all the fallout from the Penn Central's failure would take years. Fortunately, with the split of Conrail between the Norfolk Southern and CSX, the PRR and the NYC became competitors once again, and this time both properties were well-maintained and well-run. But we could not see such an outcome in 1968. I was lucky—I not only lived to see a better day, but had a hand in undoing the worst railroad merger in American history.

New Haven power at New Haven, Connecticut, 1968. EP-5 electric motors are to the right; an FL-9 lurks in the background on the left. Soon all of these engines would be dressed in Penn Central black, yet another reason to hate the PC merger.

New Haven FL-9 units at New Haven, Connecticut, 1968. The FL-9 had a third-rail pickup shoe that allowed it to run into Grand Central Station.

The eastbound "City of Everywhere East" (it was actually nameless) as seen from the cab of the Boston section at Albany, New York, 1968. The NYC had consolidated all of its long-haul passenger services into one train, an operation that I dubbed the City of Everywhere East. The times were grim and they would get much worse but there were still a lot of engines to ride.

A TRIP OVER THE MOUNTAIN

The PRR line between Harrisburg and Pittsburgh is one of the truly great railroad lines in North America. It has traffic density, mountains, rivers, and an interesting, complex infrastructure. Not long after I went to the NYC, I joined up with Bob Church, a fellow marketing trainee at the SR, to take a ride over the mountain. Bob had jumped ship and was now at the PRR. Early one dreary morning, we were at Frankford Junction (Philadelphia) for a ride in the locomotives of train TT-1, the PRR's premier intermodal train. The train had electric engines as far as Harrisburg, and this was the only time I rode an E-44 electric. My pictures are almost as lousy as the weather was, but it was still one of the best engine rides I have ever had.

At Altoona, the train stopped and two railroad policemen boarded our unit; apparently some tower operator had reported our presence. Proof of our authority to ride was duly

The Pennsylvania Railroad's hot intermodal train, TT-1, crosses Rockville Bridge at Harrisburg, Pennsylvania, 1966. This was my first locomotive ride on what is one of my favorite railroads anywhere. It would not be my last. The track was not so great but it would get worse.

presented, but the incident made the first line of the operating department's morning report the following day. It noted that TT-1 was delayed for five minutes to determine whether unauthorized people were onboard the engines. The report noted that the riders, "which included a New York Central marketing officer," had proper authorization. But given the PRR paranoia at the time, some probably thought that the NYC was infiltrating their operations for some nefarious purpose.

After the Penn Central merger, just before I left the company, I returned to make several trips over the mountain. Both of my locomotive rides—one in summer, one in late fall—were on the combined St. Louisan/Pennsylvania Limited, the morning departure from Pittsburgh.

A daylight look showed signs of deferred maintenance, although the tracks in the mountains never got as bad as the lines west of Pittsburgh, where soft subsoil hurried the process of deterioration. The signs of decay were markedly worse than the first trip that I had made across the railroad a decade earlier. It was a ride on a railroad on the edge of an abyss—a strange mixture of first- and second-generation power and of PRR and PC paint schemes. I would not ride locomotives across this railroad again for another thirty-one years.

Today the line is operated by Norfolk Southern. I am often struck by the irony of all this: the PRR used to own a major share of the Norfolk & Western, and now NS, a successor

A westbound freight on the Middle Division, as seen from the cab of an eastbound St. Louisan/Pennsylvania Limited, 1968. One of the good things to come from the merger was that my white pass on the NYC was now good on all of Penn Central, including the Broadway Limited and all locomotives and cabooses.

to the N&W, owns the main segments of the former PRR. I wrote my Wharton thesis on the then-embryonic PRR Truc-Train service, declaring that piggyback would be an important service for railroads in the future. I was right, though the process would take decades, and intermodal is now the number one commodity in terms of railroad revenues. Even more ironically, my son, until recently the vice president of intermodal and automotive marketing at NS, spent almost a decade managing the successors to TT-1.

I have ridden this line a lot—on passenger trains, office cars, and locomotives—and never tire of it. It's big-time railroading, and since NS took charge the line has been busier and better-maintained than ever.

A TOAST TO THE NYC

I loved the New York Central and believed it truly represented the future of railroading. Its investments in automotive and intermodal traffic and containerization (albeit with the wrong technology), as well as computers, traffic control, and automated yards, were needed to lead the business out of the economic wilderness. Its leaders were among the best and brightest in the industry and went on to prove their abilities in both the private and the public sectors. But in the 1960s, all that technology could not win the war against a declining traffic base, subsidized competition, and passenger deficits. It would take structural changes, both on the railroad and in

Left, **The overnight NYC mail train from Boston, ready to depart South Station, 1962.** The two-tone gray paint scheme was one of the great liveries of the streamliner era, especially when it was clean, as was the case here.

Facing, **Alco FA units at Beacon Park Yard in Allston, Massachusetts, 1962.** This picture symbolizes my experiences with the NYC; when I first met it the locomotives and track were in relatively good condition and the elegant "lightning stripe" paint scheme adorned the engines. But as time went on, both the paint scheme and the condition of the power deteriorated. The 1105 represents the NYC I want to remember.

public policy, to make railroading profitable. With so many external factors arrayed against it, there were limits to what good management could accomplish.

In the end, though, the NYC routes were survivors. More of the NYC main line is in main-line service today than is the case with its archrival, the PRR. Flat, straight, and efficient is good in a railroad world increasingly dependent on intermodal traffic.

I have worked on four "big deals" in my lifetime: the creation of Amtrak, the creation of Conrail, the Norfolk Southern consolidation, and the split of Conrail between Norfolk Southern and CSX. The knowledge of the northeastern rail network that I gained at the NYC proved invaluable in those endeavors. Although railroading in the sixties was hopelessly inefficient, and the industry and its employees would pay a heavy price for that reality, I am glad I was there to see it. It was a last brief burst of sunlight before the dark days to come. As it turned out, better days were decades away.

The southbound Silver Star at Alexandria, Virginia, 1975.
Amtrak inherited obsolete and often undermaintained locomotives from the railroads and needed new power. It bought modified freight units to solve the problem. They were built for easy conversion back to freight use, because given the uncertainty of continued funding, Amtrak did not want to take a risk on locomotives that would be surplus if Congress cut off funding for long-haul trains.

CREATING AMTRAK

I joined the newly formed Federal Railroad Administration and tackled the passenger train crisis that culminated in the creation of Amtrak.

A DECADE OF MONUMENTAL CHANGE

This chapter and the one that follows deal with the most important intervention by government into railroading since the takeover of the railroads by the US Railroad Administration during World War I. The actions taken over the decade between 1970 and 1980 profoundly changed the railroad business, both passenger and freight. First, intercity passenger service became a ward of the state, followed by commuter services. The freight business was also in jeopardy, and nationalization was widely discussed as an option. But freed from passenger deficits and burdensome regulation and aided by new markets and new technology, freight railroads became one of the greatest success stories in business history.

The pivotal point in this renaissance was the collapse of the Penn Central and other northeastern railroads. After the Penn Central merger, I joined the Federal Railroad Administration, then Amtrak, and then the United States Railway Association (not Railroad Administration—that was an earlier

time). I had a front-row seat and often participated in the massive changes that were to come.

THE PASSENGER TRAIN PROBLEM

The last time I had started a job in Washington, a uniformed guard had greeted me by name at the Southern Railway headquarters at 15th and K Streets, in the heart of the business district. My return in November 1968, days after Nixon had been elected to the White House, was not quite as classy. The Federal Railroad Administration (FRA), then a new agency, was housed in a modest four-story building in Washington's Southwest quadrant, which was then something of a wasteland. From my standpoint, the location's most impressive feature was the adjacent Penn Central main line. Freight trains to and from Potomac Yard and passenger trains to and from the South plied the route, so the train-watching was superb. I spent a lot of time looking out the window.

My first big project involved intercity passenger trains, a business that was in full retreat. Some marginal carriers, such as the Katy, had already shed their last trains, while other railroads were closing in on that goal. The US Post Office Department had supported much of the network with lucrative mail

This view, taken from a southbound Pennsylvania Railroad mail and express train, captures a Washington-bound express overtaking the mail train, 1960. The Northeast Corridor was the busiest rail passenger route in the nation but was generating huge losses that the Penn Central could not sustain. But it was a superb rail line, as this image shows. Amtrak still benefits from the vision shown by the Pennsylvania Railroad early in the twentieth century.

MY LIFE WITH TRAINS

contracts but most contracts ended in 1967. Most railroads were heading for the exit door, but the door was guarded by the Interstate Commerce Commission (ICC), which had to approve train discontinuances. The last train on a route was usually denied the discontinuance application.

In the halls of the Department of Transportation (DOT), a bigger issue was looming. The Northeast and Midwest regions' rail freight business was also in distress. Most of the passenger network was, by the late 1960s, irrelevant; the Northeast Corridor (NEC) was the exception. But freight railroads were still important for the nation. Many of us were concerned that passenger train deficits would drive much of freight railroading into insolvency.

The immediate concern was the Penn Central, the largest freight rail carrier in the nation at the time. Further, if the PC failed, connecting railroads would suffer significant losses of traffic as well. The PC was in dire financial straits, with horrific passenger losses. The goal at the DOT was not so much to solve the passenger train problem (though some of us thought that a worthy goal), but rather to avoid a broader collapse of the freight business.

DIFFERENT STROKES FOR DIFFERENT FOLKS

By the late sixties, most Americans were wedded to airplanes and automobiles. Much is made about how government subsidies aided those competing modes, but the fact was that most Americans preferred the convenience of the auto and the speed of the airplane. The fate of the passenger train evoked sharp differences of opinion. Why save the passenger train? We didn't have stagecoaches anymore, did we?

Nixon was new to the White House at the time; he and his key advisors were from California, a place where passenger trains were truly irrelevant at that time. (It's a different story today.) Still, there was a minority who believed in the rail passenger trains. Some were visionary, some steeped in nostalgia. The dispute rages even today, as some in Congress seek to eliminate funding for Amtrak, while others propose new, costly passenger initiatives. Almost fifty years since they started, the debates are the same.

In the late sixties, the "true believers" argued that passenger trains, operated correctly, could divert substantial traffic from highways and airways that even then were showing signs of congestion. Among the advocates was Senator Claiborne Pell of Rhode Island, who argued for much-improved rail service on the Northeast Corridor. His vision was very much focused on the NEC, one of the few areas in the country where short travel distances and high population density were favorable to rail. Rail passenger trains were well patronized, though they lost a lot of money. But most agreed that they made sense in this special market.

As mandated by the High Speed Ground Transportation Act of 1965, the DOT was busily engaged in building both economic and engineering models to test the potential for improved high-speed rail service. From its efforts would come both the new high-speed Metroliner and the TurboTrain.

One support group had a broader vision. The National Association of Rail Passengers (NARP) was lobbying vigorously for improved passenger service, as it does to this day. Tony Haswell, its founder and first leader, was a tireless and articulate advocate for passenger trains. While he too understood that corridors were the best hope for expanded rail passenger service, NARP supported longer-haul services as well.

For some supporters, passenger trains were about nostalgia—not just the loss of those trains but the decline of rural America, which was vanishing quickly with the changes

wrought by urbanization and the Interstate Highway System. For much of the rural United States, the loss of rail passenger service was an emotional event. Those areas were often bypassed by air service and even by the Interstate Highway System, so the loss of passenger trains seemed a stark reminder that smaller, out-of-the-way places were simply not relevant anymore. (Think of today's "blue state versus red state" cultural differences.) Of course, there were other interest groups as well, led by the thousands employed in the rail passenger business and their unions.

But there were also detractors. Most of the railroads simply wanted out of the business; once the Post Office Department pulled the plug on mail traffic, what had been a trickle of red ink became a flood. The railroads believed that if government wanted passenger trains, it should bear the financial losses. They had "been there and done that," and most had tried to run good services. But their freight business was under pressure and they had other, bigger priorities. For most (the Santa Fe and the Seaboard Coast Line were exceptions), it was now time to move on, or have someone else—the taxpayers—foot

A New York Central Empire Service train at Croton North, New York, 1968. The DOT saw services such as this as the future of the intercity passenger train. California and Washington/Oregon have proven that short-haul corridor trains can be successful.

the bill. The Nixon administration, being from California, did not care about freight *or* passenger trains; they were opposed to new, costly government initiatives. Nixon wanted to roll back, at least partly, the big government of Lyndon Johnson's "Great Society." In his view, the marketplace had spoken: autos and air had won the competitive race, albeit with a massive push from the government in the form of subsidized air and highway services.

A brief overview of passenger train economics might be useful at this point. Rail passenger services come in three "buckets": commuter rail, short-haul intercity services, and long-haul services. There is often considerable overlap among them. In the Northeast Corridor, for example, commuter rail, corridor trains, and long-haul trains share tracks, stations, and other infrastructure. Identifying the true costs of each is as much an art as a science, and disputes arise now as they did in the past.

Commuter service is characterized by morning and evening rush-hour peaks. Accommodating those peaks takes a lot of equipment, track, and people. In 1970, commuter rail

A rail diesel car is overtaken by an Empire Service train north of Oscawana, New York, 1967. This picture perfectly illustrates the linkage of short-haul passenger service and commuter service. These tracks are now owned by the Metro-North Commuter Railroad; Amtrak and CSX are tenants. The once-robust freight traffic that used to use these tracks is largely gone—the culprits have been trucks and intermodal and plant closures, including the General Motors plant at Tarrytown, a major traffic-generating point for the NYC.

operated, as it still does, in New York, Philadelphia, Baltimore/Washington, Boston, Chicago, and San Francisco. More than ten railroads had commuter services and those services produced substantial losses. In the Northeast, the commuter railroads were, for the most part, at death's door financially. But even though commuter services were a huge drain on a number of freight railroads, the DOT ducked the issue, which they deemed a local matter: if New York and Philadelphia and Boston wanted commuter trains, they should pay for them. And the Nixon White House couldn't have cared less if the people in those "blue" states got to work or not. It was a major failing on the DOT's part. Years would pass before the commuter train issue was addressed and eventually solved with huge buckets of public dollars.

Short-haul corridor service was and is characterized by high frequency and relatively high speeds, which require a robust infrastructure. By 1969, only the Northeast Corridor and a few other corridor services remained. Like commuter services, these operations lose money. In the NEC, the infrastructure costs are the culprit. (The same holds for airways and highways—government does not recover the total outlays for infrastructure from the operators, be they airlines or trucks or automobiles.) Of course, if service frequency and speeds are compatible with freight operations (in the NEC, they were not), some of the infrastructure costs can be avoided, but the passenger service is not going to be as robust. So for really good corridor service, bring lots of money and send the freight trains to some other route.

Long-haul trains have a different set of economics. They mostly use main freight routes, and generally make no more than a single round trip per day. Though interference with freight trains can be a real and costly hassle, that burden falls

MY LIFE WITH TRAINS

mainly on the freight railroads. The use of freight lines means that long-haul trains do not need special infrastructure other than stations and maintenance facilities.

The killer for long-haul trains is the above-the-rail costs, which can be huge. Short-haul services generally have high-density seating and modest food services. Because of the distances involved, a good long-haul service requires lower-density seating, food service, and sleeping car accommodations, with a lot of onboard personnel such as porters and dining car employees. And the trains are slow. The Chicago–Los Angeles train trip takes over forty hours, which translates into a lot of person-days for onboard staff. Compare that to air service between the same points: the plane can carry about as many people as the long-haul train, but it makes the trip with a crew of five in less than five hours.

All of these services—commuter, short-haul, and long-haul—had some common characteristics by 1969. All were losing money, though the amount varied by market. With few exceptions, the equipment, both locomotives and cars, was old (though much of today's Amtrak fleet is even older), and maintenance had often been deferred. Aging station facilities were usually too large for what was now a greatly diminished number of passengers. Little was more depressing in those days than to see a mere handful of travelers using some vast edifice to the passenger train's bygone glory.

DESIGNING THE NETWORK

I was hardly a passenger expert when I arrived at the FRA, but I had at least ridden much of the US passenger rail network. But given the very thin staffing at the FRA, I was thrown into the passenger issue, notwithstanding my relative lack of knowledge. First there had to be a study—in Washington,

everything seems to start with a study. The first question was, do passenger trains actually lose money? If so, how much? The agency that supposedly had the needed expertise was the regulatory guru, the Interstate Commerce Commission. It kept two sets of books. One was fully allocated costs, which included an allocation of overhead costs; many felt that set of books overstated losses. The second measurement was so-called avoidable costs—those items that might be shed with discontinuance, such as crews, engines, cars, stations, and some tracks. Actually, most railroads kept their own sets of books, which blended the two approaches on a much more proactive basis. Some trains did not show up in the red on internal accounting ledgers—at least while the mail was moving by rail. (See Fred Frailey's excellent *Twilight of the Great Trains* for a discussion of how railroads measured their costs.)

Our first objective was to determine whether the railroads were blowing smoke. There was a huge distrust of railroads and what they said—think of Citigroup, Bank of America, or AIG in recent times. Was the passenger deficit overstated? If so, why should the government step in? Further, if the deficits were real and government should step in, government needed to know the magnitude. It was hard to create a solution without good numbers.

The ICC led the study, with assistance from the FRA. As the new kid on the block, I was assigned to the task for the FRA. Dick Briggs, later of the Association of American Railroads and one of the brightest guys in the room, led the ICC effort. A very competent railroad accounting firm, Wyer Dick, did the basic accounting work.

Conclusion: passenger trains lost a lot of money. The Northeast Corridor was a money pit because of the cost of the infrastructure; the long-haul trains lost money because all of those onboard services were expensive. The ICC's first set of books, the one with fully distributed deficits, was close to the right answer if the service was infrastructure intensive, as was the case with the Northeast Corridor and commuter services. From the government's perspective, this was bad news. Forcing railroads to keep running trains, which the ICC was essentially doing, would undermine freight rail companies. But using government money was not a popular option in some important quarters, including the Nixon White House—another government agency was the last thing they wanted. The DOT was in the middle. Everyone, even the White House, understood that passenger trains made sense in the Northeast Corridor. Some believed that there were other corridors that might work. Almost no one had any belief that long-haul passenger trains were needed, or, indeed, would ever be needed. But again, our overriding concern was to find a solution that removed the passenger burden from the back of the Penn Central and the other freight railroads. The collapse of passenger railroading was acceptable; the collapse of freight railroading was not. Still, some of us hoped to save some passenger trains along the way.

Paul Cherrington, the former Harvard professor who was now head of the DOT Policy Office, led the DOT team of Bob Gallamore, Lou Thompson, and Arrigo Mongini. The FRA team was led by Jim MacAnanny, head of the FRA Policy Office and a former railroad operating executive. Bill Loftus, John Williams, Steve Ditmeyer, and I were the main FRA staff assigned to the effort. Later, Kevin McKinney and Brit Richards would play important roles.

Railpax was the working name of the project. The first task was to define the kind of network needed: should it be short-haul services only, or should long-haul routes be included? Commuter operations were excluded; they lost a lot of money but the federal government did not see them as an issue. This exclusion was a major failing, because if we wanted to save freight railroading, the commuter issue had to be addressed sooner or later. But at the time, we simply kicked that can down the road.

There was no controversy about including the Northeast Corridor in the network. In fact, the work being done by the Office of High-Speed Ground Transportation indicated that improved speeds would make the corridor profitable—which turned out to be a serious error. Beyond the NEC we thought some other corridors made sense and selected two additional ones in the Northeast (New York–Buffalo and Philadelphia–Pittsburgh), four corridors radiating from Chicago (to Detroit, St. Louis, Cleveland, and the Twin Cities), and two West Coast corridors (Los Angeles–San Diego and Portland–Seattle).

We realized the economics of long-haul passenger service but recognized that we needed to keep a few trains for political purposes. Only five long-haul routes were proposed in the initial report. In the East there would be New York to Chicago and Miami. In the West three routes would radiate from Chicago to Seattle, Oakland, and Los Angeles. Note that the DOT specified only the end points and basic service frequency, not precise routes.

It was the barest of bare bones. I agreed with the decision but was still shocked by just how much of the network would be lost. The economic realist in me knew things would have to change dramatically, but the lover-of-trains part of me rebelled at the answer. Bob Gallamore, the other closet railfan on the team, was shocked as well.

A word about the "north star" of passenger railroads: The Canadian National, owned by the Canadian government at the time, was making a major effort to increase its passenger business. It introduced fares to encourage off-peak ridership, it offered new corridor services in eastern Canada, and it even

The Abraham Lincoln ready to depart St. Louis, 1964. The Chicago–St. Louis corridor is now being upgraded for higher-speed operation but has never fulfilled the promise that I thought it had when we were creating Amtrak.

The westbound Super Continental just east of Jasper, Alberta, 1974. Although the Canadian National was successful in generating traffic growth through new services and aggressive pricing, more riders did not translate into a lower deficit and the CN, like the Canadian Pacific before it, threw in the towel. Long-haul trains are a rarity in Canada these days and perhaps the same fate will overtake them in the United States.

bought new short-haul equipment. (It also acquired a lot of equipment being shed by US railroads in their hurry to exit the business.) It is noteworthy that the other Canadian passenger carrier, the Canadian Pacific, was giving up on passenger trains at the same time as the CN was expanding.

We at the DOT/FRA were never privy to the CN's internal books, but we did know that the CN effort had reversed the decline in ridership. It seemed that if you added service and priced and promoted it aggressively, ridership would expand. Further, the CN had a national network, which provided a clue as to how the US effort might be organized. That more people could be encouraged to ride trains was a major anchor of our efforts. The CN experience gave the passenger optimists in our group some hope that passenger trains might have a future. It was only after Amtrak was launched that we

learned that while ridership had grown, the losses for CN's passenger trains grew at an even faster rate.

The DOT/FRA team debated structure at some length, but in the end focused on a single entity that would contract for passenger services with the railroads. (The railroads had initially proposed that they continue to operate the trains and be subsidized for the losses.) We felt that having a myriad of rail carriers, some still doing a good job but most not, created a huge image problem. If the passenger train was to have a fighting chance, it needed a pro-passenger management with nationwide responsibility and a nationwide identity. Again, the CN success provided guidance.

So Railpax would be a private, for-profit enterprise. It was roughly based on the Comsat model, in which the first commercial satellites were being launched by a private-sector firm mostly supported with government money. Most (including a number of us on the planning team) were dubious of the "for profit" claim, but the reality was that neither the White House nor the more conservative members of Congress were going to sign off on an entity that was set up to be a perpetual ward of the state. And the pro-passenger crowd did not object; many of them had argued that passenger trains could be profitable if they were just run right.

The "for profit" mandate haunts Amtrak to this day.

FUNDING RAILPAX

Although the Nixon White House was hostile to any bailout of passenger trains, we at the DOT/FRA were equally convinced that if Railpax were not created, the freight railroads, especially the Penn Central, were in danger of financial marginalization at best, and collapse at worst. That got the attention of the White House crowd. Here the DOT was offering two choices: a government role in passenger trains, or a government role in the entire Northeast rail operation, passenger and freight.

For the most part, Congress wanted to keep far more trains than the DOT/FRA wanted, so the White House and the Office of Management and Budget (OMB) were essentially fighting a majority in Congress as well. But the president had the power to veto any legislation, and there was no chance that Congress could overturn such a veto. So the challenge was to find a way to fund Railpax at the least cost to the taxpayer. The man who had to navigate these treacherous political waters was Secretary of Transportation John Volpe, former governor of Massachusetts. He came from a state where rail passenger service was relevant and he was a strong proponent of improved passenger service. Without him, Amtrak would not have happened.

Minimum cost to the taxpayer became an overarching objective—if the costs were too great, the White House would veto the legislation. In the give-and-take between the legislative and executive branches of government, the capital grants needed to revitalize the system were cut to the bone. It was a critical error because most of the financial projections had been predicated on new trains and, often, new stations. In the pressure to get something passed, we at the DOT did not say, "Well, if you cut the capital grants, then the operating deficits will be far greater."

To minimize the up-front public funding of operating losses, the railroads were going to have to pay an amount equal to their annual losses to exit the business. In essence, the same government that had forced them through regulation to stay in the business was now going to make them pay to leave. (When the Mafia does a shakedown like that, someone goes to jail.) The Santa Fe actually considered taking that part of the law to court on the grounds of unconstitutional taking, but it relented when it realized that the court case would linger on, subjecting it and the other carriers to ongoing losses.

The freight railroads took a hit in another important way, one that resonates to this day. Essentially, Amtrak was granted access to the basic network at fees that did not come close to covering the incremental costs, ignoring freight train interference costs and any extra costs for track maintenance. The FRA understood the issue but the drive to minimize the public cost took precedence. Amtrak had to be created, and then things could be sorted out later, or so we thought. We thought wrong, and the core issues continue to linger.

At the same time that funds were being reduced, political pressure was forcing an expansion of the Railpax network. Many in Congress, rail unions, states, and communities condemned the bare-bones long-haul network. Before all the

The eastbound Sunset Limited at Tucson, Arizona, 1962. The Sunset was one of the last trains added to the basic route structure by the DOT. Our initial plan had a huge gap between New Orleans and California, and political pressure forced the DOT/FRA to add New Orleans–Los Angeles as end points. It is ironic that the Southern Pacific, the most publicly outspoken critic of the passenger train, has passenger service on virtually all of its main-line routes. The Union Pacific inherited that burden when it acquired the SP.

political pushing and shoving ended, a lot of long-haul routes were added: Washington, DC, to Chicago and New Orleans; Chicago to New Orleans; New Orleans to Los Angeles; and Los Angeles to Portland.

The political solution was to create the far bigger network while cutting the resources needed to modernize it and keep it running. It sounds like a prescription for failure, and we now know that it was. Railpax never really had a chance. Political compromise makes for lousy economics, and Amtrak suffers to this day from the same kind of political make-believe. Perhaps the notion that you can have great trains without spending money ought to be called "fantasy railroading."

THE OMB BATTLES

Another serious conflict arose between the OMB and the DOT/FRA. We had made financial forecasts using a number of models. The Northeast Corridor ridership and economic models, on which millions of dollars had already been spent, were assumed to give the correct outcome for the NEC—wrong! New models were developed for other corridor services and for the long-haul trains, mostly by me. The assumption was that new equipment would be needed as well as new stations; corridor trains would look a lot like some of the new services on the Canadian National. The CN furnished cost estimates for cars and stations, which I cranked into my models. Long-haul trains would need new engines, modified freight power was assumed (some were already in service on the Santa Fe), and long-haul cars were mostly a best guess, though even then the bilevel cars on the Santa Fe were looking like a good bet, at least where the clearances would permit.

When all the financial models were cranked up, the result showed a profit for the NEC (all costs in) and losses for most of the other corridors and all of the long-haul trains except Chicago–Los Angeles. But the losses were modest, though all profit-and-loss estimates excluded any capital costs (again, grant money was assumed). The projected surplus from the Northeast Corridor would just about offset the losses elsewhere in the system. But it was known that Railpax would never make it as a long-term going concern able to renew its equipment, and the assumption that the government would apply up-front capital proved to be totally mistaken.

The OMB attacked the outcome, as well it should have. The DOT/FRA defended its efforts, knowing that if the financial projections were shown to be wrong, that would be the ball game: Railpax would go down the tubes, and so too might a lot of freight railroading. Arguing back and forth consumed a lot of energy and brainpower that could have been better applied to building far better economic models.

Many of the key assumptions turned out to be wrong. The NEC actually lost a whole lot of money once the infrastructure costs were included. The final political compromise excluded the capital costs of the new stations and equipment that had been assumed in the planning. But neither the OMB nor the DOT/FRA was really interested in finding the true answer.

SHOWDOWN AT THE WHITE HOUSE

Flawed though it was, the legislation passed both the House and the Senate in 1970. Now it was up to the president. Should he sign the legislation or not? A group of us, led by Jim

MacAnanny and Bill Loftus for the FRA, were summoned to the White House one evening to argue the case with the president's top advisors. It was my first and only trip to the White House in any official capacity, and it was intimidating, from the Marine guards at the door to the pervasive sense of power. Of course, the White House staffers relied on "shock and awe" to overwhelm those who chose to disagree with them.

The arguments went back and forth with a lot of focus on the numbers, and I weighed in as appropriate. When one key staffer cited a Stanford University study that showed that passenger trains lost a lot of money, I dismissed the results as biased because the study was funded by the antipassenger Southern Pacific. The Stanford study was actually pretty good, but the goal was to win the argument, not to discover the truth.

In the end, Nixon did sign the legislation, but without any fanfare. (Imagine the headline: "Republican President Announces Nationalization of Rail Passenger Service.") A quiet signature was the most we could have expected. Then it was time to implement the law, warts and all. Speed was of the essence because the Penn Central was coming unglued at an accelerating rate. It would, in fact, declare bankruptcy before Amtrak took over intercity passenger service.

THE BOARD OF INCORPORATORS

By this time, the DOT/FRA team was tired of being in the crosshairs, and many in Congress did not trust its decisions. A handoff was made to a new Board of Incorporators, which was charged with (1) determining exactly what routes and trains would be operated; (2) setting up the corporation and giving it a name; (3) negotiating contracts with the rail carriers for provision of services, acquisition of equipment, and so on;

and (4) doing the initial staffing of the organization. It was a huge task on a very tight timeline. The FRA detailed me to assist the incorporators in this start-up effort, since I had a lot of institutional knowledge of both the existing network and the thinking that had gone into Railpax.

The very bright, energetic incorporators were supported by an army of consultants. A public relations firm was charged with coming up with a name and a logo for the corporation. An accounting firm was hired to set up the necessary financial systems. Equipment experts were brought in to survey the available cars and locomotives. Because it was operating a much smaller system, Railpax could choose among the best available cars and locomotives; once they were selected, purchases or leases had to be negotiated.

Agreements had to be reached with the railroads that would actually operate the trains, using their own crews. Amtrak was to be a contracted operation with a fairly minimal management structure to set overall direction. (Now, of course, Amtrak actually owns the Northeast Corridor and is thus a "real railroad," operating with its own employees. But in the beginning, all of that was done under contract.) Negotiating those contracts was a tough task. Some railroads, including the Santa Fe and the Seaboard Coast Line, were loath to give up control to what they saw as a bunch of Washington bureaucrats. But the railroads had a strong incentive to reach a deal: the faster Railpax was up and running, the sooner most of their passenger deficits would be shed.

The anchor for all of this thankless work was a retired general, Frank Besson, who had been in charge of all of US Army logistics. Amtrak, while a formidable task, was not beyond his abilities. He was one of the real heroes of the Amtrak start-up.

All of these efforts had to proceed in parallel, and I had little knowledge of much of what was going on. Rather, I assisted a multitude of consultants from McKinsey & Company—then, as now, one of the most respected consulting firms. McKinsey was charged with deciding which specific routes and which specific trains should be run. Recall that the route structure had been only broadly defined by the DOT; obviously, without that baseline network, decisions regarding equipment needs and negotiations of operating contracts with the railroads could not be finalized.

The McKinsey crowd was bright, but most of them lacked any knowledge of the rail passenger business. They did know that the choices made would be hotly contested, so criteria were established that laid out the basics: which routes were best in terms of (1) distance and speed, (2) existing ridership, and (3) the condition of the track, stations, and support facilities.

In the end there were relatively few controversial issues. Some routes, such as New Orleans–Los Angeles, were already down to one route and one train. For the Chicago–Los Angeles end points, one route was clearly better than the other alternatives. And sometimes a tweak was obvious: between Chicago and the Twin Cities, it made sense to reroute the long-haul services from the Burlington Northern and in the process pick up Milwaukee as a station stop.

When the data did not point to a single good answer, there were some hard choices. West of the Twin Cities, the Great Northern route had superior ridership but a lower en route population. The Northern Pacific had more people but it also had an interstate highway and better air service. The

The eastbound North Coast Hiawatha in western Montana, 1977. When Mike Mansfield left the Senate, this train was a "dead man walking," so I rushed out to ride it before it was gone.

incorporators went with the Great Northern route, but soon after Amtrak's start-up, and thanks to then–Senate majority leader Mike Mansfield of Montana, a train was added to the Northern Pacific route. It survived until 1979 when Mansfield left the Senate.

I had mixed feelings about the process. I was overwhelmed by the army of McKinsey folks—at the DOT/FRA I was a relatively big fish in a small pond, and now the pond was much bigger and my participation was less important. Perhaps I resented giving up control to a group of hired guns who were not really all that interested in the outcome. But in retrospect, it was a good process, and the routes selected have, for the most part, stood the test of time.

BRIEFING CONGRESS

Once the specific route choices were decided, the incorporators presented the results to the House and Senate prior to public release. I was there to provide "technical support"—because I had actually been to places like Wolf Point, Montana, and Trinidad, Colorado. This led to one of the more interesting confrontations in my career. Congressman Harley Staggers, the head of the House Commerce Committee and the most powerful man in Congress on matters involving transportation, was at one of the sessions. He took offense at the fact that there was no train through his district in West Virginia (he was from the city of Keyser, just west of Cumberland on the Baltimore & Ohio's line to Cincinnati). We thought that running a Washington–Chicago train via Charleston, West Virginia, would satisfy the congressman. Wrong!

After the session, Staggers cornered me outside. As I recall, he asked that we take another look at the route he wanted. Ever the analyst and never particularly politically correct, I

suggested that a bus connection, or perhaps a rail diesel car, would be the right answer. No sale.

"What we need, young man," he told me, "is a train like the National Limited, with sleepers and a diner and that round-ended car." He was referring to what had been the premier Washington–St. Louis train before the C&O/B&O consolidation (when the main Washington–St. Louis train was rerouted from the B&O to the C&O). The National had been gone for a long time, but Staggers knew just what he wanted.

Of course, I thought the whole idea was silly, but Staggers pressed his case and a train dubbed "Harley's Hornet" was run for several years between Washington and Parkersburg. These days we'd call it a train to nowhere. At one time, the high-speed TurboTrain equipment was used; it was designed to run more than 150 mph, but the route of the Hornet was mostly a mountain railroad with very sharp curves—slow-speed territory all the way.

That dialogue with Staggers was not the only time that I stepped in it with a member of Congress. Silvio Conte was the ranking minority member of the House Budget Committee—not a person to be trifled with. One day I got a call from his office. I picked up the phone and thought I was simply talking to a staff person. The complaint was that the New York–Boston service was being routed via Providence, Rhode Island, as it always had been. The caller said the trains should operate through Springfield, which was both longer and slower than the route through Providence. I responded with a smart-ass remark: "If God wanted trains to go through Springfield, he would have put tracks there." Well, long story short, I was actually talking to the congressman himself, who was holding a hearing on the DOT budget that very afternoon. His leading question to the department representatives was, "Who is this McClellan fellow? I want him fired." (He would not be the last

The TurboTrain at Cumberland, Maryland, 1974. I got into an argument with Harley Staggers over this train, because I thought numbers and logic mattered. I lacked any political sensitivity at the time.

person to call for my head.) Things got smoothed over at some point but the incident did add to my reputation as something of a loose cannon.

AMTRAK BEGINS

All of the planning and contracting did fall into place for a launch on May 1, 1971. The name chosen for the public and the marketing efforts was Amtrak, though legally the corporation remained the National Railroad Passenger Corporation. The launch was bittersweet for all railfans, myself included. While some continued service was now assured for at least a while, much would be lost in the process. Amtrak would cut 60 percent of all of the long-haul passenger trains. The only service

that would remain essentially intact was on the Northeast Corridor between Boston and Washington. Many of the most storied trains in North America would ride into the sunset at the end of April. There were many farewell trips, with extra cars added to accommodate those who wanted a last ride. I knew weeks earlier which trains would be eliminated, but was working nonstop on the Amtrak start-up, so saying goodbye to some of my favorite trains was simply not possible.

A few railroads chose not to join Amtrak. The destitute Rock Island could not find the cash resources to join. The Southern was too proud to join; Graham Claytor had the books cooked to show that losses were modest, and threatened to fire an assistant vice president who chose to disagree with him. The Rio Grande was concerned about the potential

The northbound Southern Crescent at Alexandria, Virginia, 1979. The Southern opted out of Amtrak because Graham Claytor, who served in government in many capacities, did not want a government company telling the SR how to run its railroad. The Crescent was not a great train when compared to the best trains of the streamliner era, but it sure looked good compared to Amtrak's long-haul service at the time.

The westbound Rio Grande Zephyr near Rifle, Colorado, 1977. The Rio Grande did not want to take the risk that a government-run railroad would override its dispatching decisions. Like the Southern, it wanted to maintain control of its operations. As a result, railfans such as myself got a few more years of "old-time" train riding.

The Federal Express speeds through Back Bay, Boston, just a few minutes from South Station, 1962. I bid farewell to the train before it left Washington on its last journey the night before Amtrak commenced operation. May 1, 1971, marked the last hurrah for many of the name trains of the streamliner era and was a bittersweet day for many a railfan.

impact on freight operations if it lost control of passenger train dispatching (locked into a competitive battle with the better-engineered Union Pacific, the Rio Grande gave its freight trains priority).

I did make it down to say farewell to the overnight train to Boston. It was one of the few NEC trains that would not survive (though an overnight train was added later). While standing on the platform I overheard two members of the crew complaining about government bureaucrats not knowing or caring about the trains and the people who worked on them. I wanted to step up and scream, "No, no, some of us care!" But I thought better of that and simply slipped away into the darkness.

The next day, an inaugural run was made from Washington to New York and back, using Metroliner equipment. It was my son Michael's First Communion and I could not make the full trip. But my wife Joanne, Michael, and I were able to ride to Philadelphia and make the return trip to Washington. In Philadelphia, Secretary Volpe was on the platform and called me over. He asked where I had been and I told him. A devout Catholic who went to Mass every morning, he gave Michael a warm greeting and had his photographer take pictures of the two of them. It was a truly wonderful thing to do, and it is the memory I treasure most from the start-up of Amtrak. Volpe had been one of the heroes in the creation of Amtrak; he took on a hostile White House and prevailed. This attention to my son elevated him even higher in my estimation.

May 1 was not the end of my relationship with Railpax and Amtrak; I had accepted a job with Amtrak and would be working directly for the new operation. By this time, I had come to believe my own hustle and thought Amtrak had a good chance of prospering. I wanted to be part of that.

Though a lot of my railroad colleagues have given me a hard time about Amtrak, I am still proud of what we were able to accomplish. Sure, Amtrak was deeply flawed, but given the political environment—not much different than it is today—it was probably the best anyone could have done. I remain convinced that moving passenger services from the back of freight railroads and onto the government ledger (a task not fully completed until the commuter train financial "drain" was resolved years later) was a key element in the rail renaissance. The Staggers Act gets more attention, but if you run the numbers, shifting the intercity and commuter losses to the public sector was critical to improving freight railroading. I count saving the rail freight industry as the most important legacy of the creation of Amtrak.

Amtrak itself has been a mixed bag. The Northeast Corridor was always a viable market for rail passenger service; heck, the Pennsylvania Railroad crowded folks into ancient P-70 coaches and still they rode the railroad. And now the NEC is more important than ever—it has even been expanded north to Maine (though with a change of stations in Boston), something that would not have happened without ridership gains in the Northeast Corridor proper. And the NEC has also expanded south to encompass much of Virginia.

But significant issues remain. The Amfleet cars are clearly better than P-70 coaches but they do seem a bit tired. They were never all that great to start with—not all that great a ride, and those little windows are a real negative. And now the cars are getting very long in the tooth and a major rework is clearly in order. The issue, as usual, is money.

The Acela provides a very good service and while it is pricey, it is no more so than what Europeans pay for high-speed trains. But on recent trips the track seems a bit rougher and I know that huge costs are coming due for the infrastructure (new tunnels under the Hudson and through Baltimore and a few bridges along the way). We are talking billions of dollars, and I have not a clue where that will come from. Will the folks in Kansas and Iowa and Texas care about paying? Not likely. Will the states in the NEC itself make the financial sacrifice? I doubt it. So the Northeast Corridor remains a work in progress.

The other corridors have been a mixed bag. Our vision for short-haul rail back in 1969–70 has been vindicated on the West Coast. People there seem to understand that they need an alternative to crowded roads and are willing to pay the taxes needed to create a rail alternative. The willingness to invest in new equipment is a major benefit; those California bilevels are as good as anything in Switzerland. In a sense, just how far we have come is illustrated by the fact that a president from San Clemente, California, saw no need for passenger trains whatsoever and now San Clemente has service as good as that in the Northeast Corridor—or much of Europe, for that matter.

The Midwest situation is more complicated. The equipment is old. Running times have come down but are not where they need to be. Some states, such as Wisconsin, have opted out of an expanded rail network. All of which points to a critical strategic issue: if you cannot convince the voters that good rail passenger trains are desirable, then that is the ball game. Count most midwestern states in the "who cares" group—they have more pressing matters to worry about.

And then there are the long-haul services. The best thing I can say about them is that they are still with us. With few exceptions, such as the Empire Builder, they serve no real transportation need. I love them and I love to ride them but the

A northbound Acela Express at Princeton Junction, New Jersey, 2008. The Northeast Corridor has proven to be a commercial success. The challenge now is to find the money to pay for the costly infrastructure required. But the Acela's success confirms the vision that the DOT had when Amtrak was created.

cold-hearted railroader in me is annoyed when a passenger train with perhaps 250 people onboard (about the load for an Airbus 320) gets priority over a twelve-thousand-ton freight train.

I do not lose any sleep over my role in the creation of Amtrak. It did help save the rail freight industry and it offers the platform for a rebirth in rail passenger service. Whether the public or the politicians care enough to spend the money needed to make that happen remains the core unanswered question, but at least a framework is there, should the political will ever materialize.

A southbound Metroliner near Landover, Maryland, 1975. During Amtrak's first years the Metroliners were the only modern equipment the company owned. Everything else was a hand-me-down from the private-sector railroads that preceded Amtrak. The Metroliners were rough riding—but fast—and riding upfront was like riding an interurban on steroids. You did not want to think about hitting something, but the thought was always in the back of your mind.

WORKING AT AMTRAK

As a director in Amtrak's Marketing Department, I was responsible for schedules, train consists, pricing, and special moves. I gained keen insight into the gap between the plan for Amtrak and the reality of an underfunded entity struggling to provide service with hand-me-down equipment.

THE START-UP

On May 1, 1971, the first day of Amtrak's operation, services were essentially run by the pre-Amtrak railroads. On that first day, 60 percent of the train-miles were eliminated, and most of the remaining trains were run as they had been on the day prior to Amtrak's start-up. There were some exceptions, including rerouting the Empire Builder east of Minneapolis from the Burlington Northern to the Milwaukee Road route through Milwaukee. The National Limited was extended to Kansas City. And a new through service was created on the West Coast by eliminating changes between trains at Portland, Oakland, and Los Angeles. Named the Coast Starlight, it ran from Seattle to Los Angeles with connections to San Diego, and remains one of the premier trains in Amtrak's long-haul network. But overall, the changes were modest—the peak

summer travel season was only a month away. Shrinking the network was traumatic enough, so the equipment and schedules during the first months of Amtrak looked a lot like the previous private-sector operations on a much, much smaller scale.

The Amtrak start-up went smoothly, for the most part. I didn't see any press coverage saying, "This is a new day for the intercity passenger train," but there wasn't massive condemnation, either. The press was mainly focused on the nostalgia aspect: many trains were making their last trip ever.

STAFFING AMTRAK

The board of incorporators had a long list of start-up issues, and none was more important than staffing the new enterprise. The new Amtrak organization, while not operating trains directly (that would come later), would exert strong overall control of the marketing functions and create a unified model for service and equipment. It was believed that a major problem with the fragmented private-sector network was service inconsistency between the various carriers, so uniform policies on pricing, equipment, and scheduling were

An eastbound Missouri Pacific freight near Jefferson City, Missouri, as seen from the westbound National Limited, 1972. One of our creative—but ultimately failed—efforts to better tie the network together was to extend the National Limited beyond St. Louis to Kansas City.

The southbound Coast Starlight along the California coast, 2011. The Coast Starlight was made into a through train between Seattle and Los Angeles (for a brief period there were even through cars to San Diego), one of the early changes that has endured. Before Amtrak, passengers had to change at Portland and again at Oakland. The goal was not to serve the end points; air was clearly the mode of choice in the Seattle/ Los Angeles market. Rather, the target was some of the shorter origin-destination pairs, such as Santa Barbara–Sacramento or Seattle–Eugene, Oregon, where air services were marginal or worse.

important. A passenger could have a great experience on one railroad and a simply terrible experience on another.

Because I had been part of the start-up team and actually knew something about railroads, I was asked to join the Amtrak organization. Objectively, Amtrak was not a very attractive career choice. It was widely reported in the press that the Nixon White House was determined to kill it off as soon as politically feasible, and my experiences as an insider in the process confirmed that view. Given the uncertainty, there were basically three groups of Amtrak managers: those who had reached a dead end in their careers, those who were simply bored and willing to take a chance, and those who were "true believers." That third group included some from the DOT/FRA, like me, who wanted to continue what we had labored so long to produce, and a small group of railroad executives who sincerely believed in the future of passenger service.

The incorporators hired Roger Lewis, former head of General Dynamics, as CEO. He had been ousted as head of GD by Henry Crown, who was a major shareholder in the company. But Lewis had friends in high places in the Republican Party and apparently needed a job. He was certainly bright enough, but fundamentally he had no knowledge of or interest in passenger trains. Other management hirings followed. Hal Graham came from Pan American Airways to be the chief marketing officer, bringing some of his Pan Am compatriots with him. F. S. (Pat) King soon arrived from Penn Central to be vice president of operations. David Watts, who had run the Chessie System's passenger operation, became his number two. Ed Edell came from the DOT to head the public relations effort.

I was asked to join Hal Graham's staff at a director level, responsible for schedules, consists (which defines what cars go on what trains), pricing, and charter services (special trains, or special cars on scheduled trains). It was an important and interesting job. Graham was a great boss—a bit disorganized but a creative and energetic person who cared about Amtrak (again, in contrast, Lewis seemed indifferent). Working with me in this modest department were Dirk Partridge, whom Graham had brought from Pan Am; Kevin McKinney, founder of the *Passenger Train Journal*, who had worked with us at the DOT as a summer intern and economist; and Jim Dietz, who had just completed his training program at the B&O/C&O only to be downsized out of a job. Partridge was in charge of pricing, McKinney was responsible for schedules and consists, and Dietz handled special trains and charters. But we all pretty much did whatever was needed to get the job done. Amtrak was not very bureaucratic in the beginning, but even then I could see the turf boundaries forming.

NEW SCHEDULES AND MARKETS

For the first months of its existence, Amtrak was a cobbled-together system, deeply downsized from what the private railroads had run. The initial timetable reflected that fact. But the timetable change in the fall would be an opportunity to create a new image for Amtrak. We were determined to develop and promote innovative services that would convince people that there was a "new sheriff in town." As it turned out, we were creative but not very good at execution.

The Penn Central had been running six-car Metroliner trains that were scheduled for operating convenience. If a train arrived in Washington at 5:15 PM, say, and it took thirty-five minutes to turn it, the next departure would be set for 5:50 PM. We were enamored with the elegance of the airline shuttle memory schedules used for the Eastern Air Lines Shuttle: hourly service, on the hour. We informed the Penn Central people that we would like to have hourly departures all day long—trains that left on a regular and predictable basis, just like the air shuttle services so popular at the time.

The pushback was that there were not enough Metroliner cars to accomplish that.

I responded that if we ran four-car trains, the schedules would work. "What about rush hour?" the Penn Central folks asked. I suggested that with hourly service, there really wouldn't be any rush hour. Anyway, the deal was done, and it has essentially worked for forty years. This was a classic case of the new kid on the block having a different vision than the professional railroaders who had actually been running the service. It was both a generational and a cultural problem: I saw them as old-fashioned, but in their eyes I was just another of the airline and aerospace people populating Amtrak. Once I told them a bit about my background, the tensions eased. Still, it was tough going much of the time, for the railroad people and for the Amtrak people as well.

If competing with the shuttle was one objective, we also saw a lot of unmet potential in smaller markets. One of the great advantages of the rail mode is its ability to serve those markets. Routes such as Trenton–Providence and New Haven–Baltimore had little or no air service, and traversing the New York metro area by car was difficult at best.

The service Amtrak inherited was a mixed bag. Most of the trains operated between New York's Grand Central Terminal and Boston, but three trains operated through Penn Station, thus providing service between the Corridor South and the Corridor North. We doubled the number of trains running through Penn Station from three a day to six, and extended one of the Metroliner schedules beyond New York City to New Haven. Today, all Amtrak trains operate into and out of Penn Station. The through service was a success and remains so today.

Expanding the concept to the Midwest, several trains between Chicago and St. Louis were extended to Milwaukee. The goal was not the end points (Milwaukee and St. Louis), but rather the lesser markets, such as the north Chicago suburbs to Springfield. The service didn't last very long. Things got off to a bad start when the train crew on one of the new services did not have a key to the restrooms of the through equipment being used. The media headlines did not read, "Amtrak offers new convenient service through Chicago," but rather "passengers locked out of restrooms." (I still think the concept is a winner, but Chicago is a barrier to through service now as it was then.)

THE FAILURES

There were plenty of failures as well. We decided to run a Metroliner nonstop between New Carrollton, Maryland (in the north Washington suburbs), and New York. It provided a Washington–New York service of just two and a half hours, which was more than competitive with air, considering the time involved in getting to and from the airport—and those were the days before the agony of the TSA. Still, ridership was dismal, and the train was discontinued with the next schedule change—but not before Jervis Langdon, then the trustee for the Penn Central, waiting for his Baltimore–Philadelphia train, saw the largely empty Metroliner cruise right through the Baltimore station. He wrote letters to *everybody*.

Then there was the fast train between Chicago and the Twin Cities, with only one stop at Milwaukee. We were fascinated by the prospect of competing with the airlines, or perhaps it was the idea of replicating the type of service that existed when passenger trains were in their prime. Unfortunately we had ignored the fact that trains were often most competitive in smaller markets.

But the mother of all mistakes was the first Amtrak timetable. We wanted to break with the past, so while the traditional timetable displays were included, we would also produce an airline-style origin-destination timetable that would show New York to Los Angeles, or Chicago, or San Francisco, or whatever. It fit our desire to show a truly national system and break from the fragmented networks of the past.

Unfortunately, the printer, a major publisher of airline timetables, failed the proofreading part of the task. Detroit was spelled "Detriot." We had no time to reprint the timetables, so off they went, nationwide. "Detriot" appeared over and over in the timetable, as in "Los Angeles to Detriot" and "New York to Detriot," and so on. What we had hoped would be viewed as a rollout of some innovative new services with a strong national brand became a public relations disaster: a new government railway that could not spell. Hal Graham was livid. That timetable marked the beginning of the end of my career at Amtrak. Neither I nor the Schedules and Consists Department really recovered. And like it or not, that timetable reinforced the opinion that it was amateur hour at the new national passenger railroad.

THE "RAINBOW" TRAINS

We were creative in moving equipment around, trying to upgrade trains wherever possible. A lot of long-haul western trains had been abandoned on May 1, and each abandonment produced three or four train sets of equipment. Amtrak, under the guidance of Bill Edson, formerly with the New York Central, inventoried the available equipment and selected the best in terms of mechanical condition and car body. (Stainless steel was preferred because it does not corrode with age.) It was something of a buyer's market, since other than Amtrak there were few markets for rail passenger equipment.

From the large pool of equipment, we started the upgrade process—for example, moving western leg-rest coaches (similar to a reclining chair) into service on some of the Florida trains. We put dome cars on trains that had never had them before, such as the Washington–Chicago train via Charleston, West Virginia. Motive power was moved around in a similar fashion, although that function was strictly handled by Operations. (The assignment of passenger cars was negotiated between Marketing and Operations.)

While the overall quality of the fleet was improving, there were a lot of problems. For example, railroads tended to buy equipment to their own specifications, so on paper, those long-haul western coaches looked good for the Florida trains—but they would require a lot of training of maintenance personnel, something we didn't do well. The same went for parts: whatever inventory the Seaboard Coast Line had maintained at, say, Miami, was unlikely to include the parts needed for cars shifted from the West. To compound the problem, the Operating Department chose to move the parts by rail—not intermodal rail, but *carload* rail, a terribly time-consuming process. When I told them to simply hire trucks and get the job done, the answer was that we were a railroad and ought to support rail transportation.

The scheduling and consist work was a lot of fun for the railfans on our team—McKinney, Dietz, and me. We made up dream trains and put, for example, an ex–California Zephyr dome observation car on the North Coast Hiawatha next to the Northern Pacific dome sleeper. We had fun, but the overall impact was less than impressive, as trains roamed the country with a mixed bag of equipment, all in different paint schemes. It was colorful, but hardly the kind of national passenger system image that we wanted to create.

The first-year Amtrak "look" was in marked contrast to a new, private-sector operation, the Auto-Train. Gene Garfield

The northbound George Washington pauses at Alexandria, Virginia, 1972. Soon after this picture was taken a dome car was added to the train, but it did little to improve patronage. Now named the Cardinal, this train remains one of the least patronized in the Amtrak system; its triweekly schedule is a huge impediment to attracting passengers.

had created a service that carried both passengers and their automobiles between Alexandria, Virginia, and Florida. (Now operated by Amtrak, it remains a popular service.) The equipment, while reflecting different heritages, had been carefully redone to present a common image inside and outside. It was really quite a handsome train, dressed in red, white, and purple. Further, the onboard employees, all extremely good-looking young women, were dressed in the same colors. One cold night at the Auto-Train terminal in Lorton, Virginia, I was chatting with a lovely sleeping car attendant, and as we were talking, Amtrak's Florida Special roared by with a mixed consist of SCL and UP equipment. It really looked pretty down-market compared to the Auto-Train—and the Special was the best train we had in the market!

Over time, Amtrak resolved many of those early equipment problems. We then set out to redo the interior of the trains in something more contemporary, but the results received mixed reviews. Most railroad equipment interiors could only be described as variations on beige. We decided to go with chic interiors heavy on reds and purples, and so the trains' motif went from "dull" to "French whorehouse"—more up-to-date, but not exactly a good choice of colors. Traditionalists were appalled. But hey, the guy doing the work, Bob Bengston, was cool, and I thought the new motif was cool as well. (So much for my judgment.) The exterior of the cars did not fare much better, but I was not a fan of either the red-white-blue color scheme or the Amtrak logo. I'm still not.

NEW APPROACHES TO PRICING

Amtrak inherited a hodgepodge of prices; each carrier had its own approaches. Fares in the Northeast, even for long-haul

The westbound North Coast Hiawatha near Cascade Tunnel on the former Great Northern, 1973. The consist reflected the "rainbow" period of Amtrak's early years.

The northbound Silver Star near Quantico, Virginia, 1973. Both the cars and the motive power reflected the cobbled-together image of early Amtrak.

Left, **The northbound Auto-Train at Aquia Creek, Virginia, 1974.** It was a popular service when inaugurated, and with a consistent color scheme and great onboard services it was a marked contrast to Amtrak's somewhat amateurish early service offerings.

Below left, **Years before Amtrak enters the scene, the southbound Florida Special races through Alexandria, Virginia, without stopping, 1964.** The Special was a winter-season train on the Atlantic Coast Line and then the Seaboard Coast Line; Amtrak ran it for one or two seasons. We added a few new twists by routing the train around Jacksonville, further cutting the schedule time. I rode it once, and we left Washington after dusk and were in Wildwood in the morning. A lovely schedule but not one that, in the end, attracted enough riders to last. In those early years we were willing to experiment but I learned that being creative if you cannot deliver the service is simply a waste of time and money.

trains, were far higher than those in the West. We set out to standardize fares to some degree, at the same time focusing on the need to lure more people onto the trains, as well as generate more revenue wherever possible. My contribution was to attempt to bring revenues per car-mile into some sort of sensible pattern. If the economics were going to work, in essence each railway car needed to generate similar revenues per car-mile. Further, with so little capacity on the long-haul trains, we had to try to maximize revenues.

Perhaps the worst performers were the Florida trains. The SCL had been very lenient in terms of the number of fares needed to occupy a bedroom suite, so a "full" sleeping car might have fewer than eight or so passengers onboard, compared with forty-four or more in a coach.

My thinking, right or wrong, was that as a taxpayer-supported enterprise, Amtrak had to be an alternative to highways and, in some cases, air; subsidizing the sleeping car passenger was not a core mission. So sleeping car prices increased, much to the dismay of some longtime customers.

MY LIFE WITH TRAINS

But as we were adjusting sleeping car fares upward, we were taking some aggressive steps to cut coach fares, especially in the East. For example, we put a $9.90 fare in for the Boston–New York service—a dramatic reduction designed to attract new passengers. The move drew screams of unfair government competition from bus companies, those beneficiaries of publicly funded highways.

MANAGING CHAOS

I would characterize the first years of Amtrak's existence as "enthusiastic muddling-through," and my time there was mostly a blur. We did not have a truly functional Operating Department because so much had to be negotiated with the railroads. We tried a lot of new things; some worked and some did not. My consistent failing was my ignorance of just how hard it was to take innovative ideas and translate them into consistently good service.

Working with the railroads was a special challenge. Some of them, such as the Penn Central, the Milwaukee Road, and the Illinois Central, were coming unglued during Amtrak's formative years. Track was deteriorating and speeds were being reduced on more and more track miles, resulting in lengthened schedules. The poster child was the Floridian, a train forever seeking a new route as we moved it from one line to another to yet another in an attempt to find decent track. It was futile, and the train ultimately died. (Poor track also doomed the Auto-Train's effort to operate a Midwest-to-Florida service.)

The Chicago–New Orleans service was another problem child. The train that was retained, the City of New Orleans, ran on a daytime schedule. But the schedule got longer and longer as the track deteriorated; the traditional dawn-to-dusk schedule was no longer sustainable. We bit the bullet and shifted the train to an overnight schedule, in the process renaming it the Panama Limited, in homage to one of the great trains of American railroading's glory years. The Amtrak version was a pretty poor substitute, but we liked the name.

Some months after the renaming, Arlo Guthrie's song "City of New Orleans," written by Steve Goodman and telling the story of a ride on the train, became a smash hit. We had zigged when we should have zagged, missing a huge potential for free publicity. The train was soon renamed the City of New Orleans. To this day my children gather round and sing "City of New Orleans" at every major birthday, just to poke fun at their father and remind him of his lack of marketing savvy.

GETTING FIRED

Perhaps the defining moment of my time at Amtrak was my departure in the summer of 1973. I was something of a loose cannon, always pushing the envelope. For example, the operation of through cars on the Coast Starlight between Los Angeles and Seattle was a good idea that ran afoul of the Southern Pacific's Operating Department. I wanted to swap out some coaches from the daytime Los Angeles–Oakland segment, and add a sleeper or two for the overnight run to Portland and Seattle. The SP said, "Hell, no!" and argued that its main line at Oakland was too busy to permit a switch move. It was not really true, but the SP did not want to be bothered. They finally prevailed, and I was branded a troublemaker.

I did not respect Roger Lewis, the president of Amtrak; I thought he was just a placeholder until the Nixon gang could kill the company. He knew nothing about railroads and seemed not to care. I, on the other hand, was a true believer and was inwardly critical of many of his decisions—I was

The Southwest Chief heading toward Raton Pass, New Mexico, 1973. I rode this train as a "farewell to Amtrak" after I was fired (my pass was still good for a few weeks). Hanging out the Dutch door and watching the semaphores drop was a religious experience, and except for the Amtrak colors on one of the cars, I could pretend I was on the El Capitan/Super Chief.

never directly insubordinate but surely did engage in some "tone of face" criticism. (I did not recognize what I was doing until years later when my then-teenage daughter gave me one of those "you're an idiot" looks. I grounded her for two weeks. She protested, "I didn't say anything!" I told her she was grounded based on her "tone of face." It hit me then how I must have been seen by Roger Lewis.) The SP fight and other dustups were enough to get me demoted to a manager-level job in the Operating Department, where I had few meaningful duties, if any. It was clear that folks thought I was a "dead man walking." My secretary, a transplant from the UK named Holly (and as good as they come), told me as much.

And then I was terminated.

The timing was lousy—I had just bought a house. So off I went to find other employment. But before I left, we had one great blowout gathering at one of the bars down on the Potomac River. All my friends were there to say goodbye—but they left me to pick up the tab.

Destitute (or close thereto), I decided to take one farewell trip using my Amtrak pass. Jim Dietz got me space from Washington to Oakland and then down to Los Angeles and back on the Southwest Chief. I had never ridden the Super Chief but this was as close as I would get. The first-class dome was still in the consist, and the crews, all holdovers from the Santa Fe days, could not have been better. They were proud of their train even if it was now run by some bureaucrats in Washington (as they saw it, at least).

I believed in Amtrak and probably would have hung around for years if I hadn't been forced to move on. But next I got to do some exciting things in the freight business, so being fired turned out to be a very good career move.

Sunset over the Pacific Ocean as seen from a private car on the rear of
the southbound Coast Starlight in the vicinity of Surf, California, 2009.

Two westbound Conrail freight trains climb the grade to Gallitzin, Pennsylvania, 1985. MG Tower can be seen in the background.

THE CREATION OF CONRAIL

10

Fired from Amtrak, I returned to the FRA as the Penn Central was collapsing. There I was part of the effort to create a viable new railroad from the wreckage of seven bankrupt eastern railroads.

A NEW BEGINNING

The collapse of the Penn Central led to the nationalization of intercity passenger service, but the freight story is altogether happier: The PC's demise led to the creation of Conrail, which continued to lose money. But government—both Congress and the executive branch—had no stomach for long-term subsidies for freight railroading (freight does not vote!), so this led to the relaxation of government regulation with the passage of the Staggers Act.

Commercial pressures, including the deregulation of trucking, forced railroads to deal with their core economic problems: too many companies, too much low-volume track, too many employees. Railroads had to change and did, embracing technology with a vengeance not seen since the dieselization of the industry after World War II. I was in the middle of many of these changes, sometimes as an interested observer but usually as a direct participant. It took more than

two decades—roughly 1975 to 1999—to reorganize the industry into the current viable framework. (Change never comes overnight—remember that it took almost two decades for the railroads to dieselize.)

Being fired from Amtrak turned out to be a good thing. After a hard month and a half with no income, my "godfathers" at the Federal Railroad Administration, Bill Loftus and Jim Hagen, intervened on my behalf and I was hired at the FRA in October 1973. I had worked for Bill at the FRA during the passenger crisis and for Jim at the SR as a market analyst. They had a hard sell; the new administrator was John Ingram of NYC and SR fame, who later was CEO of the Rock Island. John had hired me at my first job at the SR and knew full well that I could be a loose cannon. I got a stern lecture about never, ever talking to the press again. I agreed—fingers crossed, of course.

Hiring me back was not just an act of charity, however. The "great railway crisis" was spiraling out of control, with half of the northeastern mileage in bankruptcy or headed in that direction. Judge John P. Fullam, who was in charge of the Penn Central bankruptcy case, was threatening to liquidate the company. The Washington politicians and bureaucrats finally had to pay attention to the mounting crisis. Added to the sense of impending doom was the reality that much of the midwestern network beyond Chicago was failing as well. In fact, with the Milwaukee and the Rock Island in serious trouble, some argued that the railroad crisis stretched from Boston to Houston to Denver to Seattle/Tacoma—the far limits of the Milwaukee and Rock Island railroads.

The government's initial effort to stem the mounting economic disaster—the creation of Amtrak—was not the solution. The railroad problem was accelerating.

SETTING THE STAGE

Now that freight railroads are successful and passenger service has been at least stabilized (albeit with government funding), it is hard to imagine the railroad world of 1968, when I left the PC for the FRA. There were some good railroads—the Southern, the Santa Fe, and the Union Pacific, for example. But a huge part of the industry was failing. It was not clear, especially to the Washington establishment, that railroads could or even should survive. The marketplace had spoken: failing companies should be allowed to die. That was certainly the view of the Nixon White House.

Two of the largest railroads in North America at the time, the Pennsylvania and the New York Central, had merged in 1968 to form the Penn Central Corporation. On paper, the PC was a powerhouse, with a railroad franchise serving the heart of industrial America at the time as well as the huge population along the northeastern seaboard from Washington to Boston. It also owned some of the finest hotels in Manhattan (such as the Waldorf Astoria) as well as an executive aircraft leasing company, a pipeline company, real estate in Florida,

and the Six Flags amusement parks. It was one of the largest corporations in the United States.

Two years later, the Penn Central declared bankruptcy. It was, at the time, the largest bankruptcy in US history. There were many root causes, but four deserve mention.

First, the northeastern freight business was in decline and had been for decades. Manufacturing was moving to other lower-cost regions such as the Southeast and the West. (Off-shoring would come later.) The expansion of trucking siphoned off much of the high-value freight and capped the rates that could be charged for the remainder.

Second, the track capacity needed for the booming passenger and freight business of the 1920s was now a liability. But railroads other than Perlman's New York Central were loath to cut capacity. Besides, reconfiguring a two-tracked railroad to one track with traffic control took money, something in increasingly short supply. Further, downsizing is depressing and most companies put it off. (Think of how slowly brick-and-mortar retailers have adjusted to the internet.)

Third, commuter services lost a ton of money, as public agencies would learn when they took on the financial responsibility years later. The trains were too well-patronized to be abandoned, and it was a lot cheaper to fight a railroad's abandonment case at the ICC than to actually pay the deficits. There was some grudging action—public funding of new cars here, or a station improvement there—but it was all too little and too late. Government did not "get it," and the initial response to the crisis by the DOT and then the USRA was flawed. It would take almost another decade to fix the commuter train problem.

Fourth, intercity passenger trains still lost money despite the creation of Amtrak. The biggest culprit was the Northeast

An eastbound passenger train overtakes a freight and a helper engine heading into Altoona, Pennsylvania, 1968. The bankruptcy of the Penn Central and the subsequent government intervention led to fundamental changes in the relationship between the government and the railroads.

An eastbound Lehigh Valley freight train near Bethlehem, Pennsylvania, 1975. Weeds were the norm; railroading was an ugly, ugly affair. As I walked away from taking this photo, Garry Collins of the USRA advised me never to turn my back on a moving Lehigh Valley freight train.

The Lehigh Valley double-tracked main line west of Allentown, Pennsylvania, 1975. The deferred maintenance is obvious. At this time the line still hosted six freight trains a day, and derailments were common.

Above, **A northbound Central of New Jersey freight near Bound Brook, New Jersey, with Baldwin power in charge, 1960.** The ballast was thin and the ties were rotten but things would soon get a lot worse.

Above right, **A westbound Reading freight departing Abrams Yard in King of Prussia, Pennsylvania, 1960.** Of all of the bankrupt railroads, only the Reading and the Erie-Lackawanna made an effort to maintain both their track and their equipment. Now this segment of the former Reading forms a key link in Norfolk Southern's Chicago-to-Philadelphia main line, and the Reading came out of the northeastern crisis more important than it had been before its bankruptcy.

Right, **An Erie-Lackawanna local freight at Campbell Hall, New York, 1968.** Though this railroad was once a significant factor in Chicago–New Jersey rail commerce, today only the portion of its main line between Binghamton and Buffalo, now owned and operated by Norfolk Southern, remains an important route.

A northbound Lehigh & Hudson River freight at Easton, Pennsylvania, 1960. The L&HR was a small and irrelevant railroad even when I was in college. Still, it provided variety and was charming in its own way. It joined the restructuring process but in the end was not needed and most of the line was abandoned.

Corridor, a mixed-use network of freight, commuter, and intercity passenger trains. While the accountants argued about who should pay for what, the Penn Central was still holding the bag for most of the infrastructure costs.

The story was pretty much the same for the smaller northeastern railroads: massive commuter losses (the Lehigh Valley was the exception), a declining freight franchise, and no money available for a redo of that overbuilt and collapsing infrastructure. Without the financial resources to downsize, deferred maintenance reached crisis proportions and train speeds declined, as did the productivity of locomotives, cars, and people. Deteriorating service accelerated the loss of freight traffic as customers moved to trucks. It was a death spiral with no end in sight.

Bankruptcy was no solution—some costs were avoided but the enterprise was still failing. Historically, railroads used bankruptcy to eliminate unsupportable fixed charges before returning to some sort of economic equilibrium. Not so with the Penn Central and the smaller carriers. All had tried bankruptcy: the New Haven filed in 1961, the Central of New Jersey in 1967, and the Penn Central, the Boston & Maine, and the Lehigh Valley in 1970. By 1972, the year after Amtrak was started, the Erie-Lackawanna and the Reading, as well as the smallish Lehigh & Hudson River, were also in the tank.

For the government, the choices were liquidation or providing taxpayer dollars of an unknown amount and duration. If you think of the recent meltdown of banks and auto companies, you'll get the picture: bailing out a freight railroad with tax dollars was as much a loser politically then as bailing out Wall Street or General Motors is today.

That was the situation when I returned to the DOT.

STORMY WEATHER

In the summer of 1972, Hurricane Agnes struck the Northeast, and floods took out hundreds of miles of railroad from Virginia to New England. Some carriers, such as the Southern, though hard hit, had the resources to make repairs. But for the teetering northeastern carriers, it was one more nail in their coffin. Critical lines were restored to service but not secondary lines, and even where repairs were made, the costs further destroyed fragile cash reserves.

The railroads turned to the government, and the result was a loan guarantee program. It fell to the DOT to determine which lines should be funded and which should not. For the brilliant Gerald Davies (a newly hired analyst at the FRA and later a senior executive at CSX, the BNSF, and the CN) and for me, it was a real-world education in Bankrupt Railroading 101. As was the case with Amtrak, the resources were few and the needs were great.

As it turned out, Agnes was the starting point for the dramatic downsizing of the American railway system. Armed with traffic numbers and rebuilding costs, we made decisions on a line-by-line basis. Not all lines were worth rebuilding. Even more interesting was how railroads, so hostile to government in the past, were making passionate appeals for it to restore service on many lines. The most memorable exchange I had was with Dick Hasselman, the Penn Central's chief operating officer. Hasselman wanted to restore the "Muleshoe Line" west of Hollidaysburg, which ran parallel to the main line over the Alleghenies and provided a safety valve to the route around Horseshoe Curve. But we turned him down; it seemed that there was more than enough capacity available. Hasselman challenged us: "How would military supplies move if there were another war?" We responded, "By air."

Hasselman was one of the smartest railroaders I have ever met and the glue that kept the Penn Central running. But he just could not see that the railroads were becoming less and less relevant in the transportation world. Later, when I was managing the line rationalization program at Norfolk Southern, I would hear the same passionate appeals for the status quo from both the commercial and the operating people. Railroaders love their railroads! That's normally a good thing, but it can blind them to a changing world.

GOVERNMENT ACTS, RELUCTANTLY

Soon after I returned to the FRA, the Northeast freight problem was beginning to stir. There was a high-level meeting at the DOT, chaired by the undersecretary, Jim Beggs. Beggs came from NASA and was extremely bright, a man focused on the intelligent use and analysis of data. Arrayed around the large conference table overlooking the Potomac River and National Airport were all the main players from the DOT and FRA policy offices. It was an initial scoping effort, presenting issues and options. Was the problem real or were the railroads overreacting? How big was the problem? Should the government intervene? If so, how? The pros and cons were dutifully listed. So far, this had been a standard government briefing, which normally concludes with a recommended action plan.

With his long legs up on the table, Beggs asked, "Well, what is the answer?" Jim Hagen, leader of the FRA effort and not one to mince words, said simply, "We don't know." The truth was that we were all in uncharted waters and had the good sense to say as much. Beggs said thanks and declared that he was going to go home and have a drink. It was Friday, it was late, and no one had anything of value to add.

By this time, the leadership of the DOT knew we had a serious railroad problem. But as with Amtrak, the Nixon White House was not the least bit interested in bailing out freight railroads, especially in a region of "blue" states. Besides, it was in the middle of the Watergate scandal, and the White House had other concerns.

This being Washington, there needed to be a study, of course. Congress wanted action and so did Judge Fullam. Everyone wanted answers. The DOT/FRA went into crisis mode. Deputy Secretary John Barnum and his policy team (Bob Gallamore, Lou Thompson, Russ Murphy, and Jane Holt) struggled with the broad public policy issues and politics. The pressure from Congress was intense; it wanted to avoid a shutdown and keep all of the constituent groups happy, from customers to communities to rail labor. "No pain, no gain" was not in the congressional DNA. But like the executive branch, Congress did not want to spend much on a freight railroad problem.

Meanwhile, an equally slim group of us at the FRA (Jim Hagen, Bill Loftus, Gerald Davies, Steve Ditmeyer, Jim Boone, and I) were trying to get our hands around the economics. We knew there was too much railroad but we needed numbers. So we set out to figure out just how much the system would need to be pared to produce a viable rail system. But we took the wrong fork in the road, getting hopelessly mired in data before we had sketched out the big picture.

The new secretary of transportation, Claude Brinegar, pitched our effort in the circular file and wrote the report to Congress himself. He concluded that there was a viable private-sector railroad under the rubble of the Penn Central, but that the company would have to be dramatically restructured (think smaller) and would need public funding to make the transition—a hard sell to a White House not attuned to the needs of the blue states. Next, action moved to Congress for needed legislation. Its normal tendency to dither was overcome by Judge Fullam's threat to shut the railroad down—losses were mounting, and the judge would not sanction an unconstitutional taking (the erosion of the value of the remaining assets being eaten up by the deficits). Timely and effective action by the federal government was needed.

The administration said that the railroad should be liquidated, partly to keep Congress guessing in an effort to exert maximum leverage in the writing of the law. In fact, at one point the top guns of the FRA were gone and I was left as the spokesman. (Now there's a scary image!) Ingram told me to just tell the press that a sale at the courthouse steps was the way the government was going. Then I got a call from people higher up the food chain at the DOT; their message was essentially, "Never mind—there will be no sale at the courthouse steps." Later I learned that General Motors, Ford, U.S. Steel, and Bethlehem Steel (which would later go bankrupt) got their heavy-duty lobbying into action, basically telling the White House that if the Penn Central shut down, they would have to curtail their operations as well. It was a recipe for a serious recession.

When the political dust settled, a reluctant President Nixon signed the Regional Rail Reorganization Act (the 3R Act) on January 4, 1974, creating the United States Railway Association (USRA), a private-sector, but government-funded, solution for the bankrupt railroads of the Northeast. Already deep in the passenger business, the government was now heading into the rail freight sector—with the outcome very much unknown.

In its first report, the DOT was required to describe the basic outlines of the future rail network. A joint DOT/FRA team was assembled to accomplish the task. The result, published in February 1974, was *Rail Service in the Midwest and Northeast Region*—essentially everything north of the Ohio River to the Mississippi River. The conclusion was that there were too many railroads with too much track chasing too little traffic— traffic that was declining, to boot. Our numbers showed that the network needed a fairly brutal haircut; 25 percent of the local service route-miles were declared "potentially excess"— a nice, politically correct term meaning "tear up these tracks." At John Ingram's instruction, these lines were colored a bold orange, and the report was known as the Orange Line Report.

Getting the report published by the DOT was challenging. The first challenge was self-inflicted. Gerald Davies and I made a presentation to Secretary Brinegar and his staff. We were sitting directly opposite the secretary, a bright, no-nonsense executive on loan from Union Oil. We opened the computer report, hot off the printer, and to our horror found that it had been bound inside out—to see a printed page one had to tear the perforation, a tedious task at best. As Davies struggled with the report, I grabbed a piece of paper and began to sketch the concept we had used in our analysis. John Ingram pushed his chair away from the conference table to physically distance himself from the evolving debacle. Finally, the secretary said he had seen enough and marched off to the exit door—which was locked for security reasons. He had to wait until his aide could unlock the door.

Ingram took us all downstairs, where we spent three or four tough hours trying to figure out just why we had done so badly. Ingram was not amused, but after the dust had settled we made another run at the analysis, with a better outcome. Our concepts were sound, but with the reworking we got better numbers, and a report that was printed properly.

When the report finally came together, many inside the DOT said that it was too explicit. Their view was that we should simply say there was too much railroad and that substantial abandonments would be required. Let the new agency, the USRA, define the network; the 3R Act gave them that responsibility anyway. I argued that that approach would be a cop-out. If we were out to change the railroad world— which we all believed had to be changed—we might as well get on with it. We ultimately went with the tough-love approach.

The report came out in three volumes. The first was an overview of the problem and suggested solutions, and also dealt with the level of competition needed—a very powerful driver of future rail mergers. Places such as Buffalo, Pittsburgh, and Boston made the cut; Fort Wayne, Toledo, and hundreds of other points did not. Maps of the main-line network showed corridors with too many routes. In the New York–Chicago origin-destination pairing, the DOT said two routes were enough. But unlike the local service network, the DOT did not pick winners and losers. The second and third volumes covered different geographical areas, with detailed maps showing recommendations for the local service network.

The competitive analysis and main-line findings got little attention. But the two volumes of maps that showed in orange all of those potentially excess lines created a firestorm. It is one thing to pontificate about too much railroad, and quite another to say, "And it is *your* railroad, Mr. Congressman, that needs to be abandoned." Members of Congress and governors, rail shippers and rail unions, all reacted with outrage. In some states, especially in the overbuilt midwestern states east of the

Mississippi (action on the Midwest west of the river would come later), orange seemed the dominant color. In Michigan, nearly half the mileage was deemed excess. (I was in the contingent that briefed the governor in Lansing—he was not happy.)

I was delighted that the DOT had been a truth teller. The report set the stage for restructuring the industry; decades later I cited it to justify the split of Conrail and argue why only two railroads were needed in places like Buffalo. What was once radical had by that point become conventional wisdom.

OFF TO THE USRA

The USRA was free from many constraints, such as those involving government hiring, that are desirable but that get in the way of prompt action. It was also immune from ICC regulations and antitrust, labor, and environmental laws. The railroad crisis was deemed so serious that the very laws that had contributed so much to the crisis were rescinded for the purpose of developing the plan. The USRA's plan would be subject to review by the ICC and by Congress, which could vote it down with a two-thirds majority.

The USRA had to produce two reports: a Preliminary System Plan (PSP) and a Final System Plan (FSP). The 3R Act had set out, in its preamble, a wish list of objectives for the new agency: minimize the loss of service and jobs, keep the cost to the taxpayer low, preserve competition, consider the impact of passenger service, and so on. In short, there was a nod to every constituent group, and any legislator could hide behind the preamble and declare that the outcome, if unpopular, was not their fault. (If they liked the answer, they would take a bow, of course.) These various goals assigned to the USRA were often in direct conflict with one another. But once one sorted through the debris, the tasks could be grouped around these basic issues:

- The network. Which lines would be transferred to Conrail, and which lines would be transferred to others or abandoned?
- Competition. What level of competition should and could be created?
- Profitability. Would the redesigned entity be profitable?
- Government funding. How much and what form of government financial assistance would be needed?

Of course, to answer those key questions, a lot of other information was needed. Traffic forecasts were required to estimate revenues and traffic volumes (which would impact such things as crew starts, locomotives required, etc.). The size of both the main-line and feeder networks would drive the estimate for rehabilitation. The financial statements and the need for government funding would depend on both the level of rehabilitation needed and whether the new entity would be profitable. The list went on and on.

The effort would be guided by a board of directors representing government (the Departments of Treasury and Transportation and the Interstate Commerce Commission) and rail management, rail labor, states, and communities. I have worked with many boards in my career (most after my USRA days), and I remain impressed with the quality of those board members. Each and every person worked in an unbiased fashion and there was virtually no posturing. It was an honest and largely apolitical effort to get the right answer.

Putting the board in place was relatively easy compared to staffing the operation. This would be a short-term job, but the USRA needed expertise for the daunting task ahead. An "all hands on deck" call was sent to transportation professionals in both the private and the public sectors, who were asked to pause in their careers and come to Washington. The pay would be competitive but not excessive, and the job security was nil. The message was, "Come and work incredible hours and if—*if*—we are good enough, we might just save north-eastern railroading."

A small but critical core group came over from the DOT/FRA (with no assumption that they could return). Railroads and transportation consulting provided additional expertise. Some very talented people were shamed into participating ("You have been saying that something should be done about the railroad problem—here is your chance to put up or shut up."). Like the board, the staff did not have a political agenda per se. Most had a bias toward a private-sector solution, but there was no overt hostility to government; after all, many of us had worked in government and did not see it as the enemy (as is often the case today). For the most part we were advocates for rail transportation and wanted to see railroads saved and even returned to some of their former glory. But for the short term, survival was a good answer, and if that could not be done in the private sector, then perhaps government would have to step in. Simply stated, we had a pro-railroad bias. (Well, most of us. Our vice president for finance, John Terry, a trucker by trade and disposition, thought railroads were good for hauling coal and not much else.) Our vision was that railroads could be streamlined and made competitive and financially sound. The focus was on the future—if something did not contribute to that outcome then it had to go, whether it was a track or a yard or a company.

In the USRA organization I was the director (later the assistant vice president) for strategic planning, with responsibilities for competitive issues, the light-density line analysis (what to keep and what to shed), and passenger issues. I reported to Pete Cruickshank, on loan from the Burlington, who reported to vice president for operations Jim Hagen, who reported to the president, Ed Jordan. Jordan reported to Arthur Lewis, the USRA chairman. (Lewis had also served on the Amtrak board of incorporators.) The USRA was so new and so pressed for time that the organization was fluid and reporting relationships were usually ignored. Because this was not a long-term job, the focus was on getting it done and getting out, and so corporate politics was minimal.

The Strategic Planning group consisted of three units: Garry Collins led the main-line and passenger group, Gerald Davies was in charge of the light-density line analysis, and Nelson Slater handled state and local liaisons. The key players included Jim Blaze, Jim Dietz, Mike Fox, Tom Hieber, Rick Huffman, Laurie Kent, Ed King, Tom O'Connor, Dirk Partridge, and Mary Ward. Most had prior railroad experience and most would go on to successful careers in transportation; many went to Conrail from the USRA. They were as talented a group as I have ever worked with.

SEEKING A COMPETITIVE NETWORK

Most of our time was taken up considering the competitive and branch-line issues, which were monumental (thousands of miles had to be analyzed for profitability and recommendations made for inclusion or exclusion from the final network). Passenger trains got some attention but only as much as was needed to check the box and tell Congress we had addressed the subject. The level of competition was an especially sensitive concern, and is worth some discussion here because the USRA's inability to find a competitive solution had repercussions for two decades until the showdown between CSX and NS split Conrail at great cost to both companies.

It was not that the USRA did not try. The senior staff was of two minds on the issue: One school felt that the northeastern rail system was at death's door and while competition would be nice, it was more important to simply find a core of sustainable freight rail service, with or without competition. Hagen was in that camp; he did not want the perfect to be the enemy of the good and he was keenly aware of how badly things were going out in the real world. The other view, which Gallamore and others (including me) shared was that putting all the eggs in the Big Conrail basket was risky. If it failed, there would be no rail alternative and nationalization would result, probably spreading to the rest of the industry. But if it was successful, or if CR managed to get a huge influx of ongoing public funding, then the remaining solvent railroads would be at risk.

I certainly felt passionately about the matter. I was at the New York Central when the Penn Central was created and I thought it was a huge mistake. My hostility to the PC carried forward to my involvement in the DOT Orange Line Report, which came out in favor of limited but balanced rail-to-rail competition at a limited number of high-volume points served by two carriers only.

Given the importance of the issue, Hagen directed Strategic Planning to start with a blank sheet of paper and look at all of the options that we could think of. Jim Dietz worked day and night (writing in penmanship that would have made his grammar school teachers proud) to create a number of scenarios:

- Simply ignore competition and put all of the bankrupt carriers together in one company (Big Conrail)
- Split the Penn Central into its component parts that existed before the merger
- Create further subdivisions to create "many Conrails," thus avoiding the problem of "too big to fail"
- Make the Penn Central the core of the new Conrail, and merge the smaller bankrupt carriers to create an alternative to Conrail
- Merge all lines of bankrupt carriers east of a line through Buffalo and Pittsburgh, and operate them with ongoing government subsidies
- Have the government own the infrastructure as it did for highways, and permit open access to all railroads
- Encourage the solvent carriers to absorb the lines of the Penn Central and other bankrupt carriers

If an option had a multiple-carrier solution, revenue and costs had to be developed. If, say, some lines were to be sold to solvent carriers, or if Conrail itself were to be split east and west, then the financials had to be developed accordingly. Essentially, Dietz would define an option, and Newt Swain, the marketing guru, would then estimate the appropriate revenues. Chuck Hoppe and Hugh Randall, the operational planning experts, would generate the operating statistics (miles of road, car-miles, etc.), and John Terry, head of finance, would produce financial statements, assisted by Russ Murphy and Jane Holt. It was a huge amount of work because the time pressures were intense; every day the bankrupt carriers were getting weaker and service was getting worse.

A couple of the options did not make it far in the review process. For example, the kiss of death for the idea of "many Conrails" came at a public meeting of carriers and shippers. Jim Hagen outlined the USRA's thoughts on the options and the audience responded. Yale professor Kent Healy, one of the towering intellects in transportation education, observed that the head of one of the private British railways (there were individual companies in the UK until they were all combined into British Railways after World War II) had said that the firm's size should be such that the CEO could meet with each of its employees at least once a year. To which Jack Fishwick, CEO of the Norfolk & Western, replied, "Professor, if that was the standard then there would never be a British Empire." End of discussion and end of the concept.

A government-owned, government-subsidized infrastructure (a concept the USRA called Confac) had some appeal in some circles, mainly among economists and public policy wonks. In theory, government funds would flow freely to the infrastructure company, just as funds were freely flowing to highways at that time. The USRA rejected the concept overall but did apply a derivation to the Northeast Corridor. My penetrating glimpse into the not-so-obvious came one evening at Georgetown University, when I was addressing a group of law students. One of them pushed hard for the public infrastructure option, arguing with great passion (as befitted a lawyer-to-be) that such ownership would assure an ongoing source of funds and thus a robust track structure. I responded, "I just drove over here on publicly-owned and -maintained streets and had to dodge potholes all the way. So maybe public ownership does not equate to good infrastructure." Going home (dodging potholes once again), the issue became clear to me:

once railroad funding was in the public domain, then it would be competing with every other claim on the tax dollar, from wars to social programs. (This was the era of the Vietnam War and the War on Poverty). My instincts were right: Amtrak has to beg for money every year, and now even highways are underfunded.

In the end, the idea of using the Penn Central as the core for Conrail and shifting the other bankrupt carriers to solvent carriers was the basis for the competitive solution outlined in the Preliminary System Plan. It was cooked up one night in a bar and drawn on a napkin by Garry Collins and me. The Erie-Lackawanna would be offered to the Norfolk & Western, and the Central of New Jersey and the Reading would be offered to the Chessie. If either solvent carrier chose not to bid, the package would be offered to the other solvent carrier.

Not surprisingly, the N&W pretty much said, "You have to be kidding." The ICC had already forced them to take the E-L in order to consummate the Wabash/Nickel Plate deal; the N&W kept the E-L at arm's length lest its poor financial performance sink the N&W. We had anticipated that reaction from the N&W, but believed that if they were offered something reasonable and then refused, they could not then cry foul. (The restructuring process was as much about politics as it was about economics.) The Chessie response was positive; they were interested in the Reading/CNJ (a natural fit and the Chessie's historic "friendly connections" into the New York area) and would look at the E-L as well. The expanded Chessie would be an effective counterweight to Conrail (a.k.a. the Penn Central rebuilt).

Negotiations began, led by Pete Cruickshank for the USRA. The Chessie would take both the E-L and the Reading/CNJ. Some thought the Chessie was just playing games, but some of their best management brainpower, such as Ray

Lichty, worked on the project, and a company does not commit those kinds of resources unless it is serious.

But in the end there was no agreement. The Erie-Lackawanna unions insisted that past labor agreements be honored, and the E-L still had six-man crews in Ohio. The Chessie, fearing the costs of labor claims without end, opted out of the deal. A time would come for labor to be reasonable, but not yet. Politics always lags behind economics.

CONTROLLED TRANSFER

While Cruickshank was negotiating with the Chessie, Hagen called me in for a special assignment. Hagen was being pressured by Bill Coleman, who had become secretary of transportation in March 1975, to simply sell the bankrupt carriers to the N&W and the Chessie. Called controlled transfer, it was a version of the earlier DOT approach of selling assets at the courthouse steps, but this time the DOT proposed a substantial "bounty" for potential buyers: $500 million in government grant money would be available to both the Chessie and the Norfolk & Western. The solvent carriers would split the bankrupt carriers and then use the federal grant money (free money, if you will) to rebuild their portions of the bankrupt properties.

The key issue was splitting the Penn Central; if that was accomplished, then the smaller pieces of the puzzle would fall into place. Emotionally I favored a split (rooted in my long-standing hostility to the Penn Central merger), but I was at a loss as to whether it could be accomplished. Faced with this monumental problem I turned to one of my best friends, John Williams. Now back at the Southern Pacific, Williams and I had worked together at the FRA. He was a network expert, and with his FRA background, he knew a lot about the Northeast.

(When I know I'm in over my head, I always seek out smart people to help, a trick I learned from Jim Hagen.)

With John's help, I worried about the issue for several weeks and still could not decide which way to go. But undecided or not, I had to give my conclusions at the next meeting of the USRA board. I put together one of the worst presentations of my entire life—much too long and inconclusive, a classic "on the one hand, on the other hand" that makes economists a target for derision. It was so boring that Gus Aydelott, the CEO of the Rio Grande, read his *Wall Street Journal* as I babbled on. After I spent an hour presenting the pros and cons of controlled transfer versus doing the Chessie deal (which was very much in play at the time), Bill Scranton, no longer governor of Pennsylvania but still a board member, asked, "Well, what would you do?" Cornered, I said that the Penn Central was simply too fragile to split; the risk was that the process was so perilous that it could sink the PC and the solvent carriers as well. I let my gut do the thinking instead of my head, and that was a good thing. Decades later, when CSX and NS split a very healthy Conrail and still stumbled badly, I knew I had given the right answer to Bill Scranton's question.

Looking back, I probably had already reached my decision. Several weeks earlier Jack Fishwick called—the only time he called me directly. Secretary Coleman had offered the N&W the deal outlined above: $500 million in grant money, and the N&W would take half of the northeastern bankrupt network (essentially the former PRR). Fishwick asked my view, and without any hesitation I said it was not nearly enough money and was not worth the risk. I should have been as decisive in my presentation to the board.

Controlled transfer would have been an utter and complete disaster. Coleman was not at the meeting but was very upset to hear that his pet solution had been voted down by the

A westbound Delaware & Hudson freight near Oneonta, New York, 1975. When the Chessie deal fell through, the smallish D&H became the default competitive solution in the Northeast. It was simply a stopgap measure designed to keep the creation of Conrail on track.

USRA. I got caught in the fallout—I had planned to go from the USRA to Conrail, but Coleman put a stop to that.

THE SHINY SILVER SPHERE

Meanwhile, the Chessie deal was falling apart, and the USRA was left without a competitive solution. Hagen called me into his office and, arms outstretched, asked if I knew what he was holding. I did not have a clue. "Jim," he said, "it is a shiny silver sphere and your job is to take it out and let people feel it. But never let them poke it because it is full of shit."

Hagen knew that the clock was running and Conrail had to be launched. So he had a press conference and sold the Delaware & Hudson as a competitive solution: the D&H would be given trackage rights to connect with solvent carriers at Buffalo, Philadelphia, and Alexandria, Virginia. Gallamore and I, both opposed to this sham, were allowed to come to the press conference on the condition that we not utter a single word publicly or privately. And damned if Hagen did not pull it off! Using a map of the Northeast, he waved his pointer around vaguely to describe the grant of trackage rights. It was smoke and mirrors, but he convinced most of the press that the D&H was a viable substitute for the Chessie System.

It was the right decision—a classic case of never letting the perfect become the enemy of the good. The D&H faltered and provided weak competition at best, but Conrail was launched. Federal dollars began to flow to rebuild the network, and rebuilding the bankrupt carriers was far more important an objective than some notion of balanced competition. Still, the pain and cost involved in the split of Conrail decades later could have been avoided had the issue been resolved in 1976 and had the Chessie taken the USRA offer. But the competitive structure that now exists is just about perfect, because it corrected the core competitive issue created by the merging of the Pennsylvania with the New York Central.

SHRINKING THE NETWORK; OR, ORANGE LINE REDUX

Strategic Planning devoted most of its time to deciding which lines of the bankrupt carriers should be included in Conrail, conveyed to other carriers, or simply scrapped. The DOT had already declared that huge portions of the northeastern rail network were "potentially excess." Now it was up to the USRA to do further analysis and make the call on the fate of thousands of miles of line. Using data obtained directly from the railroads (a far more accurate measure than the 1 percent waybill sample used by the DOT), the USRA analyzed all light-density lines of all the bankrupt carriers and made its decision.

It was tedious number-crunching. A line-by-line description of the action recommendation, complete with a map, was published in the Preliminary System Plan. The Rail Services Planning Office (RSPO), part of the independent Interstate Commerce Commission, was a creation of Congress, and was designed to provide a critical review of both the DOT's and the USRA's plans for the Northeast. Always looming in the background, the RSPO did keep the DOT and USRA somewhat honest, though our main focus was on the congressional reaction. The RSPO held hearings at various locations, and while there was a lot of wailing and gnashing of teeth, few fundamental mistakes were found.

The Final System Plan dropped over six thousand route-miles from the Conrail system. Subsequently, Congress added a federal subsidy program amount equal to 100 percent of the losses on a line in the first year, tapering off to zero after five years. The subsidy was a lure for many serious entrepreneurs and more than a few rail buffs who hankered to have their own railroad. As the subsidies declined so did the mileage operated, but there were some success stories. States, most notably New York and Pennsylvania, stepped in to provide subsidies in some instances.

The USRA did an adequate but not great job of trimming the system. A few years later, new legislation was passed to give Conrail automatic abandonment authority under certain conditions, and a second round of abandonments ensued.

The Orange Line Report and the FSP gave legitimacy to the elimination of redundant rail lines as a tool for solving the railroad problem. It was timely, because by 1976, the railroad crisis had moved west. Using its power of the purse to deny federal funds to projects that it deemed unworthy, the DOT extended the rationalization process to the granger states. And in 1980 when the passage of the Staggers Act forced railroads to operate more efficiently, solvent carriers joined the rationalization bandwagon. Some lines were transferred to short-line carriers, while others were abandoned outright. From the passage of Staggers until 2000, when downsizing was about over, Class I carriers dropped from almost 196,000 route-miles to 99,000.

AMTRAK BECOMES A "REAL" RAILROAD

The Final System Plan had a major long-term impact on the relationship between freight railroads and passenger operators. Passenger deficits were dragging down the Penn Central and the other bankrupt carriers. Amtrak had not resolved the deficit issue. The culprit was the cost of the fixed plant.

A New Jersey Transit commuter train at Princeton Junction, New Jersey, 2008. The USRA transferred facilities primarily used for passenger service to the appropriate public entity, whether Amtrak or a commuter authority.

Commuter operators had contracts with the Penn Central and other bankrupt carriers, but isolating the costs of the infrastructure was extremely complicated. Not surprisingly, under pressure to keep subsidies as low as possible, Amtrak and commuter authorities found that it was easier to argue about a charge than to pay it. The "hole in the doughnut" amounted to millions of dollars annually.

The USRA recommended that all lines where passenger services were the dominant user be transferred. The Northeast Corridor between Washington and Boston (less some segments already owned by state agencies) was designated for transfer to Amtrak, while commuter lines were to be conveyed to commuter agencies, such as Metro-North, the New Jersey DOT, and the Southeastern Pennsylvania Transportation Authority. Those conveyances did not totally eliminate the losses on commuter services. After Conrail was in operation, further legislation shifted passenger employees to the commuter agencies and to Amtrak. But the transfer of the infrastructure was a critical first step in relieving Conrail of the hidden costs of passenger operations. It is a model that has now been used almost everywhere, but there are exceptions. For instance, Chicago's METRA railroad still contracts with the BNSF and the UP to supply employees under contract, and the infrastructure remains with the freight carrier.

THE LEGACY OF THE PENN CENTRAL

The failure of the Penn Central and subsequent government actions (the creation of Amtrak, subsidies for commuter services, the Staggers Act) marked the starting point for the rail renaissance. If the public wanted passenger service, the public was going to have to pay. Similarly, if customers wanted better freight service, they too would have to pay. And if railroad managers wanted railroads to survive, they would have to find more efficient ways to operate their business.

It took roughly a decade for all of the pieces to come together, but the ultimate success of Conrail spared the rail freight business the curse of nationalization. If the freight business had been forced to endure the vagaries of the political process to obtain funding, railroads would not have endured. Nationalization was a very real threat but thanks to some smart decisions and some very good luck, freight railroading dodged the nationalization bullet. It was a better outcome than most of us involved in the process would have predicted at the time.

Facing, **A westbound Conrail freight on Horseshoe Curve, just west of Altoona, Pennsylvania, 1985.** Conrail did a remarkable job rebuilding and reenergizing a moribund northeastern rail network. Its success ultimately led to its being divided between CSX and Norfolk Southern.

The Southern Crescent ready to leave Peachtree Station for New Orleans, 1979. I was a frequent passenger on this train during my second tour with the Southern; we were required to take the train to and from Atlanta.

LOOK SOUTH, AGAIN

11

I returned to the private sector in the Southern's Corporate Planning and Development Department as the SR was seeking to expand through merger. But CSX moved first, and the SR was forced to play catch-up by merging with the Norfolk & Western.

GETTING BACK TO BUSINESS

"Well, Jim, welcome back to the private sector," was the way Arnold McKinnon—the Southern's vice president for law and later the CEO of Norfolk Southern—greeted me soon after I joined the Association of American Railroads. "I never thought that I left," I answered, but Arnold assured me that I had.

Getting back to the private sector had been a hard slog. With the publication of the Final System Plan, the work of the US Railway Association shifted from planning to the legal work of transferring the properties to the entities designated in the plan. It was an essential part of the process but it was not my thing. I thought my best career move at that point was to go to Conrail. After all, I had gone to school in Philadelphia and my wife and I loved the city. We even found a house in the Philadelphia suburbs. But I had been blackballed by Secretary

Coleman—apparently Jim Hagen, Gerald Davies, and I had offended him during the USRA process, and he declared that our going to Conrail would be a conflict of interest.

If Philadelphia was a nonstarter, then we wanted to stay in the Washington area. The options were limited. The Southern had hired Hagen back and did not need another planner with government experience. I wanted to get back to the private sector if I could, which meant trying to find a job at the Association of American Railroads (AAR). The AAR was the industry's trade association and as such did lobbying as well as think tank work to support its lobbying effort.

Shef Lang was the head of the AAR's think tank group. When he was head of the Federal Railroad Administration, he had given me a job when the Penn Central was imploding; now he came to my rescue again. But my hiring had to be approved by the AAR board of directors, all of whom were railroad CEOs. Apparently I had made a lot of enemies during the northeastern rail crisis. The final vote was six to five in favor, with those who did *not* know me voting "aye" and those who did voting "nay." It was not exactly a resounding vote of confidence. I suspect McKinnon cast the winning vote.

It was now 1977, and Conrail was up and running but still losing buckets of money. Still, the Northeast was no longer in crisis mode. But the "railroad problem" persisted; it had simply moved to the Midwest. The Rock Island, the Milwaukee, the Chicago & North Western, and the Illinois Central were in varying degrees of financial angst. None would survive as independent companies. Government was once again in rescue mode, but the FRA, not the USRA, was the point agency for this crisis. For most of these railroads, obtaining funding was a matter of economic life or death.

The AAR provided an interesting vantage point from which to view this ongoing drama. The monthly board meetings gave insight into the concerns of the CEOs. Basically, the industry was split between the haves and the have-nots. The Santa Fe and the Union Pacific were suspicious of government intervention, fearing that it was a prelude to nationalization. Their fears were not unfounded; intercity passenger service had been nationalized. And Conrail was, after all, a ward of the state as well. The weak roads, meanwhile, needed federal aid and to hell with the consequences. Drowning men have no time to argue philosophy.

Sometimes the arguments got downright silly. When the FRA and various states requested traffic density maps, showing which lines were busy and which were not, there was a pushback from some on the board. John Reed of the Santa Fe declared that if the maps got into the wrong hands, terrorists would know what rail lines to sabotage. (There had been some instances of terrorism even then.) Of course, terrorists could figure out which lines were busy simply by sitting at trackside and counting the number of trains—but I kept my mouth shut. A larger concern was that competitors would use the maps to gain commercial information. The SR thought it had solved that problem by submitting maps cut along state boundaries, but the states (and, I presume, the SR's competitors) simply got together and glued all the pieces back together to get a complete map.

If most railroads were deeply hostile to government, they were also ambivalent about me, even the ones that had supported my being hired. Some state planners, knowing of my role at the DOT and the USRA as an advocate of streamlining the network, saw my role at the AAR as an industry plot to abandon lines on a nationwide basis. That was not the case, but such was the paranoia of the times. Railroads were in retreat almost everywhere.

My stint at the AAR was brief. I learned that Jim Hagen was leaving the Southern to take the top marketing job at Conrail, which created an opening at the SR, though not at the same level. After my tours in government and at a trade association, I was anxious to get back to an operating company. But I have some fond memories of my time at the AAR from 1976 to 1978. Lang was one of the smartest men in the railroad business and I learned a lot from him. There were other benefits, too: free from the pressure of crisis management, I was able to see and study more of the industry and fill in some gaps in my knowledge. Better still, interaction with railroad CEOs gave me insight into how various rail leaders viewed the industry and how they approached problems—and let me see who was smart and who wasn't.

RETURN TO THE SOUTHERN

Returning to the SR was not exactly a slam dunk. I called Stan Crane, then the Southern's CEO, directly and said I wanted to come back. Crane balked, citing Hagen's compensation to the nickel and indicating that his departure would reduce overhead costs. Finally he relented just a bit and told me to

A northbound Missouri Pacific freight train at Osawatomie, Kansas, 1980. The Southern's second effort to merge with the MP led the Union Pacific to make a strong bid for the MP. That was the start of the UP's march to prominence in the West.

call Bob Hamilton—the man who had hired me on my first tour, who was quite angry when I jumped ship for a job with the New York Central.

But Hamilton offered me a job as a director in the Corporate Planning and Development Department, reporting to Phil Dieffenbach, the assistant vice president who headed the small department. Rail mergers and acquisitions were a key task. Given the industry's financial turmoil, I was convinced that mergers were where the action was going to be. I was more prescient than I could have ever imagined—much of the rest of my career would be focused on restructuring the SR network and that of Norfolk Southern.

In fact, shortly after I arrived in the fall of 1978, I was told to take a look at the file on the aborted SR–Missouri Pacific merger. The first effort had failed when they could not agree on who would be in charge (always a key issue in mergers) as well as the respective values of the two companies (often a

consideration secondary to that of who would be in charge). Now the SR was making another effort. A bid had been made and I was gearing up for the kind of action I had seen at the FRA and the USRA. But a day later I was told to stand down; the Union Pacific had trumped the SR's second offer by a wide margin. One can only speculate about how the industry would have aligned if a successful east-west merger had been accomplished.

I learned later that John Kenefick, the CEO of the Union Pacific Railroad (the UP Corporation was far more than a railroad at the time), had designs on the MP. Kenefick, with whom I had worked at the New York Central, was as smart and aggressive as they come. He understood that the UP was vulnerable to the Burlington Northern, newly created in 1970. But the corporate leaders in New York were not convinced that railroading was a good place to invest. The second SR bid played into Kenefick's hand; he argued that if the SR and the

MP merged, the UP would become a marginal franchise. For the UP, a deal with the MP was a make-or-break proposition, and New York relented.

Meanwhile, the Seaboard Coast Line was moving to better integrate its expansive empire, including the Louisville & Nashville and the Georgia Railroad/West Point Route. The SCL "network" (which had been the Atlantic Coast Line network originally) was much larger than the SR, but, unlike the SR, it had never been operated as an integrated system. With a more unified commercial and operating structure the SR was at risk of being marginalized. The SR's paranoia about being outclassed by a larger carrier was a theme that would drive SR's—and then NS's—decisions for years to come. In fact, the eastern railroad story is largely one of the SR and then NS playing catch-up with its larger competitor, the Seaboard System. And soon after I returned to the SR all hell broke loose on the merger front, as we shall soon see. I find it interesting that the SR was one of the first railroads to propose an interterritorial merger. But when it failed to consummate the MP deal the action shifted to other carriers.

BACK IN THE LINE RATIONALIZATION BUSINESS

It seemed that I had spent a lifetime abandoning trains and tracks, first with the creation of Amtrak and then at the FRA and the USRA with the creation of Conrail. The USRA excluded thousands of miles from the final Conrail network; entire railroads disappeared. I had no interest in tearing up more railroad lines, but Stan Crane ordered me back into the rationalization business anyway. Crane and other senior executives were inspecting an abandonment candidate in South Carolina when their hi-rail bus derailed, sending some to the hospital with cuts and bruises and sprains. Crane called me up to his office a day or two later and said, "The lawyers aren't getting the job done—I want you to get involved in these abandonment cases." I said I was tired of doing abandonments. Crane reminded me that he had made a decision and that what I wanted to do was irrelevant. As I had learned in the military, I said, "Yes, sir," and moved on.

The SR needed a lot of trimming; it had too many lines serving low-volume markets. Based on my USRA experience it was far overbuilt for current, post–interstate highway market realities. Apparently I was a bit too aggressive. One day I was sitting in the anteroom waiting to see Earl Dearhart, executive vice president for our department. I could hear Dearhart and Crane talking. Crane said, "He is going too far—take him off the job."

"He is doing what you told him to do," Dearhart replied.

Crane said, "Well, I did not want him to do this much."

I made a quiet exit.

Crane really loved the railroad and hated to see any of it go away. Interestingly, once he went to Conrail, he was very supportive of line rationalization efforts. I think Crane, with his long career with the SR, thought of it as family and all of those lines were part of its heritage. Conrail was another matter, at least emotionally.

While I was not happy at the time, the new responsibility turned out to be a good career move. New leadership at Norfolk Southern—Bob Claytor until 1987, and then Arnold McKinnon—had a much different perspective on downsizing, which took place under both. I would have a leadership position in the largest downsizing in the company's history, shedding some six thousand route-miles (about a third of the railroad at the time). Transfers to short-line carriers and outright abandonments were the tools of the rationalization trade both at NS and at other railroads.

A Southern Railway inspection train in Andalusia, Alabama, 1981. The train had two F units in green and off-white on the point, followed by ten or so office cars. At the end was the SR's test car and then the theater car. It was pretty much a train out of the 1960s, and I have fond memories of hanging out the Dutch door as we trundled through the Alabama night at 20 mph.

THE SR LOOKS AT THE ILLINOIS CENTRAL GULF

The Southern needed to reach new, important markets, but insisted that it be the dominant partner in any consolidation. The SR was very proud of its corporate culture and believed that it was the best-maintained, best-operated, and most innovative railroad in the country. Mythology can die hard in the corporate world. The SR might often be wrong but it was seldom in doubt. However, it was wise enough to understand that other carriers were consolidating, and the SR needed to respond.

The Southern was approached by the Illinois Central Gulf: Would the SR be interested in acquiring the ICG? A merger study was launched, and Phil Dieffenbach and I were part of the study team. By 1979, the ICG was a sick railroad. Created from a merger of the Illinois Central and the Gulf, Mobile & Ohio, its main line ran from Chicago to New Orleans, while secondary main lines reached out to the east and the west of this core—to Kansas City, Indianapolis, Birmingham, and Shreveport. Illinois Basin coal, grain, chemicals, and wood products were its most important commodities. The IC had been one of the premier railroads in North America.

The "Main Line of Mid-America," it had operated one of the classiest passenger trains in the land, the Panama Limited, an all-Pullman service, for many years. Its City of New Orleans was the inspiration for one of the greatest railroad songs ever written. Its City of Miami provided a high-class service between Chicago and Florida. In Illinois, it operated passenger trains at 100 mph. As a flatland, coal-hauling railroad, it stayed with steam longer than most other railroads.

The Gulf, Mobile & Ohio, meanwhile, was a second-tier railroad that duplicated much of the IC's route structure, and its market coverage and infrastructure were second class. Putting the two railroads together was classic 1960s strategy: a parallel merger that would permit the elimination of redundant tracks, yards, and people. But the savings proved too small to save a declining traffic base.

The ICG was a good fit with the SR network. With the IC, the SR could strengthen its existing coal and grain franchise and add a base of chemical traffic—an area where the SR was relatively weak. The main ICG routes lay to the west of the SR system, broadening SR coverage in Mississippi, Louisiana, and Tennessee. The SR was weak in Illinois and had no lines in Iowa and Missouri; it would gain access to Baton Rouge (rich with chemical traffic), Shreveport, Kansas City, Indianapolis, and Chicago. Chicago was especially important: the expanded Seaboard Coast Line's Family Lines had good access to Chicago while the SR had to depend on Conrail or the Chessie, neither of which was very interested in short-haul traffic from the Cincinnati gateway anymore. The SR needed single-system service to stay competitive with SCL.

In merger terms it would be an end-to-end merger: while the SR and the ICG served some of the same markets, the routes went in different directions (the SR went east from St. Louis, Memphis, and New Orleans; the ICG went north). It was a perfect fit. The proposed merger would be a takeover of the ICG by the SR, thus assuring that the SR would be in charge, a key objective of any merger deal from the SR's perspective. The sticking points were profitability (lacking) and rehabilitation (hundreds of millions of dollars required). Track, locomotives, cars, and yards would all require a massive upgrading.

The SR wanted to do the merger but the numbers simply made it too high-risk. In retrospect, a takeover of the ICG would have been possible but for two factors. First, the ICG needed a severe haircut, and at the time—before the Staggers Act—it was hard to see a way to downsize the ICG, especially when the SR was seen as a "rich" railroad able to subsidize a weak ICG. Second, and more importantly, the SR was unable to think outside the box. As was the case with the Penn Central, there was a viable core inside the ICG waiting to get out. But rather than think creatively, the SR simply applied the same formulas that had worked in modernizing the SR in the fifties and sixties. The plan was to turn the ICG into a mirror image of that era's SR, with automated yards, welded rail, modernized shops, new engines, and new cars—all of which came with a huge up-front cost.

Further, there was no strategic plan. The ICG reached Kansas City, Indianapolis, and Shreveport—places where its market position was weak and its infrastructure a disaster. In this pre–Staggers Act environment, neither abandonment nor transfer to a short line was deemed an option. In that, the SR was correct. However, the reinvestment was not required; the SR could have just limped along in these noncore markets just as the ICG had been doing for years. But that was not the way the SR operated. Its culture was far too rigid to consider another course of action. Nor were the new boxcars and a new hump yard in Memphis needed—the traditional carload market was in decline, though the SR did not really understand that. Of course, the ICG later proved that with the right plan and a far better regulatory climate, it was possible to downsize the railroad.

I was certainly no stranger to a downsizing effort, because of my FRA and USRA experience. But I did not speak up; as the new guy, I lacked the confidence to take on the rest of the SR merger team. And I too thought that the regulatory environment would be hostile to the kinds of changes needed. (At the USRA we were operating outside of the ICC regulations.) My sense is that the course of merger history would have been far different had the SR acquired the ICG, just as it would have been different had the MP merger been consummated. A combined SR/ICG would have reached west without a doubt.

STRIKE DUTY

Soon after I returned to the SR, a strike was called. I marched down the hall to see Paul Rudder, vice president for transportation. I volunteered to help. "What can you do?" he asked.

"Well, I have switched cars," I said, based on that one night of switching passenger cars at Grand Central Station. "And I have run locomotives." (Three hours at the controls of the Rio Grande Zephyr.)

Rudder called the Greensboro Division's superintendent and told him, "I have an engineer for you." At this point I said that my experience was limited. Rudder said, "Just put him on in the daytime."

Fortunately the strike was over before I could get to the airport to catch my plane.

Fast-forward some months. In 1982 there was another strike. I got a call in the evening and was told to "report to Inman Yard by tomorrow morning."

Again, my military training kicked in: "Yes, sir." I later learned that once I had declared that I could run locomotives, my name had been entered into the SR computer database as an engineer. Be careful what you wish for, as they say.

I caught the last plane from Washington National to Atlanta, arriving just before midnight. I spent the night sitting in the airport, and then got a cab to Inman Yard. At the gate to Inman, my taxi was met by a row of picketers. Not knowing where I needed to go, I asked them where crews reported for duty. They directed me, and there was no hostility—but you know there was a lot of talk once the cab drove off. ("How about that, they're sending people to run the railroad who don't even know where to report!"). But the strikers directed me to the right place.

I went into the office and said I was there to be an engineer. Blank stares. No one was expecting me. Someone said, "We need an engineer on the pullback engine—let's put him there." The van pulled up and off I went to my assignment. There sat my engine, a cow-and-calf switcher (one engine powered, and the second one with just traction motors, getting its electric power from its teammate). I climbed onboard and asked the engineer to give me a quick rundown on the controls. He demurred, saying, "I'm retired, I just came back to help out, and I just want to go home and get some sleep!" I thought to myself, now you've done it. But there was no going back, and somewhere deep in my brain was enough information to remember what all of the controls did. Once I got the hang of it, I had a ball. The weather was great, and the only drawback was that we were on duty more than twelve hours—not quite kosher—and my lodging was downtown, which meant a long walk to the gate and a long bus ride. It did not leave much time for sleeping.

The strike was over in four days, and I was sorry to see it end. A year or two later, an engineer's training course was offered at the training center in McDonough, Georgia. I signed up and actually learned all of those things that I should have known earlier. I stayed qualified for years until I decided that running a simulator once a year for half an hour did not really make me an engineer. Of course, once I was actually trained, there were no more strikes.

Looking back, I am appalled at how casually we treated safety. I was hardly qualified to run an engine, though I was sufficiently scared to avoid doing anything stupid. My Navy training was helpful; ships, like trains, do not stop on a

Above, **This was my locomotive for the first two days of the strike of 1982.** It was the pullback engine for the Inman Yard hump. Inman is now an intermodal terminal.

Left, **The hours were brutal but I had a ball during the strike of 1982.** Here is yours truly at the controls. The photographer was one of my crew whose name I no longer remember.

Facing, **The view of the yard from my engine, 1982.**

dime, and you learn to think and plan ahead. I think fear was what got us through, because I was hardly the only person out there with limited skills and experience.

When I ride locomotives today I am always impressed that "safety first" is now a culture and not just a slogan.

BUYING A LINE TO NOWHERE

With the ICG study done, I grew bored. Long lunches with my friends at the FRA became a frequent occurrence. But I needed a project, and went searching for one. Conrail had a line along the Indiana-Illinois border that ended at Cairo, Illinois. It crossed the SR's St. Louis line at Mount Carmel, Indiana. The line had substantial coal mines and coal reserves, though the ICG enjoyed the business. The SR was "coal poor" and did not have the on-line coal to support all of the power plants on its railroad. The line no longer fit the CR system but it was a good fit with the SR.

So in 1982, off went the "band of brothers" (Bob Cooney, the lawyer; Steve Evans, the planner; and I), heading west in search of a new project. Reaching the Cairo line was a challenge; it was three hours by car from St. Louis, Memphis, or Evansville. Once we got there, the Holiday Inn at Muddy, Illinois, was the only source of lodging, food, and alcohol in this dreary part of the world.

The track was in terrible shape from Mount Carmel to Harrisburg and essentially out of service from there south to the Ohio River. But a huge amount of coal was available; a number of major mines were or could be served from the line. We interviewed customers, who, anxious to encourage competitive rail service, assured us that they would use Southern service. The SR would have two ways to handle coal: north to its St. Louis line at Mount Carmel, or south to Cairo for barge transportation beyond, provided that rebuilding the south half of the line could be justified. (The SR had been in the barge/rail business for years over at Pride, Alabama.)

It was one of the dumber projects I ever attempted. The effort was overtaken by events: the NS consolidation was approved, and the N&W coal department took charge of coal marketing. They were not the least bit interested in developing new coal production out in the boonies. The line was never improved and ultimately most of it was abandoned. But Illinois Basin coal is now in favor again; it is relatively cheap, and for power plants with the scrubbers that are now the norm, it is a desirable boiler fuel, whereas central Appalachian coal, the bread and butter of the old N&W franchise, has fallen into disfavor because of its cost. My concept was not all that bad, but my timing was off by two decades.

From this episode, I learned that a solid concept (which this was) needs a rabbi—someone who has clout, can pull strings, and can protect a project from hostile forces. Unfortunately we didn't have one, and the project went nowhere. Doing the deal is the easy part; the follow-up is not, unless someone in charge cares. With NS now in its start-up phase, there were a lot more interesting projects to work on.

CSX FORMS AND THE SOUTHERN RESPONDS

While the SR was studying the ICG, the Seaboard Coast Line was engaged in expansion plans of its own. One trigger was the SR-MP merger talks, to which the Southern Pacific responded behind the scenes with an overture to the Chessie, but the routes did not mesh—the only common point was East St. Louis. Next, the SP approached the Seaboard Coast Line, but the SP's overbearing Benjamin Biaggini turned off the Seaboard's genteel (but very bright) Prime Osborne. Then Osborne and Hays Watkins, head of the Chessie, made contact, ultimately structuring a deal to consolidate the Chessie and the Seaboard Coast Line under the name CSX (Chessie and Seaboard, tied together) in November 1980. The original concept was a holding company: the two railroads would keep separate marketing and operating organizations, but would consolidate joint facilities and reroute traffic for the benefit of CSX. (Nor did the SCL ignore its own backyard: in 1982 the Seaboard System was formed with the formal merger of the SCL and the Louisville & Nashville.)

As an interesting side note, I got early knowledge of the planned merger from John Snow, with whom I had worked at the DOT/FRA and who was now in the Washington office of the Chessie. He and I had lunch one day and I suggested that the Chessie and the Southern would make a great fit. As I recall, I even had the maps to show John. He responded that he thought a north-south merger made sense but that the "other carrier made more sense" for them. I thought I had scored an intelligence coup and reported back to the SR that a Chessie–Seaboard merger might be in the works. I was widely rebuked as being an alarmist. As a new hire and an outsider from the government I was treated with a fair amount of suspicion.

CSX was the first meaningful crossing of the historical north-south boundary, and it presented a huge challenge to the Southern. Substantial traffic diversions from the SR to CSX were predicted. Jack Fishwick, the CEO of the Norfolk & Western, came to Washington to discuss a common defense, though I am certain that a merger was on his mind. That he came alone was instructive; where the SR was run by a senior management team, Fishwick was a lone wolf. But that was good for me because Phil Dieffenbach and I were in the meeting despite our being lower on the totem pole.

The traditional counterpunch to a merger was to propose a series of conditions to the merger: keeping competitive gateways open, providing switching access to segments of the proposed network, and the like. Under the guise of maintaining competition, such conditions also restricted the ability of the new entity to make many commercial and operating changes in their new system.

In this case, the SR would seek access to the west coast of Florida, where the merger of the Atlantic Coast Line and the Seaboard Air Line to form the Seaboard Coast Line years earlier had created a rail monopoly. Our plan proposed that the SR acquire the former ACL from Jacksonville (the end of the SR System) to Tampa. The area south of Tampa would be turned into a neutral terminal company, owned by CSX and the SR, similar to terminal companies such as the Belt Railroad of Chicago and the Terminal Railroad of St. Louis. (Our choice for a name was the whimsical Naples, Venice and Florence, all towns in the proposed switching area.) The concept was not implemented at the time, but was the germ of a concept that will appear later in our story.

The SR also wanted to purchase the former Monon Railroad (acquired by the Louisville & Nashville in 1971) to give the SR its own access to Chicago. The SR had had a chance to purchase the Monon earlier but now decided that it was critical to the SR's future. Finally, both the N&W and the SR proposed that a new, neutral company be formed to provide open access to the Seaboard System's coal origin points around Corbin, Kentucky (formerly Louisville & Nashville lines, and once the stomping grounds of the L&N's handsome "Big Emma" locomotives). This entity would be called the Eastern Kentucky Railroad.

The proposal had to be backed with complete commercial, operating, and financial details. Support had to be developed and local interests courted. For example, if the SR obtained the Monon, it would increase the number of freight trains rumbling through Hammond, Indiana. This did not go down well with Hammond's mayor and I was unable to bring him around. Score another point for the opposition.

The SR had no access to the properties involved or to traffic records, so our marketing and operating plans were a bit shaky. Much of our "research" had to be done on the sly; rental cars were our stealth mode of investigation. One of our consultants did score a major coup when he talked his way onto the locomotives of Amtrak's Floridian, then running on the Monon. There were screams from the opposition, as there should have been.

Preparation of the case was an intense, fast-paced effort, similar to what I had experienced at the FRA and the USRA. In the end, I felt that we had made a good case and that we would get at least some of what we wanted. I was wrong. The decision came promptly (at least by ICC standards), and the SR and the N&W got absolutely nothing, except for one minor condition granted to the N&W. Essentially the ICC ruled that it would protect competition, not competitors. The N&W and the SR were admonished to find a proactive solution to the challenges of CSX—in essence, "Go do your own deal."

Our merger team was shocked; clearly the ICC was no longer playing by the rules that had governed its decisions for decades. We should have known better, since our application came just after the passage of the Staggers Act, and much of the debate leading to that law had been critical of the ICC for

A Norfolk & Western coal train on Blue Ridge summit, Virginia, 1958. I spent time photographing the N&W in the fifties (mostly chasing steam engines). With the SR-N&W merger, I became reacquainted with the railroad, and this time I got to stay in the Hotel Roanoke rather than the YMCA.

protecting the status quo. Indeed, many of the ills of northeastern railroading had been laid at the ICC's front door. The SR and the N&W got caught in the crosshairs of a new regulatory world.

CSX had won a stunning victory over the N&W and the SR. So now what would the SR do? Crane called to pick my brain. First he launched into a rant about the Seaboard System, arguing that it simply was not fair that he would be a loser. "Hell, I run a better railroad than they do," he said. This reflected the attitude of many CEOs at the time. They were

living in a static, regulated world, and believed that if you ran a good railroad, you should do fine.

Crane was adamantly opposed to a merger with the Norfolk & Western. And he did not like Fishwick, for whatever reason. Crane suggested that we reactivate the ICG talks, but I told him that buying ICG would make us weak financially and an easy prey for a larger railroad such as the Burlington Northern. That was not what he wanted to hear. He said, "God, save me from the planners and thinkers!" I had the good sense to leave his office.

But in the end, the SR really had few options except to merge with the N&W. Much of the negotiation was beyond my pay grade at the time. But talking to board members years later, it seems that the board essentially forced Crane to do a deal. I was in the room for one classic exchange. Our investment banker insisted that the exchange rate be changed in the SR's favor. It was a minor point in the scheme of things but the banker darkly hinted that it might be impossible to certify that the exchange rate was fair to the SR shareholders. At which point the SR's CFO said, "Well, I guess we will just get another banker who sees things our way." Needless to say, the necessary opinion was forthcoming soon thereafter.

The two management teams were suspicious of each other, though with less intensity than had marked the Penn Central merger. The SR was a broad-based merchandise railroad that took pride in operating its sprawling network efficiently. The N&W was more focused: utility and export coal, vehicles and vehicle parts (especially for Ford, a legacy from the Wabash part of the N&W), and grain and grain products, also a Wabash legacy. The systems did not mesh all that well. The SR was oriented north–south, the N&W east–west. The SR needed a route from Cincinnati to Chicago, and fortunately the N&W had acquired the former Penn Central line from Cincinnati to Richmond, Indiana, thanks to the foresight of Louis Newton of the N&W. With this former PC line, and with a lot of rebuilding of Nickel Plate branch lines, a more or less direct route to Chicago could be cobbled together— but not one as good as the CSX's line through Nashville and Evansville, an advantage CSX enjoys to this day.

Nancy Fleischman—one of the finest attorneys I have ever known—and I had to develop a consolidation plan. (That's technically the legal term, but I will use "merger" from here on in.) There were many commercial and operational issues to be resolved. What new traffic might be gained? Were there improved routings? What yards would close? What lines abandoned? How many jobs would be added or lost, and where? What about environmental impacts, such as more trains running in proximity to schools and hospitals? It was a balancing act; the applicants needed to show benefits (otherwise, why do the deal?) but also wanted to minimize the harm, lest a political backlash unhinge the merger.

I recall our first meeting of the merger team in Roanoke. All of the major groups were gathered around a conference table—Marketing, Law, Finance, Transportation, and Engineering. Nancy and I had a leadership role; our job was to produce a credible story for the ICC, backed up with facts. We said that we needed the group's input and suggested that everyone get together with their counterparts, brainstorm, and come back with their ideas. The request was met with indifference and some hostility—not many in the room were enthusiastic about the merger. Finally, in frustration, I suggested that Nancy and I would prepare the submission for the ICC and if they did not like it, they would have to live with it. I figured they'd rather cooperate with the "other side" than trust a lawyer and a planner. A couple of hours later, we had enough ideas from the marketing and operating people to create the beginnings of a very good story.

DISSECTING A MERGER

This is a good place to pause and consider how mergers have been structured. What are the benefits and what are the risks? Most have worked well, but some have not, and of those that have worked well, many got off to a very rocky start.

A northbound freight train descends the grade between Ridgecrest and Old Fort, North Carolina, 1980. The Southern's merger with the Norfolk & Western permitted much of the traffic on this tortuous line to be rerouted to the more direct and far better-engineered N&W main line.

For simplicity's sake, economists have put mergers into two boxes: parallel and end-to-end. Parallel mergers seek to improve efficiency by eliminating duplicate facilities—lines and terminals especially—and creating new, combined routes that reduce train-miles, engine-miles, and car-miles. It is all about doing more with less. Along the way, a lot of overhead functions can be eliminated: shops are consolidated and the headquarters function is slimmed down, eliminating a lot of costly vice presidents in the process.

End-to-end mergers seek to expand market reach, extending hauls by accessing new markets for one or both of the partners. Diversifying the traffic base is another main objective—you always want to hedge your bets. The key is to have new routes *and* new markets: one plus one equals more than two. End-to-end mergers do permit downsizing of the overhead functions and shop consolidations, of course, but expansion, not shrinkage, is the name of the game.

Most mergers are a blend of parallel and end-to-end concepts. The Penn Central merger is widely considered a parallel merger, though it had elements of an end-to-end combination; for example, it provided the Pennsylvania Railroad with a route to New England. The NS merger was more end-to-end than parallel, but with some major parallel-merger benefits as well. For example, the SR was moving a large volume of traffic between the Cincinnati gateway on the one hand, and Virginia and the Carolinas on the other. Traffic moved due south on the SR to Harriman Junction, Tennessee, then turned east to cross the Appalachians. The route was rugged, with heavy grades and curves. It was high-cost railroading. By contrast, the N&W provided a shortcut from the Midwest to the Virginia and Carolina markets over a double-tracked, well-engineered railroad; the route was essentially the hypotenuse of a triangle. In addition to consolidating overhead functions, these reroutes produced substantial merger benefits and were something we simply had not anticipated until we worked the numbers.

From the Southern perspective, the N&W allowed the SR to reach some important midwestern markets such as Cleveland, Detroit, and Chicago—all places already served by CSX. The routes were often inferior to those of CSX, but at least now the SR would have a substantial presence in the Midwest.

Another big winner: N&W states produced a lot of grain, while the SR served a lot of chicken and hog producers, most of whom got their grain locally (some by rail but most by truck). Soon trainloads of grain were moving from low-cost producing areas in Indiana and Illinois into the Southeast, displacing higher-cost grain produced in Virginia and the Carolinas. Short-haul movements, always under cost pressure from trucks, were now long-haul moves impervious to truck competition. (This is called geographic competition.)

All of these benefits were dutifully written down and put in a thick application to the ICC. With CSX already approved, there was little chance that the proposed NS consolidation would be rejected or burdened with any serious conditions. The decision came down quickly, and Norfolk Southern became a reality on June 1, 1982.

The lawyers and the planners were having a victory celebration when someone came in with a press release announcing the creation of the new company—and also saying the headquarters would be in Norfolk, Virginia. We were devastated. After all that hard work, we were facing uprooting our families to Virginia's Tidewater region, a place that we sophisticated Washingtonians were convinced was a total backwater. (Ah, the arrogance of the inside-the-Beltway crowd!) I did not want to go to Tidewater, having been there several times while in the Navy, and I started serious negotiations with Burlington Northern in Seattle. But in the end, I made the move after Phil Dieffenbach, my boss, had had enough of my constant grousing and said, "Go or stay, I don't care. But make up your mind and stop complaining." I bought a house on the water in Virginia Beach, complete with a dock—for a longtime boater it was a perfect location, and we stayed there after I retired. Moving to Tidewater proved one of the best changes in my life.

CREATING A NEW COMPANY

It was not a merger made in heaven. In the Southeast, NS missed virtually all of Florida. In the Northeast, CSX served Baltimore, where it was the dominant railroad, and Philadelphia. The NS network ended at Buffalo and just east of Pittsburgh. To reach the important markets on the coast, NS had to rely on a largely indifferent Conrail or a combination of weak railroads (the Delaware & Hudson and the Delaware Otsego). NS would spend the better part of two decades, on again and off again, on efforts to improve its northeastern access.

Norfolk Southern went to only one important market not served by CSX: Kansas City. But Kansas City was a one-way gateway. The western carriers did not like to be short-hauled, so NS took loads originating on NS to them, but nothing much came back. And there were other issues as well. On the map, NS appeared to be a midwestern powerhouse. In reality, it was a Potemkin railroad: there were lines on the map, but precious

Bob Claytor in the cab of the 611, 1980.
Under Claytor, Norfolk Southern had a robust steam program featuring the 611 and the 1218. He was the right man for handling the conflicts between N&W and SR executives following the creation of NS.

little traffic on many of those lines. Many would be abandoned within the next decade (for more on the NS network's deficiencies, see chapter 12). The shortcomings in the NS system were a strong impetus for its efforts to acquire Conrail.

Flawed or not, though, it was time to bring the companies together. Following a merger, the choices essentially are to move rapidly and achieve the benefits of the merger as soon as possible, or to move slowly and avoid serious failures. The Penn Central, given its desperate financial condition, moved quickly. Burlington Northern took a more patient approach and its merger went smoothly. (Had the BN merger failed, that would have spelled the end of mergers for a number of years.) CSX was too cautious; the subsidiary railroads and their management stayed in place for months. Indeed, one of the complaints that the SR and the N&W heard from customers

was that it was impossible to get a consistent answer from the CSX commercial people—the Seaboard System representative would give one answer and the Chessie representative another, and they would even argue with each other at meetings with customers.

Norfolk Southern followed a middle course. It merged most functions early, allowing its sales and marketing people to speak with one voice—a direct slam at the CSX approach. But it kept the transportation functions separate. In retrospect, NS did it right, though it was costly. There were too many staff people for too long, and several years after the NS merger, a thorough housecleaning was required to eliminate redundant staff.

Integrating two cultures takes the right kind of leader. Bob Claytor was made CEO, a very astute choice. A real

A Norfolk Southern inspection train at Roanoke, Virginia, 1982. The merger was only a few months old at this point and I was invited to ride from Roanoke to Chicago and return. It was a great way to see the N&W and to meet many of their senior management. The paint scheme was an experimental effort but was rather attractive. In the end, NS adopted a basic black scheme that survives to this day.

gentleman, he soothed many a bruised ego. (In mergers, lots of egos get bruised. It is rather like musical chairs: half of the senior positions are eliminated, and those with no place to sit tend to complain.) Most of the SR senior team had worked for Bob's brother, Graham, a man greatly admired by the SR executives.

Norfolk Southern avoided the Penn Central mistake of layering the different players (such as a vice president from the NYC and an assistant vice president from the PRR). Rather, N&W executives dominated the Law and Finance Departments, as they should have. The merchandise arena went to the SR, the coal to the N&W—again, logical choices. Maintenance of Way went to the SR, which was absolutely the right decision. The N&W did not have a Corporate Planning and Development Department, so there was no conflict there. It

did have a line rationalization effort, though, and that was an issue. The matter went to Bob Claytor, who penned a note stating that I would head the Light-Density Line Committee "for now." It was hardly a ringing endorsement, and fair warning that I was on probation.

Creating a common culture took a long, long time. In fact, when NS was born, the N&W itself did not have a common culture. On the N&W, there was a schism between the merchandise railroad (the former Nickel Plate and the former Wabash) and the coal railroad (the former N&W). Coal was king and accounted for well over half of N&W's profits, a fact well known to former N&W executives. The coal railroad was a tonnage-based operation: accumulate cars until you can launch an efficient train to Ohio or Tidewater. Merchandise traffic needed to be run on a more rigid schedule, but

The Norfolk & Western's Pier 6 as seen from a plane departing Norfolk, 2003. The substantial profit margins from export coal propelled the fortunes of the N&W for decades, but in the end the company had to move beyond its dependence on coal.

frequently cars were held for tonnage on the merchandise side of the railroad as well.

One story captures the tension between the two camps at the N&W. On a postmerger inspection trip between Chicago and Norfolk that stopped in Portsmouth, Ohio, for the night, we had a nonalcoholic happy hour that included shrimp cocktail. Somebody said, "Hey, we did not get anything this good on the Western Region!" (That was the merchandise railroad.) To which Mike Irwin, the Eastern Region general manager, retorted, "That is because you're on the Eastern Region now—we make all the money, and the Western guys just spend it."

These cultural differences carried over to NS. On the N&W, the company fortune was tied to the coal business. The export coal piers are visible from NS headquarters, and many an executive still keeps an eagle eye on the number of ships being loaded—if there are none for a couple of days, it

is time to adjust the budget downward. The SR was more like the Nickel Plate and the Wabash; it had to hustle for each and every carload and take what it could get, including short-haul grain business, pulpwood, paper, and furniture (which was sometimes reduced to kindling by the time it got to its destination in a boxcar). Holding for tonnage simply could not be tolerated on the SR, which has run a scheduled railroad for decades.

Past experience was perhaps the greatest barrier to creating a cohesive culture. The SR was in a growing region and was willing to roll the dice and spend money, betting that increased traffic would ultimately justify the investment. The N&W was in a declining region—think the Ohio Rust Belt—and saw the world as a glass half-empty. It was, by necessity, far more risk-averse. Neither carrier was wrong, per se; they just viewed the world through different prisms. But those different

PAINTING THE ENGINES

A new railroad deserves a new paint scheme, and NS was no exception. CSX chose a handsome blue, gray, and yellow livery, spending months making the choice. (I heard that there was even a committee created to address the issue.) For NS, the decision was no more than a footnote in the merger process. N&W engines were black with a large "NW" stenciled on the side; it was plain Jane, reflecting the N&W culture as a no-frills company, and perhaps harking back to its legacy as the last major steam-powered railroad in the United States. The SR locomotives were black as well, but with a wide off-white band outlined with gold stripes above the running boards. That scheme now adorns the F units that NS uses on its executive train.

As I heard the story, the NS paint scheme was decided almost as an afterthought by some of the senior management. General Motors needed to know how to paint the new engines they were to deliver. The GM salesman had a model in black, and that was the choice except for one minor detail—NS had adopted a black Thoroughbred horse as its corporate symbol (as in "The Thoroughbred of Transportation"). A black logo on a black engine would not work. So the GM salesman painted a white band on the model's nose, and that was that—no fuss and no need for a committee. (The horse was a rearing stallion, but was missing its stallion "equipment." A rash of artistic types in shops and elsewhere went to work painting a penis on the horse until firm orders were given to cease and desist.)

Engines are one thing; getting the transportation function to mesh was another matter. The SR ran a scheduled railroad, something that Bill Brosnan had started. Not everything was scheduled, but there was a network of corporate trains, and local supervision messed with them at their peril. The N&W was oriented to the bulk trade of coal and grain, and other than the auto business, schedules were often ignored.

The operating vice president, Ed Burwell, was an SR man who quickly brought discipline to the N&W merchandise side of the network. I recall being in the division office in Brewster, Ohio, when the superintendent took a call from Burwell. All I heard was, "No, sir," over and over, followed by, "It will never happen again, sir." The superintendent had annulled a corporate train. Burwell chewed him out, and, as word got around, reliability did improve. But the efforts to operate a truly reliable network would ebb and flow over the years, and running to plan is an ongoing challenge even to this day.

CONRAIL IS FOR SALE—NOW WHAT DO WE DO?

Norfolk Southern was launched in 1982. In 1983, the USRA proclaimed that Conrail was profitable, and soon thereafter, the Reagan administration wanted to divest Conrail as part of its goal to reduce the size of government. Conrail was now in the black, thanks to the efforts of Stan Crane, Jim Hagen, and others (Crane had retired from the SR and was now Conrail's CEO—a hard-nosed operating man, he had tackled the Conrail cost structure with a vengeance). The Reagan crowd pushed first for liquidation but, with CR making money, decided to sell it intact. Its criteria involved a lot more than price, however—it was interested in the staying power of the buyer, because it did not want to deal with another northeastern railroad crisis. From my days at the USRA I knew the potential of the CR franchise; if NS owned CR, it would be the strongest railroad east of the Mississippi.

A westbound Conrail intermodal train at Mifflin, Pennsylvania, 1986. This was once a very busy passenger route but now only one round-trip passenger operation remains.

The announcement came at a bad time for Norfolk Southern, which was still putting its own merger together and did not yet have a cohesive management team or philosophy. The internal discussions at NS were intense, with each side, the SR and the N&W, holding different views of the future. Both were legitimate, but they reflected different cultures and different experiences. The SR was a merchandise railroad with a long history of working with northeastern carriers over both the Potomac Yard and the Cincinnati gateways. The SR regarded Conrail as an opportunity—they saw merit in tying southeastern production centers with the population of the Northeast. The N&W had a different vision. They had operated in

the Northeast for decades (since the acquisition of the Nickel Plate and the Wabash) and had seen the relentless decline in the industrial base and the attendant loss of traffic. In fact, N&W chairman Jack Fishwick had declared earlier that the solution to the northeastern railroad problem was to establish a firewall (the "Fishwick firewall") east of Buffalo and Pittsburgh. East of the firewall, the network would become a ward of the government, and the cancer of deficit railroading could be contained. When pressed by the USRA to take the Erie-Lackawanna, the N&W said, "Hell no!" Later, when Transportation Secretary Coleman offered half of the Penn Central to the N&W with a dowry of $500 million in grant money (taxpayer dollars), Fishwick said no again. Fishwick was still on the NS board, a fact that would play an important part in what was to follow.

After much internal haggling (with former N&W folks generally against and former SR people generally for), NS reluctantly decided to bid. The bid was partly defensive, aimed at blocking any move by CSX. We planners had used the fear of CSX as a reason for action, and we showed that the risks were modest so long as our bid was not too high. Norfolk Southern essentially tiptoed into the battle and lacked a strong will to win. This ambivalence about Conrail would come back to haunt us, and ultimately doomed our effort.

I strongly advocated making an aggressive bid—I thought that the acquisition of Conrail would greatly strengthen the relatively weak NS route network and was an opportunity that might never come again. Now, years later and far from the passion of the hour, I can see that the naysayers had a point. Conrail was not, at the time, making very much money, and it was unclear that it could ever make enough money to justify even a modest price. The Staggers Act was now law, but who knew how that new regulatory freedom would play out? It might just prove the prelude to a race to the bottom as carriers cut prices to hold volume—hardly a new concept in railroading. Most significantly, a newly deregulated trucking industry was tearing a broad swath through traditional rail merchandise markets.

THE BATTLE BEGINS

Norfolk Southern won the nod from the secretary of transportation, Elizabeth Dole. When Bill Loftus, my old boss from the FRA, told me that we had won the bid, I was amazed. (Loftus and I met at Danker's, a smoke-filled bar where much of the plan for Amtrak and the northeastern rail crisis was cobbled together.) I thought the Alleghany Corporation had the stronger bid, simply because it avoided the competitive issues that came with a CR-NS merger. But Dole was convinced that Conrail would be better off as part of a larger rail system and a company with deep pockets.

With her pick of NS, the first battle of the East began. CSX was adamantly and aggressively opposed to the merger and was joined by Conrail, which did not want to be taken over and certainly not by NS. (Conrail's chairman, Stan Crane, simply didn't like the N&W—recall that when he was with the SR, his distaste for the N&W had almost tanked the NS consolidation.) I was not on the front lines in this effort; I was more a resource than a decision maker. I was hauled out to support senior management and make presentations because I was one of the few people at NS who understood the northeastern rail network, thanks to my years at the New York Central, the Penn Central, and the USRA. Though I was in the middle of the fight, I was a sergeant in the process, brought out to take the hill after the leaders had chosen the hill and made the decision to attack.

In retrospect, NS had a lousy plan, and the opposition, which only had to play defense, made our lives miserable. CSX and Conrail launched a classic negative campaign, the kind so common in today's political arena. For example, CSX would say, "If NS gets Conrail, thousands of CSX jobs will be lost in [name the state]." I'd fly in and present numbers to show that the claimed job losses exceeded the total CSX employment in that state, so clearly the CSX claim was a distortion if not an outright lie. Or CSX would go to Seattle and tell the port folks that NS planned to take all of their international trade to Los Angeles, and then they would go to Los Angeles and say NS would favor Seattle. The only good thing for me was that I got good at public presentations and accumulated a lot of frequent-flyer miles. (When the battle was over, I would use these for trips to Europe and Asia.) It was hard duty—up before dawn for a trip and back late at night, only to repeat the process the next day.

At one point during this time, I almost lost my job, thanks to some loose talk to Dan Machalaba of the *Wall Street Journal*, who cornered me after a public meeting in Baltimore. I thought we were off the record, but with Dan you had to be super careful, and I failed that test. I had gotten back from a trip to the UK to find myself at the center of a firestorm. The *Journal* had a lead article about the fight for Conrail. I was widely quoted in it, most famously for saying that NS and CSX were long-standing rivals and that Richmond, a mere hundred miles west of Norfolk, was "close enough to throw hand grenades." I was warned that I was likely to be fired, so when Harold Hall, Norfolk Southern's president (Bob Claytor was chairman), called me to his office, I feared the worst. But he gave me a hearing. I apologized, saying I had been making the NS case for two years in the public arena, and this was my first serious stumble. Hall, who was part Cherokee, looked at me with those dark eyes and warned, "If you ever do this again, you are gone." As I walked around the halls for the next couple of days, folks would do a double take when they saw me, clearly thinking, "What is he still doing here?"

There were two major flaws in NS's strategy for acquiring Conrail. First, NS plus all of Conrail would have made it a much larger system than CSX. Clearly some divestitures were in order, but the NS solution was to expand Guilford Transportation, a small New England carrier, between the Northeast and Chicago. NS would divest the lines of the former Erie-Lackawanna between New Jersey and Buffalo and the lines of the former Nickel Plate between Buffalo and Chicago to Guilford. Guilford's vision for the future was to operate a nonunion intermodal railroad between New York/New England and Chicago. That did not sit well with either the unions or existing NS customers along the lines proposed to be divested. It was a silly alternative and smacked of recreating the failed Erie-Lackawanna (or the USRA scam that expanded the D&H to compete with Conrail). The proposal gave CSX and Conrail a lot of ammunition to be used in their attacks on NS.

More importantly, NS failed to play the money card. It was getting hammered by CSX and CR for trying to buy CR on the cheap. Dole asked NS to raise its bid, but Fishwick called for another study, which would take time, as Fishwick knew. Essentially we dithered, and as we did, the political pressure mounted.

And so it went, charge and countercharge; NS never got ahead of events. After more than two years of arguing and lobbying, the NS effort sputtered and finally failed in 1985. The coup de grâce came when Congressman John Dingell, the House's "transportation czar," declared that the NS effort was dead, though the Senate had endorsed the NS plan.

In my opinion we failed because we were timid: slow to raise the financial bid and slow to deal with the competitive issues. In fairness to NS, the financial projections for Conrail were dicey at best. We were fearful that raising the bid or spinning off more of CR's routes would simply leave us with a perpetual loser. When it was over, I was convinced that the "CR dream" was gone forever. Losing after two years of intense effort really hurt badly.

Norfolk Southern did not lick its wounds for long. The railroad business was in the doldrums, and traffic had stagnated even on the SR side of the system. The company had to change direction. One objective was to find new markets outside of the railroad business; the other was to cut costs. I was deeply involved in both.

The company was sitting on a huge amount of cash, and after the Conrail bid failed, our investment advisors—always on the hunt for another deal and the fees that went with it—put us on to North American Van Lines (NAVL). Owned by PepsiCo, NAVL no longer fit the corporation's business model, and the truck company was for sale. NAVL was a huge moving company, so there wasn't much synergy with the railroad there. But at the time it was the nation's largest truckload carrier, and linking a big truckload carrier with a railroad seemed to have promise. After all, the Southern Pacific owned a motor carrier, which from all reports seemed to be a good business. In retrospect, we should have done a lot more due diligence.

We went to NAVL's Fort Wayne headquarters to hear their pitch, and quite a pitch it was—smooth-talking MBAs with fancy slide presentations. We were impressed. It turned out that the core competence of the NAVL management was in giving slick presentations. I cannot even claim "I told you so," because I was as captivated by the NAVL story as the rest of the NS management.

Using some of its cash, NS bought NAVL. It was a marriage made in hell. The truckers resented being owned by a railroad, thinking railroads only hauled coal and grain and were otherwise irrelevant in the transportation world. Indeed, from their perspective, that was true; their customer base

rarely used a railroad. (This was before intermodal service had gained significant market share.) And the railroaders were not pleased that money earned from railroading was being diverted to buy a truck line.

And this truck line was in deep trouble. Commercial Transport was NAVL's truckload subsidiary, and its business model had been a winner in a regulated environment (for-hire truckers needed a certificate from the ICC, and the NAVL lawyers were good at getting those certificates). About the time that NS acquired NAVL, that business model failed for two reasons: first, trucking regulation had ended when the Staggers Act became law in 1980, and second, new operators, such as J. B. Hunt, created a lower-cost business model. With no restrictions on entry, any trucker was free to roam the land looking for traffic, which put a lot more competitors in the market. Prices came down. Costs came down as well, and Commercial Transport soon faced a tsunami of lower-cost truck lines.

Norfolk Southern struggled to make a success of NAVL, but in the end simply sold the company. We did get one good thing from the transaction, though many at NS would disagree. Tom Finkbiner, an aggressive and mercurial but brilliant executive, came from NAVL to run NS's intermodal department. Over the next decade he would make intermodal an important part of NS's services. He fought with just about everyone at the company (one vice president threatened to throw him out the window), but intermodal needed a booster, and Finkbiner was a focused, if abrasive, advocate. Intermodal was hard to manage and operate; the traffic was highly competitive and service quality was critical. The old-time SR transportation folks, trained by Bill Brosnan, got it. The N&W people, steeped in the tradition of a tonnage railroad, were less receptive. Of course, those with experience with the Wabash and Nickel Plate understood the game, but they were no longer in charge.

The only reason Finkbiner survived was that Arnold McKinnon, who became CEO after Claytor retired, recognized that in order to prosper, the company would have to find and grow new lines of business. Some core business on the SR, including furniture, paper, and pulpwood, had been hit hard when trucking was deregulated. On the N&W side, both grain and coal traffic were erratic, and that much concentration on a few markets is never a good thing.

NORFOLK SOUTHERN SLIMS DOWN

Railroads have been downsizing since before World War I. The pace was glacial, however, because regulation made abandonment difficult and because railroaders were slow to grasp the fact that the world had changed. The network was essentially static from 1929 (229,000 route-miles) until 1970 (206,000 route-miles). It was a very modest retrenchment, considering how the railroads were savaged first by the Depression and then by the growth of trucks and automobiles after World War II.

Then all hell broke loose. Mileage declined by 41,000 miles in the next decade (1970–80) and an additional 45,000 miles in the decade after that. The downsizing ball got rolling with the northeastern rail crisis. Jervis Langdon, the Penn Central's trustee, proposed cutting back to a core network, a term that would become part of railroad lingo in the coming years. Concurrently, most of the midwestern railroads west of Chicago were in distress and wanted to shed thousands of miles of their light-density lines.

The downsizing process at NS got off to a slow start. Although there had previously been some downsizing initiatives, a valid starting point was June 1983, when NS filed to abandon the line from Brunswick, Missouri, to Council Bluffs, Iowa (discussed below). But downsizing was not a one-size-fits-all proposition. On the SR side, there were lots of little squiggly lines reaching out to minor markets. The tracks were in good condition—the SR culture simply would not tolerate a badly maintained railroad—but most of the lines were laid with light rail, and wooden bridges were the norm. There was an assumption that sooner or later these lines would be needed because the South had been growing. That turned out to be a false hope.

The N&W side of the house presented a far different profile: many of the branch lines had been former main lines made redundant after the N&W took control of the Nickel Plate and the Wabash. Both of those carriers served many of the same markets, and once traffic was concentrated on the best lines, a lot of fairly empty railroad remained (such as the Cloverleaf District of the former Nickel Plate, which ran from central Ohio to East St. Louis, Illinois). The N&W was deferring maintenance, and with carload traffic declining, there was little hope that tomorrow would be any better than today.

The reality of deferred maintenance brought rationalization front and center: bad track made for an operations headache in the form of speed restrictions and derailments. The poster child for the problem was the Omaha line, which wandered from the Wabash's Detroit–Kansas City route to reach Council Bluffs, Iowa. The Operating Department wanted to abandon the line, but it was more than two hundred miles long and there were a number of on-line traffic points. The Law Department did not want to tackle the case, except for

Wabash train number 214, the overnight train from Council Bluffs, Iowa, arriving in St. Louis, 1962. Years later I would lead the effort to shed the two-hundred-mile line between Brunswick, Missouri, and Council Bluffs.

Bob Cooney, a very aggressive attorney from the N&W side of NS. Cooney and I petitioned CEO Bob Claytor to give us a shot at the problem. He gave us a green light to try, but said we were going to fail—he was a good lawyer, and he knew the difficulties we faced. He even said he would buy us a steak dinner if we were successful.

After inspecting the line, visiting customers, and grinding out reams of revenue and cost information, the normal abandonment application was generated. But instead of just filing it with the ICC, we took the draft document to each and every customer on the line. We met them at their place of business and laid out the economics. We declared, with more conviction than we felt, that NS was going to win the case. Our pitch was, "We are going to win, but know that it will drag on for the full statutory eleven months needed to get a decision. All of

this is just wasted effort for everyone." Then we suggested an alternative. Norfolk Southern would (1) guarantee continued operation for the full eleven months, and (2) help find ways to bring other railroads in at the crossing points (the solution that was used when the Rock Island was liquidated). Some rail service would be saved, and even those without hope of continued service would have time to prepare for the change that was coming.

These visits were usually confrontational in the beginning, but the customers were businessmen and understood economics. It took time, but eventually everyone signed on. The filing drew no protests other than pro forma complaints from rail labor. As the case proceeded through the ICC process, Cooney and I set out to get agreements with a short line to assume service on the first forty miles of the railroad. And

A local freight on the Ohio Central near Sugar Creek, Ohio, 2008. Now part of the Genesee & Wyoming, the Ohio Central was pieced together from remnants of larger railroads by Jerry Joe Jacobson.

we arranged to open up access at other stations where other railroads had existing operations.

Claytor never did buy me that steak dinner, but I had gained the attention of the Operating Department, which was anxious to speed up the abandonment process. One of the best compliments I ever got was when Ed Burwell, vice president for operations at the time, introduced me to some other transportation officers with, "This is Jim McClellan. You can count on him to get the job done." In the railroad culture, that was better than being seen as a planner and a thinker.

The line rationalization effort was certainly a boost to my career. While I do think about the future a lot, planning is not really my thing; I'd rather go out and cut deals and make things happen. And the Omaha line case became part of a template for future cases: create teams of planners and lawyers, inspect the property on the ground, talk to the customers, formulate a plan (which might well be abandonment), and then talk to the customers again and again—as many times as it takes. We never got a customer protest during the entire process.

JERRY JOE JACOBSON BUYS A RAILROAD

The next crisis was the Zanesville, Ohio, line, a branch line of the former Wheeling and Lake Erie and then the Nickel Plate. There was yet another wreck, and Dick Dunlap, the N&W vice president for transportation, declared that he was going to embargo the line. The lawyers said he couldn't do that—you could embargo a line but you had to restore it to service within a reasonable amount of time. At a high-level meeting called to resolve the matter, it was push and shove for over an hour, as the lawyers insisted that NS had to have an abandonment certificate, which would take a couple of years to obtain. Dunlap pretty much said to hell with that idea; the line was an operating nightmare right now.

Cooney and I declared that we would like to try to find a buyer for the line. A sale would be a lot faster and a lot more certain than a protracted ICC abandonment case. I do not recall how we found Jerry Joe Jacobson or how he found us, but he had one short line in east central Ohio and was looking for other lines. A deal was struck: we sold the line to Jacobson for fifty cents on the dollar. Later I would realize that such discount sales provided an incentive to an operator to simply abandon the line and cash it out for its scrap value. So from that point forward, most of our deals were leases rather than discount sales.

It's a wonder that we ever cut a deal. Jacobson was a devout Mennonite, while I liked my bourbon and was known to swear a lot. Not knowing that he was deeply religious, I did not modify my behavior; only later did I realize how badly I had behaved.

But Jacobson stayed with the process and acquired the line. He got some grant funding from the Ohio DOT for a modest rehabilitation effort and then found new sources of traffic. From there he went on to create a short-line empire in eastern Ohio from lines that NS and CSX no longer wanted. Ultimately he sold his empire to the Genesee and Wyoming for several hundred million dollars.

Jacobson was, and is, an avid steam fan. At first I just thought he was a railfan who wanted to play trains. But he was a very astute businessman, and in the end made more money from the railroad business than many a Class I CEO. The substantial profits from our deal permitted him to create one of the finest steam locomotive collections in the nation, housed in a brand-new roundhouse near Sugar Creek, Ohio.

THE GREAT RETREAT AND THE THOROUGHBRED SHORT LINE PROGRAM

Norfolk Southern had a five-year plan that was updated annually. Producing the plan was one of the primary duties of the Corporate Planning and Development Department. The plan's 1985 update indicated that NS's profitability was going to decline. Growth in the Southeast had slackened, and the Northeast and Midwest continued to diminish as well. While we had been pruning the railroad, it was pretty much on a case-by-case basis. McKinnon, by this point the CEO, decided that the railroad had to get its costs in line with the new market reality. An early buyout was offered to reduce the ranks of nonunion personnel. NS had never really streamlined its staff after the merger, and there was a lot of redundancy.

McKinnon and I discussed the need to reduce the size of the network on a systematic basis. Armed with data from a new analytical system that the Planning group had created, I suggested that we could shed 3,000 to 4,000 miles of railroad. McKinnon then told Wall Street that NS would shed both people and rail lines, with a target reduction of 3,500 route-miles to be achieved within thirty-six months. McKinnon designated me the project leader. Line rationalization became an all-consuming task for our group for almost three years.

The project almost went into the ditch on day one. Virtually every suggested abandonment or transfer to a short line was rejected by the Marketing Department. In frustration, I went to McKinnon and told him that I was unable to get the job done given the pushback from the commercial people. (In their view, the traffic would come back in the near future, but my experience with the creation of Conrail made me a skeptic.) After listening to the complaints, he told the Marketing leadership that he had made a commitment to Wall Street to downsize the railroad. He said he did not care whether they used my list or not, but if they didn't, they had to come up with their own plan that must total 3,500 miles. Within two days, Marketing signed off on our list with only one exception.

Now the challenge was to get the job done. The universe of problem lines included some where abandonment was the only solution; there was simply not enough traffic to support even a short line. A few lines could be sold, but most lines were in a gray zone. They had enough traffic to ensure that we would face a lengthy abandonment case with an uncertain outcome, but seldom had enough traffic to support a sale for cash. As former main lines, many had relatively heavy rail, and their scrap value was too high for a short line to fund with a conventional loan. I came up with the solution: lease the lines at no cash cost to the new operator. The name was obvious (to me, at least): the Thoroughbred Short Line Program.

There was one hitch in the lease terms: the short line had to deliver as many carloads to NS as the line had generated for NS in the preceding year. If that objective was met, the cost was zero. There was a provision for a cash payment for each car short of the goal. The short-line carrier had the option of buying the line at any time for net liquidation value. There were no restrictions on interchange with another carrier, but if, say, a short line sent all of the business to CSX, the penalty for the shortfall in cars would be due. My logic was that these lines were at death's door, and we ought to give them the best possible opportunity to succeed—and it was better that CSX get traffic than let it go to a trucker.

The finance people were not enamored with "free leases," nor were the unions, who took us to court to stop what they saw as illegal contracting out. I made the case to McKinnon that NS had plenty of cash; what it needed was as much traffic as possible, so it was better to try to keep the traffic base and forgo the cash. He agreed, and the Thoroughbred Short Line Program became the core of our rationalization effort.

To move the process along, we divided the universe and assigned lines to teams of two people, a planner and a lawyer. In all cases, "missionary" work was done with the shippers and there were joint meetings of the customers, the operator we had selected, and the team. We talked in blunt terms to customers, telling them that the short line was a last chance to save the line; NS had the option of trying a new operator or simply filing for abandonment.

The program was reasonably successful. We got the job done; the 3,500-mile goal was achieved six months ahead of schedule. But in retrospect, we often got the outcome wrong. Lines we thought could never be successful were saved, and others that we thought should be winners did not survive in the long term. Perhaps that was the beauty of the program: it permitted other operators to take over the lines at minimal cost and give the lines—and the customers—a second chance. Let the market, not some planner in Norfolk, decide what would work or not.

A lot of railroad history fell by the wayside during the rationalization process. Bill Schafer, a certified railfan, drew the short straw for three high-profile lines: one was a portion of the first rail line to be operated by steam power (the

Augusta–Charleston line, of Best Friend of Charleston fame); the branch line to Warm Springs, Georgia, that had been used frequently by Franklin Roosevelt; and the Richmond–Danville line immortalized in the Joan Baez hit "The Night They Drove Old Dixie Down." Schafer got all of this done in one year, and not a single railfan picked up on the fact that these bits of history were being abandoned.

Many of us in the Planning Department doing all of this dirty work were railfans and were aware of the history of many of the lines. But we also were worried about the future of railroading. Our belief, our hope, was that by taking aggressive action to prune the network, the rest of the network would survive.

A SPEECH AND A PROMOTION

Once a year, NS had a meeting of some three hundred or so of its senior executives. Both an educational and a social event, its goal was to bring the management up to date on important initiatives. Over the years, I was a presenter at many of these gatherings, but my first appearance was the most important.

For this particular meeting, held at the Cavalier Hotel in Virginia Beach in 1994, I was assigned the task of giving a strategic overview of the industry and NS's position in it. I presented comparative information on the growth and efficiency of the major rail carriers. Long story short, I declared that not only was NS a slow-growth carrier compared to railroads in the West, but it was a high-cost railroad as well (measured in cost per ton-mile). In fact, I declared that based on the numbers, NS and CSX were dead even on the cost side; what put NS on top was higher revenue per ton-mile. I then suggested that everyone should hug a marketing guy, because

their ability to produce high revenues provided NS with the lowest operating ratio in the railroad business at that time.

Now, having the lowest operating ratio was one of those things that NS bragged about year after year. It was ingrained in the corporate culture. A low operating ratio proved, or so we believed, that NS was the best operating railroad in the business. But the facts did not support that claim. Norfolk Southern was a disciplined operating railroad with superb infrastructure, but it was not as good as it thought.

The head of operations at the time, Paul Rudder, stood up and declared that he did not believe the numbers and was incensed that I might imply his team was incompetent. About one hundred members of his team stood up with him in protest. Now, my normal style when challenged is to get into an in-your-face argument. But the new CEO of NS, David Goode, was sitting in the first row and looking right at me. It was one of those bet-your-career moments, so I settled back and thought before I opened my mouth. I said that no one was accusing the NS operating folks of incompetence; it was just that they had a far more difficult task than their counterparts in the West. The reality, I added, was that the Burlington Northern was hauling (at that time) twelve-thousand-ton trains out of Wyoming, loading those trains on a loop track in a couple of hours. To accumulate a train of that size, NS had to do a number of mine runs up into the "hollers" to assemble tonnage, a costly and inefficient process. It was not about the quality of the operating people—it was about a fundamental difference in operations in the East versus the West. Longer hauls out west and a lot less switching gave the western railroads an inherent cost advantage.

But myths die hard and some harsh words were said after dinner. In a stage whisper heard by many, Rudder said I ought to be fired. After dinner, Goode invited me back to his suite and asked how I felt about the confrontation. I said it did not bother me very much. (After all, much of my career had involved doing and saying things people did not like.)

Some months later, I was called up to the executive dining room and introduced to the board as the new vice president for strategic planning. It was an exciting moment and a position that I had never thought I would achieve, given my erratic career path. Indeed, when the former CEO, Arnold McKinnon, congratulated me, he added, "You know, I never had the courage to promote you." My reputation as a loose cannon was no doubt central to his thought process.

That night I was off to New York for a meeting with our investment bankers. I took the last plane to Newark and the bus to Midtown, climbing over the drunks and panhandlers outside the Port Authority Bus Terminal en route to my hotel. The next day I visited a clothing store next to the J. P. Morgan offices to buy a tie. The salesman, an Indian gentleman, came over and took a hard look at my suit. "Sir," he said, "these rack suits never do look quite right." That trip to New York proved to me that having a title was no ticket to either good travel experiences or sartorial splendor.

I did not need a suit salesman to confirm that I might be in over my head. So in choosing who would fill the assistant vice president slot, I looked outside the Strategic Planning group for someone who could handle all of the day-to-day business that I so disliked, someone who was not a loose cannon, someone who would push back hard when I got a goofy idea. I reached out to the Law Department to Nancy Fleischman, with whom I had worked on merger and abandonment projects. That caused a lot of internal problems within NS—the Law Department was a nation unto itself, and lawyers simply did not make lateral moves to other departments. (Promotion *up* was all right, of course.) The vice president for law was furious, and Goode even made a pitch for me to change my decision. I dug in. It turned out to be the right thing to do, given what lay ahead.

By 1990, the downsizing effort was largely behind us, and it was time to find other projects. I had started the decade with a hard-fought failure, when NS's effort to acquire Conrail was thwarted by determined opposition from both CSX and Conrail. But the decade ended on a high note: the line rationalization had been a success, and both my reputation and that of the Planning Department improved in the process. We had moved on from being just "thinkers and planners" to become a team that, in Ed Burwell's words, "could get the job done." That was important, for Strategic Planning would soon face its toughest test, as the eastern merger battle between NS and CSX played out.

A westbound Conrail intermodal train leaves Altoona, Pennsylvania, heading for Slope Tower and Horseshoe Curve, 1985. The Pennsylvania Railroad had been a pioneer in the development of intermodal traffic, starting in the late 1950s. Conrail was the successor to the PRR. Now this line is owned by NS and hosts a never-ending parade of intermodal trains.

A westbound Conrail intermodal train just east of Gallitzin, Pennsylvania, 1986. Conrail got off to a poor start but thanks to the efforts of such leaders as Stan Crane and Jim Hagen it built a valuable franchise that dominated the populous Mid-Atlantic states. Norfolk Southern and CSX battled for years to acquire Conrail until they reached a compromise to split the company.

THE QUEST FOR CONRAIL

12

After Norfolk Southern failed in its multiyear attempt to acquire all of Conrail, CSX and NS engaged in a costly high-stakes bidding war, resulting in the restoration of balanced competition to the Northeast after twenty-five years of a Conrail monopoly.

AN IMPERFECT MERGER

When Norfolk Southern was born in 1982, most of us at the Southern were not enthusiastic about the combination—we thought that the N&W was simply a rich coal road with few advantages other than a strong balance sheet. At a management meeting just before the merger, Ed Burwell, then the SR's chief operating officer, was asked how the N&W made so much money. He replied, "They haul coal downhill." He was pretty much correct, as we would learn when we saw the financial reports.

The N&W and the SR were blindsided by the formation of CSX but got lucky. CSX dithered in integrating the Chessie and the Seaboard System, giving NS the time it needed to create and integrate its network. Luck trumps smart almost every time. But NS was a flawed system; CSX had a better network, and those of us who paid attention to such things

knew it. For the next two decades NS sought to catch up to its larger competitor.

Norfolk Southern sought to improve its market position over a period of twenty years. Finally, there was an ultimate showdown when CSX inked a merger agreement with Conrail. Its back to the wall, NS, with the far stronger balance sheet, played the money card. After the expenditure of billions, the battle ended in a stalemate and CR was split between NS and CSX, with NS getting the larger portion. From an overall industry standpoint it was a good outcome that produced a balanced eastern rail network, and customers and investors were both well served by the new structure. But the outcome was hardly preordained.

In railroading, the network is all-important. When most companies sit down to discuss a merger, they whip out their financial statements. When railroaders sit down, they unfold their maps—for very good reasons. A railroad company is tied to where it goes and how it gets there. New rail lines are a rarity due to their cost and huge environmental hurdles. (Had the EPA been around in 1865, there probably would not have been a transcontinental railroad.) In economist-speak, there were huge barriers to entry. A company that goes to the right places

Above, An empty CSX coal train at White Sulfur Springs, West Virginia, 2012. Not only did the Chessie System and the Seaboard System merge before the Norfolk & Western and the Southern did, but the resulting CSX franchise was superior to that of NS.

Left, A southbound Norfolk Southern merchandise train near Lexington, Kentucky, on the Cincinnati, New Orleans & Texas Pacific route, 2008.

with good routes—direct, fast, low grade, adequate capacity, and so on—will be a long-term winner. Short of buying another railroad, a competitor can do little to change the equation.

If the route structure is destiny, CSX had the upper hand. Compared to CSX, NS had some serious flaws. First, CSX had a virtual rail monopoly in Florida. Norfolk Southern stopped at Jacksonville, where it was dependent on the Florida East Coast to reach farther south. Worse, NS had no access to

Florida's west coast, either directly or by a friendly connection. It was the west coast that generated the high-margin traffic, including phosphate.

Second, NS had no access to the Northeast east of Buffalo and Pittsburgh. By comparison, CSX served Baltimore/Washington and Philadelphia directly, and from Philadelphia, CSX could dray intermodal traffic to and from the New York market. The NS end points—Pittsburgh and Buffalo—presented

A Burlington Northern grain train climbs Crawford Hill, Nebraska, **2005.** Norfolk Southern never considered the BN as a serious merger partner; the traffic flows simply did not mesh.

An eastbound Union Pacific merchandise train leaving Rock Springs, Wyoming, **1988.** The UP would have totally dominated a merger with NS, and thus was rejected by NS as a potential partner.

major competitive challenges. Norfolk Southern had inferior access to local industry, and where it did have such access, the industry was declining. More importantly, there were no friendly rail connections east of Pittsburgh, and at Buffalo only the weak D&H/Delaware Otsego route was available. The NS routes to Buffalo and Pittsburgh were not quite "tracks to nowhere," but it was close.

Finally, NS's midwestern network was adequate but hardly overwhelming. Its access to Chicago from the south was in part made up of upgraded branch lines, and was circuitous compared to CSX. Norfolk Southern did reach Kansas City

and CSX did not, but western carriers much preferred to interchange traffic at Chicago, a junction that gave them their long haul. Kansas City was not exactly a railroad dead end but it was not a powerhouse interchange point either. Much of NS's midwestern network looked impressive on a map but there was often no "there" there in terms of traffic. As I discussed in the previous chapter, my job involved eliminating many of these lines from our network.

Most of the NS management did not lose much sleep over these issues—they had a railroad to run. But some of us in Strategic Planning worried a lot about the structural

An eastbound Santa Fe intermodal train at Siberia, California, 1990.
NS did study the Santa Fe as a potential merger partner but to create
a viable network any deal would have had to include the Kansas City
Southern. A three-way deal was simply deemed undoable at the time.

weakness in our network, and we conveyed our concerns to senior management.

LOOKING WEST

While efforts to streamline the network were underway (consuming almost three years), NS continued to look for other opportunities. The purchase of NAVL (discussed in chapter 11) convinced us that we were railroaders: if we wanted to grow, we needed to expand *in* the railroad business. At one time or another NS studied all the western carriers. It kept me busy but I accomplished little, other than to hone my presentation skills for the board. The UP and the BN would have dominated any merger, and the NS management was unwilling to

play second fiddle. The Santa Fe had poor connections with NS to the West and the Southeast, so there was not much there unless the Kansas City Southern (KCS) could be brought into the deal. That seemed unlikely at the time. The Southern Pacific was an excellent fit in terms of routes and markets, but was in bad shape physically and financially, and getting worse by the day. It was clear that the potential pain exceeded any potential gain. And the likely countermove would be a UP-CSX merger that would have left NS/SP in the dust. Mapping out the moves and countermoves was a serious part of any merger analysis.

We always came back to Conrail. It fit our network and the combined markets had huge potential. Most truck traffic moved short distances and, if we could do it right, the

A northbound Southern Pacific intermodal train (actually east-bound in the SP vision of the world, which began and ended in San Francisco) near Caliente, California, 1988. Southern Pacific was a good fit with NS from a route and market-coverage standpoint. But a huge rehabilitation effort was required and, as was the case with the Illinois Central Gulf, the rewards were not worth the risk.

prospects for increased traffic were enormous. But so was the degree of difficulty—rail intermodal service requires a commitment to both cost control and service quality. Seamless service is required, and for an interline service the partners have to be working as one. A strong alliance is essential, but effective alliances are hard to achieve and harder to sustain.

ATTEMPTING AN ALLIANCE WITH CONRAIL

Norfolk Southern wanted better access to the Northeast for intermodal traffic. There were two choices: work with Conrail or use the highway. NS did truck some freight from Alexandria, Virginia, but the costs of rail plus the extended dray were not competitive with trucks. Working with Conrail was the only real way to increase traffic.

In 1995, Conrail completed the project of clearing its main line through Pennsylvania for double-stack trains (partly funded by the Commonwealth of Pennsylvania in an early public-private partnership). That cleared route went through Harrisburg, not far from the end of NS's Shenandoah division at Hagerstown. On an inspection trip out of Hagerstown, I suggested to Arnold McKinnon that, with CR's cooperation, we could create a double-stack route from New Orleans and Memphis all the way to the New York area. He agreed, and I set out to gain Conrail's cooperation. The process was helped by the fact that Jim Hagen, who had been my boss at the SR, the FRA, and the USRA, was now CEO of Conrail. I teamed

A northbound Triple Crown train near Lexington, Kentucky, 2008. As part of the effort to create a stronger alliance with Conrail, NS sold half of its interest in Triple Crown to CR. That allowed Triple Crown to reach the large New York and Philadelphia markets.

A Conrail inspection train on NS's Front Royal–Manassas line, 1996. The train operated from Newark, New Jersey, to Manassas and permitted CR and NS officials to see the north–south double-stack route being developed at that time.

up with Les Passa, my planning counterpart at CR, and set out to make a deal. Before we had finished, we had not only created a new double-stack route but had also sold a half interest in our retail intermodal company, Triple Crown, to CR. For NS it was a big deal: the expansion of both double-stack and Triple Crown service into the Northeast.

We decided to celebrate the first double-stack train on this new route with an event in Manassas, Virginia. It was raining but there were tents and an excellent buffet luncheon. Our guests—customers, politicians, and government officials— were in a good mood. But the appointed arrival time came and went with no train in sight, and the crowd grew increasingly restless. Several hours went by. Tony Ingram, NS's vice president for transportation, was storming around cursing Conrail. It seemed that one of the packers used to load containers at Kearney Yard in New Jersey had broken down, and the remaining packers were used to load east-west traffic first. The inaugural train was not a priority, even though the CEOs of CR and NS and a number of lesser officials and their guests were waiting for the special train. Finally, some three hours late, the train arrived and broke the banner. The Conrail engines needed a good wash, and "Clinton Sucks," scrawled on the dirty fuel intake of the lead unit, was a less-than-elegant touch. Late, dirty, and crude was not a good omen for the new service. On the company jet heading back to Norfolk, David Goode, NS's CEO, asked, "Whose idea was this, anyway?" He already knew the answer but got me to publicly admit that I was the culprit.

That botched beginning was noted by the NS management team. If CR cared so little about the service that it could not get it right for the inaugural train, would it ever care enough to get it right over the long term? Increasingly we thought not, and that would guide our thinking going forward.

The inaugural Newark-to-Atlanta train about to break the banner at Manassas, 1996. The train was hours late and this poor performance convinced many at NS that an alliance was not going to work—we would have to merge with Conrail to create the kind of quality service necessary to compete with trucks.

If Conrail could not be counted on in an alliance relationship, perhaps it was time to think of mergers. Hagen, Goode, Passa, and I met in Washington on a fine spring day in 1996, and after some preliminary issues, Les and I were dismissed. Taking a walk around the Connecticut Avenue area, we both felt that the vibes from the top guys were favorable. Les and I even talked about options for headquarters—someplace neutral would be important—and I recall that both of us thought Baltimore would be a good choice (the Chessie System, later part of CSX, had been based there, then had left Baltimore for points south).

That evening I sat on my back deck overlooking the Lynnhaven River and pondered the future. A deal seemed likely, so I might not be enjoying this view much longer. The goal that I had been pursuing for years was not without its downside: I did not want to leave Virginia Beach.

But the deal was never consummated. Conrail wanted more money, and NS was slow to raise its bid. I think Hagen had lost his zeal for the merger; it was going to take a huge effort to negotiate divestitures with CSX (if it could even be brought to the negotiating table), and without a deal with CSX, the merger would face substantial opposition from shippers and a number of government entities. One night I called Hagen, and his wife Mary answered the phone. Now, I had known Mary for decades—the Hagens were our daughter's godparents. Always one to speak her mind, she said, "Why don't you silly boys just give it up?" She very much wanted Jim to retire, and an NS-Conrail merger effort would mean he could not do that for several more years.

Goode and Hagen met a few days later. Just what occurred is mired in controversy to this day: Goode said he met the price Conrail wanted, and Hagen said he did not. I am fond of both of them and do not know where the truth lies. But the deal was off. Today, with hindsight, I think Hagen and Goode each saw the exchange through a different prism. Meanwhile, I went back and tried to find more cooperative ventures, but the effort had lost its steam at both CR and NS, and would soon be overtaken by other events.

THE KINGSMILL NEGOTIATIONS

Not long after those talks broke down, John Snow, CEO of CSX, called Goode and suggested that NS and CSX sit down and develop a plan to split Conrail. This would be done without any input from Conrail. Just how we were going to convince Conrail to do a deal was to be decided later.

I was opposed to this because I still believed that the alliance strategy would work. Goode thought differently, so small, high-level teams from NS and CSX assembled at Kingsmill, a resort in Williamsburg. The NS contingent was led by CFO Hank Wolf. John Friedmann (then a director in Strategic Planning and now the VP heading the department) and I handled the proposed split of the CR network. Norfolk Southern, always in the shadow of the larger CSX, wanted to level the playing field—and then some. With its stronger balance sheet, NS tried to force a somewhat one-sided deal in its favor.

The proposed split would have transferred CR's St. Louis line (rich with chemical traffic from the Southwest), the NS line between Cleveland and Buffalo (former Nickel Plate), and CR's Southern Tier line to northern New Jersey (the former Erie-Lackawanna) to CSX. The proposal would give NS the strongest intermodal franchise in the region. Snow accepted the split and compensated for its relative weakness by negotiating a very favorable price. (In theory, the money saved on the purchase could have been used to upgrade the Nickel Plate and E-L lines.)

With the basics in place, the negotiating team was expanded: labor relations, accounting, equipment experts, and others were brought into the process. Inevitably, CR got wind of what was being plotted. Conrail CEO David LeVan called for an urgent meeting with Goode in New York. Goode and I met with LeVan and Passa in the NS apartment at the Essex House, with its magnificent view of Central Park. LeVan pleaded with Goode: "Don't do it!" Passa brought charts to show that the alliance was working; traffic between NS and CR was increasing at a faster rate than for other interline partners. But Goode rejected LeVan's overture and refused to terminate the talks with CSX.

But in the end, CSX and NS simply drifted apart. There were too many issues to resolve, and it was clear that Conrail was going to fight any split with all of the political and legal weapons it could muster. Not only was CR a tough nut to crack, but I sensed that many of the senior CSX executives felt the deal was too one-sided in favor of NS. After a decade of being the largest carrier in the East, they were simply unwilling to accept the number two position that the proposed deal would mean for them.

The talks with CSX ended the special relationship with CR that I had labored so long to create. But not all was lost: what I learned about Conrail in the process would prove invaluable in the future.

On notice that it was a target, Conrail made a countermove to strengthen its position as a stand-alone railroad by expanding its network to Texas and Louisiana. The proposed UP-SP merger would create major competitive issues on the Gulf Coast. The UP and the SP were the big guns in the Gulf Coast chemical market (the BNSF and the KCS had a much smaller presence), and the merger would give UP-SP an overwhelming market position. Conrail seized the opportunity, proposing that it acquire the eastern portion of the SP (East St. Louis down through Arkansas to Texas and Louisiana) as a condition of a UP-SP merger. It was a great fit, but it was hard for CR, with its near monopoly in the Northeast, to argue that regional rail monopolies were a bad thing. Further, CR failed to gain much-needed customer support.

In the end, the UP cut a deal with the BNSF to solve the competitive issues. With the SP at death's door, the Surface Transportation Board (STB) was justifiably reluctant to introduce a new, complicated issue into the pending case. The UP-SP merger led Conrail to believe that the STB no longer considered rail-to-rail competition an important issue. But CR was completely wrong.

Later in 1996, just as we were taking a breather from the Conrail efforts, a new opportunity was presented. Rob Krebs, CEO of the BNSF, called Goode and proposed a merger. A team was appointed to study the potential economic benefits: Krebs's assistant Carl Ice and CFO Tom Hund led the BNSF negotiators, while John Friedmann, Nancy Fleischman, and I represented NS. We met in Pittsburgh at a hotel near the airport to keep the matter secret.

Krebs had told Goode that NS would be in charge of the combined company because he, Krebs, was going to retire. The NS negotiators did not believe that was true, given the huge size advantage of the prospective western partner. In the end I made a lengthy presentation to the NS board at the Forest, the NS hunting preserve in South Carolina. I think I presented the pros and cons fairly, but I was not an enthusiastic supporter of the proposal, which the board no doubt picked up on. As I recall, the issue was tabled for further discussion.

An empty northbound BNSF coal train at Palmer Lake, Colorado, 2006. Rob Krebs, the BNSF's CEO, contacted Goode and suggested that the BNSF and NS merge. After a serious study, NS concluded that Conrail was still the better merger partner.

We did not want to slam the door on the BNSF, but there was no need for us to act precipitously.

A JURY OF OUR PEERS

Soon after that meeting, Goode created a group of vice presidents to review NS strategic merger plans. There was some precedent for "outsiders" getting involved in strategic planning affairs. Over the years, as is common in many large organizations, silos had developed at NS, with people being very protective of their prerogatives and hostile to outsiders messing with "their" turf. In an effort to create a more open culture, Goode was creating teams to look into broad problems such as cost reduction and infrastructure needs. It was a license for outsiders to get inside the silos, which created a lot

of tension and even bad blood. But it was a good thing for the company.

Now it was Strategic Planning's turn to go under the microscope. A group of eight vice presidents, dubbed the "Gang of Eight," was appointed to conduct a review of our merger strategies. Nancy Fleischman was upset, but I was more relaxed, reasonably confident that we had done our homework—if others had access to our data and our thinking, we would be just fine. After the long review, vice president and treasurer Bill Romig and I presented our findings at the September 1996 board meeting. That report and the date would turn out to be very important.

Romig presented the financial findings, and I weighed in with the strategic considerations. Essentially the "jury of our peers" agreed that NS needed to focus on Conrail. I argued that an NS-BNSF merger would leave CSX free to acquire CR and then either merge with or form an alliance with the UP. The CSX-CR-UP network would have roughly 60 percent of US rail traffic, leaving NS-BNSF 40 percent. That endgame would put NS-BNSF at a competitive disadvantage, especially in the all-important northeastern intermodal market. No effective competitive countermoves would be available.

A board member questioned whether CSX and CR might merge. One of the lawyers observed that the STB would never approve the deal. I suggested that CR might hold a different view. Les Passa had said as much to me in a one-on-one discussion in New York, and added that in light of the UP-SP decision, even a CSX-Conrail merger would pass regulatory muster. A warning bell went off in my head when I heard that. To counter the lawyer's observation, I simply said that what we believed was not as important as what Conrail believed. Indeed, at the very time of this board meeting, CSX and CR were in serious merger discussions. A board member then asked Goode how things were going on the Conrail front, and he acknowledged that David LeVan was not answering his calls. That was another warning bell.

A DUEL TO THE DEATH?

The next month was one of the worst of my life. I came into work early one lovely morning in October 1996, in order to tie up loose ends before a short trip to Los Angeles—a train-chasing expedition, naturally. Well before 8:00 AM, I got a call from Debbie Wyld, our director of shareholder relations, who asked, "What are you going to do now?" I had not a clue what she was talking about. She dropped the bomb: CSX and CR had announced a "merger of equals." I was stunned. And as the news spread, shock and disbelief were the dominant feelings. Goode called his senior staff together, and I have never seen such a depressed group—some were essentially catatonic, and simply sat and stared at the commanding view of the Norfolk harbor. We all knew that a CSX-CR merger would greatly weaken NS and, further, make us an unattractive partner for a western or Canadian railroad. For more than a decade, some of us at NS had feared being marginalized—the day we had dreaded had finally arrived.

Throughout that day of hand-wringing, Goode remained a beacon of strength and calm. He had a prior speaking engagement scheduled at noon, at which he simply said that NS would find a solution to this new challenge. It reflected more confidence than he or anyone else felt, but it was important to rally the troops.

A few days later at a shippers' conference in Atlanta I was further jolted when a shipper observed that it was too bad about NS because "it has been a good railroad." When a major customer talks about your company in the past tense, you are in trouble. And it seemed obvious that the customers were not going to the mat to protect NS, any more than the chemical companies had rallied to stop the UP-SP consolidation. Clearly, we could not count on the STB or the customers to save us, and that was an important part of our strategy going forward.

Still, all was not lost. While John Snow characterized the CSX-CR deal as "bulletproof," it was not quite the slam dunk he might have wanted. There were some major holes in the proposal:

· The offer was for a combination of cash and CSX stock, so the value of the deal depended on the price of CSX stock.

- CSX-CR would completely dominate railroading east of the Mississippi, something that the regulators would notice.
- Unlike the SP, CR was not a failing railroad, and the Surface Transportation Board would not be under pressure to approve a merger lest Conrail collapse. The STB had glossed over some of the anticompetitive aspects of the SP-UP merger because the SP was a sick carrier—that wasn't the case with Conrail.

The regulators would play an important part in the drama that was unfolding. I caught a lucky break in that regard. Some months earlier, STB chair Linda Morgan announced the creation of an unofficial advisory board to deal with current issues in a nonlegal, nonadversarial forum. Large and small railroads, shippers, and rail labor were all represented. I tossed my hat into the ring, because it sounded interesting and would give me an excuse to get to Washington and make the rounds with government contacts as well as members of the press.

I got an appointment, and found the group to be an interesting one. The conversations were open and often contentious. In the process, I grew to like and respect Morgan, and I think the feeling was reciprocated. As luck would have it, we had an advisory board meeting two days after CSX-CR was announced, and while I could not and did not say much, Morgan could certainly feel my pain.

A few days after the CSX bombshell, Goode met with Snow in Washington. I flew up with him and handed him my memo suggesting that CSX thought we were too genteel and too cheap to spend the money needed for a sustained fight. After all, NS had been reluctant to play the money card in prior negotiations. I feared we might settle for some low-cost solution such as trackage rights to major markets. The questions

he raised on the flight ("What would be wrong with just taking trackage rights?") fueled my fears, though in retrospect he knew that was a bad idea and was probing to see where I was coming from.

The meeting was held at the former SR building at 15th and K Streets, NW, in NS's congressional affairs offices. I was in the next room, but try as I did, I could not hear a thing, so I was on pins and needles wondering about the outcome. Having worked with Snow at the DOT, I knew just how charming and persuasive he could be. Would Goode fall for a "Snow job"?

I need not have been concerned. Goode came out mad; he said Snow had been arrogant and had offered nothing meaningful. Snow had declared that the deal was done and there was nothing Goode could do about it. The memo I had written as a call to arms paled in comparison to Snow's handling of the meeting. I knew Goode had a temper, but I had never seen him as ready to fight as he was that morning. CSX had clearly underestimated the resolve of its opponent. As it turned out, it might have been one of the greatest misreadings of an adversary in the history of railroading.

It would be war—but war with a very uncertain outcome. If not bulletproof, CSX-CR did hold the high cards: they did have a deal, they did have a Pennsylvania law against hostile takeovers, and they did have the entire CSX-CR organization at their disposal. It would be an uphill battle, and I and many others at NS were pessimistic about the outcome.

THE MONEY CARD AND BALANCED COMPETITION

A few days after CSX made its move, NS held an emergency board meeting in New York. The senior management was there, as were our investment bankers, J. P. Morgan, and our law firm, Skaddan, Arps. Bill Ingram and I were there from Strategic Planning. The lawyers and the finance people were front and center in the process but when it came to strategy and public policy issues, Strategic Planning was a participant from the start. This was in marked contrast to our first effort in 1984, when Strategic Planning was clearly in a peripheral role.

As it turned out, the merger review we had conducted at the board meeting at the end of September was incredibly fortuitous. At that meeting the board had been told that CR was the right strategy, and the arguments for and against had been vetted. Because the presentation had been made when there was no gun to NS's head (the gun was being loaded as we met but we didn't know that), it was an objective assessment of options. At this October meeting, the board, to a person, signed on for a bet-the-company decision. It felt that the NS franchise would be marginalized if CSX-CR became a reality. NS's former chairman Arnold McKinnon, a man who knew railroading and commanded a lot of respect from other board members, summed up the NS situation best, saying, "We do not have a choice." The challenge now was to decide what to do.

Wall Street bankers get a lot of abuse, but I had great respect for their performance in the CR fight. Norfolk Southern had a balance sheet far superior to that of CSX, and the bankers used that balance sheet boldly. J. P. Morgan, led by its vice chairman, Roberto Mendoza, proposed that NS make an all-cash tender offer for CR stock at ninety-five dollars a share. To prove that we were deadly serious, the final decision was to raise that to a nice round one hundred dollars a share. This strategy focused on a weak point of the CSX bid: its use of a combination of CSX stock and cash. The Morgan team was certain that the arbitrageurs (the "arbs"), sensing a bidding war, would scarf up much of the outstanding CR stock. If that happened, CR would be owned by shareholders whose only loyalty was to the money; the highest offer would buy their support, and cash usually trumps any alternatives. Recognizing that any deal by either CSX or NS would have to pass regulatory muster, the NS announcement vowed to bring balanced competition back to the New York metropolitan area, something the New York market had not had since the formation of Conrail. Hank Wolf wanted to save that argument for later, but I said we needed to open with a strong position on both the financial and the public policy fronts. A promise to restore rail competition to the New York market would resonate with some powerful interests in that city and the state.

Norfolk Southern reaffirmed its proposal for the establishment of neutral terminal companies in northern New Jersey, in Philadelphia and southern New Jersey, and in Detroit, and also proposed that the Monongahela coalfields south of Pittsburgh be opened to competition. These "open access" areas put NS on the right side of the competitive argument, and also gave NS an argument for competitive conditions should CSX prevail. "Balanced competition" was an easy concept to understand and became a powerful argument for NS, generating support from shippers, states, and communities.

So NS had the money and public policy issues covered. The third leg of the NS offensive was to challenge Pennsylvania's antitakeover law on the grounds that shareholders should not be denied the right to choose which offer to accept. (The Pennsylvania law essentially allowed the CR board to ignore higher offers.) The NS position was pro–shareholder rights, another simple and powerful concept. Like any political campaign, which this certainly was, sound bites made a difference. (NS had learned that from the master: CSX had used simple sound bites to defeat our earlier bid for Conrail.)

Bill Ingram and I went back to the Essex House for a nightcap and pondered where NS might be going next. We had both been through the earlier CR efforts and agreed that this one felt different. The commitment was clearly there; the question was whether NS could overcome CSX's substantial head start.

The battle was joined the next morning when the stock market opened. J. P. Morgan had it right: the arbs moved in and acquired a majority of CR shares.

Norfolk Southern's aggressive actions took many by surprise, including people at Conrail and CSX. I was at a major rail conference in California a few days after NS announced its bid. Les Passa was there and said something to the effect that when NS got mad, all hell broke loose. At the same conference, Bob Gallamore (my good friend from my DOT/USRA days, who at this time was at the UP) suggested that NS ought to be less aggressive lest the CSX-NS fight bring some form of reregulation down on the entire industry. My vocal response, which I partly believed but partly staged for the other railroaders standing around, was, "I don't give a fuck about the rest of the industry; my concern is the survival of NS!"

The next couple of weeks were traumatic. I honestly thought that CSX was going to prevail, which would mean the end of NS as an important part of the industry. I hosted a dinner to boost the morale of the Strategic Planning group, but I was trying to boost my own morale as well.

At one point my longtime friend and frequent advisor John Williams came east to discuss strategy. He declared that NS would win because we had the money and CSX did not. He was a financial expert who truly understood the power of the balance sheet much better than I. I hoped he was right. I was scared and the NS management was scared—CSX seemed to have Conrail locked up.

Suddenly the game changed, or so it seemed. I was going out to dinner and got a call from David Goode. "What are you doing tonight?"

"Walking out the door with Joanne to go to dinner."

"No, you are not—you need to come downtown right now!"

John Snow had blinked. The fight was getting very costly, and CSX did not have the balance sheet to continue. I think Snow finally realized that once NS decided to protect its franchise at all costs, CSX did not have the financial firepower required to win the battle. So Snow and Goode talked—who called whom remains uncertain—and then met in Williamsburg. Goode told me that Snow proposed that NS take about 60 percent of Conrail, focused on the lines of the former PRR. I was as stunned as I had been when the CSX-CR deal was announced. Rather than looking at Armageddon, we were looking at a balanced system that would allow NS and CSX to duke it out on equal terms.

Goode told me we were meeting with Snow and others the next morning in New York City and he needed a plan. I called Strategic Planning's experts John Friedmann and Bill Ingram. (I knew the northeastern network pretty well, but these guys knew more and I needed all the help I could get.) Fortified with Kentucky Fried Chicken, we pulled out the maps and laid out a preliminary split of the CR network. After a few hours' sleep, I was on the corporate jet headed for New York along with Goode, CFO Hank Wolf, and chief operating officer Steve Tobias.

Pete Carpenter and Bill Hart were there for CSX. Snow was not. We started the meeting without him. After reviewing

A westbound NS intermodal train ducks into a tunnel on the PRR route, 2009. The tunnel was enlarged to accommodate double-stack trains. Had the PRR not already been cleared for double-stack traffic, the CSX-NS negotiations would have been far more difficult and might have failed.

our proposed split with CSX, they and we were satisfied that we could do a deal. CSX would take one-half of the Conrail *X* and NS the other half. The *X* was the guts of the CR network, and was sacred in Philadelphia. The fundamental issue was how to split the *X*. The Penn Central merger had combined the two premier east–west railroads in the Northeast—the PRR and the NYC. When Conrail was created, it integrated the Reading–Central of New Jersey, along with a segment of the Lehigh Valley, into its core network. But balanced competition

now required splitting the Conrail *X*. Earlier, NS had rejected such an even split and demanded that it retain three legs of the *X* (with CSX getting only the St. Louis line). But now that CSX was in the driver's seat, there was no way NS was going to get such a one-sided deal.

A fair split of the *X* was the only solution, and CSX and NS were now willing to consider radical surgery to avoid a costly battle. Of course, that Solomon-like solution would not go down well with Conrail, and therein lay a serious problem.

Conrail was, of course, opposed to this solution, which is why the battle continued for months after the October meeting in New York, with billions more spent before a settlement was reached. But the general agreement to split the *X* held to the end.

Months later, when Bill Hart and I were at dinner, he outlined CSX's thinking: CSX was convinced that sooner or later NS would put up the money needed to acquire Conrail. If CSX made a preemptive strike, they might get all of CR, but in any case, they would get more of CR than had been negotiated at Kingsmill. Snow later avowed that CSX knew a settlement would have to be reached with NS. I am not so sure that in the first moments of the battle he didn't think CSX might not win it all, but once NS put the all-cash offer on the table, he knew compromise was the only solution. It took many months before David LeVan came to that understanding.

As NS and CSX sketched the route structure that morning in New York, CSX would get the half of the *X* from Boston and the New York metro area through to St. Louis, via Albany, Buffalo, and Cleveland. Norfolk Southern would take the other half of the *X*: the CR route from the New York metro area to Chicago via Allentown, Harrisburg, Pittsburgh, and Cleveland, and the former NYC from Cleveland to Chicago. Thus the NS main line would include portions of the Central of New Jersey, the Lehigh Valley, the PRR, and the NYC. This southerly route was shorter between New York and Chicago, while the northern route was faster and avoided the mountains.

Under this plan negotiated by NS and CSX in the New York meeting, NS would acquire more than half of Conrail in terms of traffic volume. The deal provided three things that NS wanted very badly: access to the Monongahela coalfields, access to the booming Harrisburg intermodal hub (within an easy dray from most of the Northeast), and the premier line into Chicago from the east. The split would require that CSX double-track the Baltimore & Ohio line from central Ohio to Chicago. (The project was feasible because the B&O line to Chicago had formerly been a double-tracked railroad, but it would be costly nonetheless.) Likewise, NS would have to substantially upgrade its Wabash line to the St. Louis gateway. Ironically, Conrail's public-private partnership with the state of Pennsylvania was a powerful factor in working out a deal. Under the program, the former PRR main line had been cleared for double-stack service. Without that project, whoever took the PRR route would be at a huge competitive disadvantage. That fact made the ultimate split viable for both parties.

Over the years since the split, I have been lauded as a genius for choosing the PRR line to Harrisburg over the NYC line to Albany, and branded a traitor to my NYC heritage for ignoring the Water Level Route east of Cleveland. But the split was so logical that I told someone my dog could have figured it out. I credit Steve Tobias for insisting that NS acquire the former NYC west of Cleveland; it had the best access to Chicago, and as an operating man, Tobias understood that better than I did.

As noted, the southern route tied neatly into NS's north–south route at Hagerstown, for years the route of a joint PRR-N&W passenger service between New York City and Roanoke. Operationally, that was a huge plus. More importantly, had NS taken the northern route, achieving a balanced system would have required that it also take the Baltimore & Ohio from central Ohio to the Northeast. In that scenario, not only would CR be split but some key CSX routes would be dismembered as well. The regulatory and operational challenge of splitting Conrail was daunting enough without disrupting even more of the northeastern network. Logic dictated that NS take the south route and CSX the north route.

THE TENTATIVE DEAL COLLAPSES

Our initial excitement about striking a deal, at least from a route structure standpoint, was soon dashed. Snow never did show up at the meeting in New York. That led NS to believe that it had been set up, and that the real CSX goal was to signal to the arbs that a deal was in the works and the bidding war was over. That would mean that the allies NS had gained with its hundred-dollar-a-share cash offer would be spooked, fearing that the ultimate deal would be done at the lower price proposed by CSX. That is exactly what happened: the trading in CR stock opened lower the next day.

But NS was not being set up. Snow was proposing a deal he could not deliver, because LeVan was adamant that Conrail not be split. Conrail was not about to surrender its *X*, nor was LeVan willing to sacrifice the CR management by splitting the company.

Now we were back to all-out war. The next months were an intense roller coaster ride as each side made move and countermove, and it was never clear who the victor would be. Norfolk Southern believed that it could lose the fight, and that was a good thing—its back to the wall, NS exhibited none of the tentative behavior seen in the earlier fight.

Goode, Wolf, and vice chairman Ike Prillaman set the overall strategy. Goode and Wolf focused on the critical legal and financial aspects of the battle, while Strategic Planning supported the overall strategy and had two primary tasks: continue to define just what parts of Conrail we would want,

and build and communicate the arguments for balanced competition. Internally, there was constant interaction with Goode and the key NS officers. Externally, the case for balanced competition had to be explained to other railroads, large and small; to states and communities; and to the Washington establishment. "Balanced competition" was a great sound bite, but various audiences wanted to know just what it meant for them.

Back in 1996 the internet was not the powerful communication tool that it is today; this was still the newspaper era. Rather than fragment our efforts, as we had in our first fight with CSX over CR (more than a decade earlier), we focused on some key publications: the *Washington Post*, the *Wall Street Journal*, the *Journal of Commerce*, the *New York Times*, and *Traffic World*. The people who would influence the outcome would be reading one or more of those periodicals.

Mustering the needed resources was a challenge. Strategic Planning was a small group without the horsepower for the battle already brewing. But money was no object; speed and firepower were. Back in the USRA days, Jim Hagen employed what he called the "U-boat commander" strategy: hire as many smart, knowledgeable people as possible. They would support your effort but just as importantly they would be unavailable to the opposition.

I engaged an army of consultants. Some, like John Williams and Judy Roberts of Woodside Consulting, had worked on prior mergers in the West. Former Conrail employees were another source of expertise: Gordon Kuhn was formerly CR's top commercial officer; Bob Haddon was assistant vice president for transportation; and Michael McClellan, my son, had been in both the Carload and the Intermodal Marketing groups at CR. Roy Blanchard and others helped us reach out to short lines, and Mike Mohan and Declan Brown of the Kingsley Consulting Group provided general backup and operational expertise. Larry Kaufman, a public relations veteran, helped us craft the message. I continued my long-term relationship with Don Phillips, who was a conduit to Linda Morgan—direct contact with her was off limits. (CSX used Phillips as a conduit as well.)

The assistance of former CR people was critical in understanding the exact boundaries of the split. For example, my son Michael told me to get the bypass route through Pittsburgh; it was cleared for double-stack trains, and the alternate route wasn't. Of course, CSX could have done a far better job of precisely defining the lines it wanted simply by using the expertise at CR. But using Conrail staff would have signaled to LeVan that CSX was seriously considering a split, and that would have confirmed LeVan's worst fear: that CSX would throw Conrail under the bus to get a deal with NS.

As in any political campaign, there were claims and counterclaims, and one goal was to discredit the "facts" presented by the other side. Norfolk Southern had by far the stronger story: it was willing to create a balanced system, and CSX-CR was not, at least as long as CR was adamant about preserving its *X*. We got wind that CSX-CR was considering offering the former Baltimore & Ohio and the former Erie-Lackawanna in the state of New York to NS and then declaring that the competitive issues were resolved. Now, most railroaders knew that the former E-L was inferior to the NYC and that the B&O was inferior to the PRR. But for the general public, the routes looked quite viable on a map. CSX-CR was setting NS up: they would offer these inferior routes, and when we said no, we would be the ones playing defense.

To get the story out, Larry Kaufman set up an interview with Rip Watson of the *Journal of Commerce*. I showed him the route comparisons, noting that while routes were important, so too was a balance of originating and terminating traffic. The goal was wider than just a focus on the routes per se. The ultimate audience for the public policy case was the STB—we needed to convince them that balanced competition was a good idea, and that NS was prepared to address the issue and CSX-CR was not. But this effort spilled over into the financial and legal arguments. NS had to be seen as the most credible buyer.

Throughout this period, NS continued the battle on the financial and legal fronts. Norfolk Southern spiked the concerns of the arbs by making a guarantee that the price would still be one hundred dollars a share, should a negotiated settlement be reached. That put further pressure on CSX to up its bid, which it did (partly to compensate for a decline in the value of CSX stock). Norfolk Southern immediately raised its bid and also announced that it had secured a $15 billion line of credit to support its bid. There was a final round of bidding, and Goode and the CR acquisition team (which included his senior Commercial, Operating, and Legal officers along with support from Strategic Planning and others) responded with an aggressive bid. While some of the team wanted to wait a week, we decided that an immediate raise in our bid would signal to the other side that resistance was futile. The timid NS of the past was gone.

I was part of the team tapped to sell the NS plan to potential investors. I was amazed at how few questions I got about the viability of the proposed plan. We at NS knew there were massive risks involved, but the banks seemed uninterested in performing due diligence; they were focused on making loans to NS. If there were risks, they seemed not to want to know about them, and it certainly was not my job to tell them.

A westbound Canadian National freight rolls through Dorval, Quebec, 2010. Norfolk Southern offered some Conrail routes and markets to the CN or the CP if CSX did not move to close a deal with NS.

All of this effort took place in the fog of war. (For the best account of how the battle played out, see Rush Loving Jr.'s book, *The Men Who Loved Trains*. Loving interviewed the key participants after the fact and the book provides an excellent account of what the various participants were doing.) Goode, Wolf, and their high-powered financial and legal consultants could only guess at what was going on in the CSX-CR camp. I certainly did not know, and assumed that they were winning. The legal battle was a back-and-forth affair, with CSX-CR doing all that they could to restrict the vote. Finally, on January 17, 1997, the shareholders voted. Norfolk Southern prevailed with 65 percent of the shares voting against approval of the proposed CSX deal.

I had been at a meeting in New York and ran into one of our vice presidents in the USAir Club at LaGuardia Airport.

He told me NS had won the vote. I was as excited as I had ever been, and quickly called Jim Hamilton, my contact at Morgan, to confirm that it was true. He said the issue was never really in doubt. (I didn't order a round for everyone in the club, though I was tempted.) It had been an emotional roller coaster, but it was not over. Conrail remained stubbornly opposed to dealing with NS.

THE CANADIAN CARD

Despite winning the shareholder vote, NS was still unable to get CSX back to the bargaining table because Conrail was refusing any deal. (We did not know that LeVan was refusing to cooperate with CSX.) So I contacted the Canadian National and the Canadian Pacific and offered to let them outline how

A westbound Canadian Pacific inter-modal train just west of Lake Louise, Alberta, 2008. The CP responded to the NS overture with a realistic set of desired divestitures, while the CN overreached.

they would solve the competitive issues. Acquiring part of Conrail would dramatically improve the market coverage of either company. The CN was skeptical; Gerald Davies, now the CN's chief commercial officer, with whom I had worked at both the FRA and the USRA, thought it was just a ploy, and that NS would come to terms with CSX in the end. I replied that the odds were that we would make a deal with CSX, but could the CN refuse to participate? To add to the credibility of the overture, there was no announcement of the talks whatsoever. They were wrapped in strict secrecy at NS because I was convinced someone would leak the information and thus increase the paranoia at CSX that NS was moving behind their backs.

The Canadians did submit their wish lists: the CP was reasonable but the CN simply wanted too much of the Conrail franchise. But ploy or not—and faced with the possibility

that it would get nothing from its Conrail initiative—CSX pressured Conrail to face reality and acquiesce to being split.

In the end, Don Phillips and Linda Morgan played a crucial role in changing Conrail's thinking. Phillips interviewed Morgan, who affirmed that the STB wanted two balanced systems in the East and would much prefer to have the parties work it out rather than have the STB staff create a plan. John Snow worked behind the scenes to convince a reluctant LeVan that Conrail would have to be split—no other scenario would produce the balanced solution that Morgan said the STB wanted. The CSX and NS offers were melded to provide for the purchase of Conrail for $115 per share.

The "balanced competition" theme had been a winner. On February 3, 1997, the Conrail board voted to accept the joint proposal.

With the battle concluded, NS and CSX faced the daunting task of making good on their promises. No carrier of the size or complexity of Conrail had been unmerged and then re-merged. The Rock Island had been liquidated, and relatively small or little-used lines had simply been attached to larger, stronger systems. But CR operations in the Northeast were larger than those of either CSX or NS. It was complicated, and the potential for failure was high. Billions of dollars had been borrowed to pay for CR, and earning a return on that huge investment was urgent.

The number of issues to be resolved was enormous, and every time the teams met there were more and more challenges, including the following:

- How would CSX and NS divide the costs of acquisition and such additional expenses as labor protection, the STB case, and the community and environmental measures needed to gain regulatory approval?
- With the Monongahela issue resolved, how precisely would the infrastructure (defined by exact mile post) be conveyed to CSX, to NS, and to the shared asset areas (neutral switching areas now known as "little Conrail")? Included in the infrastructure decisions were such things as the system shops at Altoona and the Philadelphia office building.
- How would CR's equipment be allocated?
- How would employees be assigned after the split?
- How would the Conrail data and management systems, the heart of modern railroading, be integrated with existing CSX and NS systems?
- What charges and operating protocols would be used for the three shared asset areas?

This is only an abbreviated list of the questions that had to be resolved before operations could be shifted to the new owners.

Teams were established to resolve the issues. Strategic Planning was involved in most of them, if only to set forth what was agreed to in the negotiations. Most of the problems, while difficult, were solved with a minimum of contention. With the big battle over, the need for speed was paramount. Every minute, money was going out the door.

While the basic parameters of the split had been established, some thorny details remained. Precise cut points had to be decided, and some of those decisions had very real commercial and operating implications. For example, most of CR's coal traffic originated on the former Monongahela Railroad south of Pittsburgh—who would control that operation? Should it be turned into a joint company like the other shared asset areas? Steve Tobias and Pete Carpenter went round and round on that one. Finally CSX agreed that NS would control the lines and give CSX trackage rights.

Another question: which carrier would take which intermodal terminal in northern New Jersey? There were four, not counting one operated by the Port Authority. Normally the Strategic Planning team simply made the call, because we did not have time to bring the commercial people into the discussion, knowing that the arguments would go on and on. But in this instance, the heads of intermodal for each company were included in the decision. After all, bringing competition back to the New York area had been one of our key arguments. Nothing is more competitive than intermodal, and terminals are critical to providing quality service. For that reason, while access to northern New Jersey was over shared asset area tracks, the terminals themselves would go to either CSX or NS.

Another tricky matter was where to draw the boundaries of the shared asset areas. On one side, industries would have access to two line-haul railroads; on the other side they would be captive to a single carrier. We made a pragmatic judgment, driven partially by historical switching limits, always making the cuts so that there was substantial distance between those industries inside the shared asset areas and those outside their boundaries.

One of the toughest challenges we faced was deciding how much NS and CSX would pay for their portions of Conrail. The final price for the CR stock was over $10 billion, and to that was added debt assumed, the cost of implementation, and other up-front administrative costs. The carriers agreed to split the cost based on the share of CR's traffic that each was likely to obtain; it was up to Bill Hart of CSX and me to settle on a procedure and sign off on a number. MultiRail, based in Princeton, New Jersey, the acknowledged leader in making traffic diversion studies, was given the task of predicting how the post-split traffic would be routed. Traffic diversion studies had been used for decades to make such predictions in prior merger cases. The models were run, and the outcome was that 58 percent of the traffic was predicted to accrue to NS and 42 percent to CSX. The logic was straightforward: for instance, a car originating on the current NS and terminating on what would be NS's portion of Conrail, or at a shared asset station, was assigned to the NS side of the ledger. If a car moved from a gateway, such as Chicago, to a shared asset station, it was assumed that each carrier would have a 50 percent chance for the traffic.

I had a lot of experience in the use of traffic diversion models and knew just how unreliable they could be. The stakes were significant: each 1 percent shift in the traffic split was worth more than $100 million. Some other advisors said the split was more in the range of 50–50, not 58–42; the difference between the two opinions was about $1 billion. Hank Wolf was certainly nervous about the outcome and checked with some sources at Conrail, who said, "Well, McClellan knows about as much about the Conrail system as anyone." When I expressed my own concerns to Tobias, he asked if anyone else was better able to make the decision.

Each of the other areas had similar multimillion-dollar implications for the two companies. That said, the pressure from the top to keep the process moving meant that the various teams were able to work in relative harmony. They were professionals and did not want some planner or lawyer making, for example, a locomotive decision for them.

THE REGULATORY CASE

Almost concurrently with these planning activities, lawyers were developing the case for the STB. There was never any question about ultimate approval—the board had publicly lauded the competitive solution we had negotiated, and was no doubt happy to avoid having to decide the outcome of a long fight between CSX and NS. But the pressure was intense. As NS's army of lawyers was busy drafting the case and all of the related verified statements, the same process was underway at CSX. It was the responsibility of Strategic Planning and the lawyers to review all of these documents and make certain that they were internally consistent and that they meshed with both what had been negotiated and what had been said to shippers and various governmental entities. This effort consumed the Planning staff as well as many of our outside consultants.

A westbound Union Pacific steam train just east of Glenwood Springs, Colorado, 2006. After the intensity of the fight with CSX and the split of Conrail, I was ready for a break. The battle for Conrail had put my railfan activities on hold, so this trip was special.

Even though there was no risk that the STB would reject the application, there were still risks from the imposition of conditions. Recall that the Penn Central merger included a condition that the PC acquire the destitute New Haven—that was probably the final nail in the PC coffin. So imposed conditions could have huge economic consequences.

Meanwhile, we learned just how disruptive well-organized opposition could be. Cleveland was ground zero for changes in operating patterns. Because of the split, considerable volumes of traffic that had moved south of the city would now go through Cleveland proper. Fortunately, the tracks necessary to do that were in place, thanks to a New York Central line that bypassed the passenger line along the lakefront. That bypass line was no longer heavily used, but with the split, the line would become very busy once again. For the people living near the line—mostly in inner-city, poorer neighborhoods—the increased traffic would be a nuisance.

The mayor of Cleveland took the lead in condemning the proposed plan and led a focused public relations effort to bolster the city's case, but there was no alternative to the use of the Belt Line route. Linda Morgan signaled that the issue was too hot for the STB; the railroads would have to come up with a solution. Weeks later, a costly mitigation package was announced, including some grade-crossing elimination, payment for soundproofing trackside homes, and several new fire stations. The clock was ticking, and submitting to blackmail was the only alternative.

Given my deep involvement in the negotiations, I was a prime target for opposition lawyers. No one was opposing the overall package, but there was a major attempt to gain a concession here and a concession there, with those concessions worth millions overall.

As a witness, I spent a day and a half being cross-examined, and I had a ball once the first butterflies were overcome. No one else in the room knew as much about how the northeastern rail network had evolved. The opposition lawyers either knew that going in, or soon got a sense of the depth of my knowledge, so they tended to go carefully in their questioning.

The case went on for months until a decision was issued on July 23, 1998, but by that point there was no longer any doubt about a favorable outcome without too many harmful conditions. When the regulatory phase was over, I took a breather. It just so happened that Union Pacific steam locomotive number 844 was running in Colorado, and my good friend John Rebensdorf, the UP's strategic planner, even got me a ride in the cab for part of the trip. It was a great reward after three very trying years.

There was no breather for many others, however. The teams were busy putting the finishing touches on plans to run the "new NS."

A BOTCHED BEGINNING

Conrail ran for more than a year while all the planning and regulatory work was underway. The agreement between NS and CSX required that CR maintain the status quo; new market initiatives and changes in operations were all frozen in place. With CR's headquarters essentially shut down, there were no orders to change this or that. The CR operating officers said that the railroad had never run better. Perhaps the lesson was that a railroad runs better when changes are minimized, or maybe that railroads run better if senior management takes

a holiday. Regardless, Conrail was running well until NS got there. That would change.

I was in Philadelphia on June 1, 1999, the start date for the operational split. The night before, Don Phillips and I went to a bar not far from CR's headquarters, where we drank a toast or two to Conrail. He and I had both been there for its creation, and now, some twenty-three years later, we were there for its end. It was a bittersweet moment for me.

The next morning I was up early to get a status report. The news was not good: the Information Technology people in Atlanta had failed to load the CR operating information properly. The mistake was corrected in a matter of hours, but it was a harbinger of far more serious IT problems to come. As I walked in the door of Conrail headquarters, Ron Conway, formerly CR's vice president for operations and now in the same job at CSX, was coming in. I congratulated him on a smooth start-up for their team, acknowledging what he already knew: NS had botched day one.

Things went downhill from there. Despite all the planning, the NS and CR computer systems were not in sync. The modern railway runs off computers: the assignment of motive power and the trip plans for cars (essentially which cars go on which trains and which cars get switched at which yard) are all computerized. The NS/CR systems had failed. Cars were routed to New Jersey and then routed right back to their origin. Yards were plugged; trains could not get into them and were parked on the main lines, so the main lines were filled with stopped trains, creating a domino effect. Crews had to be relieved as they reached the federally mandated limit on work hours, and suddenly NS was short of crews.

Things were spiraling out of control, and by the end of the first week NS was in deep, deep trouble. Initially, the outside world was unaware of the depth of the problem. This was, after all, Norfolk Southern, a company with a reputation for operating excellence. But inside the company we were well aware of the problem but not sure what to do about it. Goode called for 7:00 AM meetings with the leadership team seven days a week, to review problems and make changes as necessary. At the meetings, calls were made to the key yards for status reports, but the reports were seldom encouraging. One morning Goode asked Steve Tobias, the COO, about the condition of the railroad. Tobias replied, "Chunky." It was that and more. On another morning, one of our local public relations representatives said they were getting a lot of pressure from some town on the railroad—engines had been sitting there for several days, idling, and their noise kept people awake at night. Jon Manetta, our vice president for transportation, bolted from the room. The engines had been lost and were now found, thanks to the complaint.

Personally, I was as depressed as I had ever been. In my view, the acquisition of our part of Conrail corrected a defect in the rail system that had started with the Penn Central merger. I had played an important role in correcting that defect, and after all those years and all of that work, the outcome so far was a disaster. I had my sixtieth birthday on June 10, and my wife had organized a surprise party. Some of my very closest friends were there, some of whom had come hundreds and even thousands of miles to attend. But I was so immersed in NS's meltdown that I really did not enjoy the celebration. Joanne was terribly disappointed at my lack of enthusiasm, but the failure of the start-up was a huge emotional downer.

Things didn't get better for months. I hit the road to explain our problems face-to-face with some key customers and government agencies, such as the Pennsylvania DOT, where the service failures had been most acute. I also kept Linda Morgan apprised informally of just how bad things were. The auto companies were simply livid. The service was so bad that many of their plants were threatened with closure due to a lack of parts. Further, assembled vehicles were delayed leaving the plants. Norfolk Southern, with its part of CR, was a huge factor in the automotive supply chain, and at times it seemed that we were about to shut down an entire industry. The meetings with them, which Steve Tobias and I were handling, were ordeals.

I was hardly the only person at NS depressed about the turn of events. Norfolk Southern thought of itself as the most competent operating company in the business, and many NS people could not come to grips with our failure. I personally came in for some blame, since many believed that if we had never done the Conrail deal, this meltdown never would have occurred. Still, everyone soldiered through. Many people, including most of the Planning Department, were sent to Atlanta and Roanoke to trace cars manually and deal with irate customers. The company even chartered air cargo planes to move auto parts to plants that were about to shut down.

At the first board meeting during those dark days, one of the members got up and gave a pep talk—something to the effect that he and the board had confidence in the management team and were certain we would work our way out of the problem. Later he admitted that we all looked so glum that it was clear to him we needed support.

I could do little to fix the problems and could not stand to be idle, so between visits to angry customers I went out to see firsthand what the meltdown looked like. On my first trip, I was coming east on Amtrak's Three Rivers, a Chicago–New York train via Pittsburgh (now defunct). I rode the locomotives out of Pittsburgh. It was depressing. As we went east, we passed train after train, both east- and westbound, very few of which were moving—they were idle on the main

The eastbound Three Rivers as seen from a westbound NS freight train, 2003. Norfolk Southern flubbed its takeover of its part of Conrail in the summer of 1999. To get an unvarnished view of how the railroad was performing, I took a ride in the cab of the Three Rivers.

line waiting for crews. One of the busiest railroads in North America was essentially a parking lot.

An Amtrak road foreman was in the engine, and as we approached Horseshoe Curve, he turned to me and, more in sadness than in anger, said, "I don't know what happened, but it sure worked fine before you people showed up." I think that summed up the attitude of most of the Conrail operating employees as well. They had gone through the trauma of splitting their company, to which many felt a great loyalty, and this was the result? Who were these braggarts from the South who strutted around thinking they were the best operating people in railroading?

As we were coming down Horseshoe Curve, the one train moving was grinding up the grade at perhaps 5 mph, clearly underpowered. At Altoona, I went back to the train, where the

conductor told the passengers that I was an NS vice president, and NS was the reason the train was five hours late and they would not get to New York until well past midnight. After the conductor decided that I had taken enough abuse, he gave me an empty roomette in which to hide out.

At Harrisburg, a very angry station agent greeted me. He had been struggling for weeks with a train that was routinely four to seven hours late. Finally, he had someone onboard to whom he could vent his frustration face-to-face. I was relieved when we finally made it to Philadelphia and I could get to the safety of the USAir Club at the Philadelphia Airport.

The problems lasted through the summer and into the fall. In October I was the dinner speaker at the Detroit Auto Club's annual dinner, which I had committed to months before the split. It was a large group, well over three hundred people. I laid out what was wrong and what we were doing to fix the problems. But given our actual performance, the words had little credibility. I did open by stating that it had been a bad summer: "I turned sixty, my favorite dog—a Lab—died, and my railroad came unglued." I went on to suggest that neither my youth nor my dog would ever come back, "but the railroad would return." (What kind of coward evokes the image of a dead Labrador to get sympathy from an audience?) Some of our automotive customers got up and said what a bad job NS was doing. I did get out alive, but it was another painful and very public encounter during the meltdown era. (At another meeting months later, a woman came up and said, "I know you—you were the man whose dog died. That was so sad.")

The railroad did come back. The day after the speech I rode the engines on the Three Rivers from Chicago to Pittsburgh; we passed or overtook over seventy trains, and all but two had crews. The trip was timely—a few days later I got a call from a very worried Linda Morgan of the STB. Norfolk Southern had been in trouble for months, and now CSX was faltering. Pressure from politicians and shippers was intense. Her reputation and that of the STB were at risk, thanks to the lousy job NS and now CSX were doing. I suggested that she hold off on any action for a couple of weeks—I told her I had ridden the railroad the day before, things looked very, very good, and my gut told me that the problems were largely behind us. I think she trusted my assessment, thanks to our interaction at the STB advisory board years before, and she gave us a few more weeks.

And I was right. By Thanksgiving the railroad was operationally sound. But although revenues were coming in as expected, the financial performance was lagging badly. Goode decided that NS needed a new approach to improving efficiency.

Companies tend to ossify over time. From my experience, failure to change is the number one obstacle in railroading. But slow change can be a good thing; railroads work best when they do the same thing at the same time in the same way day after day.

One of the criticisms of John Snow—and I have seen him in action—was that he could think up new ideas, many of them good, faster than they could be implemented. At the other end of the spectrum are organizations, such as the PRR and Kodak, that fly their business plan right into the ground. Norfolk Southern was somewhere in between.

The N&W was not exactly an agent of change either. It was the last big railroad to dieselize—a change that had to be forced on its then-CEO, lawyer Stuart Saunders, which says something about its culture. Now it was up to another N&W lawyer, David Goode, to get NS to focus on the future. Morale at NS was a mixed bag after the exhausting multiyear effort to acquire part of Conrail. Yes, NS had checked the CSX expansion plans, and yes, it had acquired the larger part of CR. But it had stumbled badly in integrating its part of CR. While the railroad was now running well, it was not making much money. Clearly something was amiss, and fundamental changes were needed.

The teams that Goode had created a few years earlier to work outside the traditional silos had achieved some success, especially in the cost area. For example, NS had an entire shop dedicated to making switch frogs. (The switch frog is the crossing point between two rails.) The Birmingham frog shop was the result of the SR Maintenance of Way Department's tradition of controlling every aspect of the MOW process, which they felt, with some justification, was the best in the industry. But when the company was being stretched financially, could NS do the work in-house with union forces? Or could an outside vendor be found who could produce the frogs more cheaply? The answer was the latter, partly because the frog shop, in order to keep its unit costs low, was producing more frogs than the railroad needed, and the excess was piling up in inventory.

After the CR transaction was completed, Goode expanded the concept and I was drawn into the effort. I was half-asleep at a management meeting, listening to Goode outline how we needed to do a better job of making infrastructure investment decisions, when I heard him count off the members of the new team, concluding with, "Jim McClellan will lead the effort." (It was like daydreaming in school and having the teacher suddenly call on you to answer the question. It was definitely time to wake up.) The assignment proved an interesting one. The team was made up of representatives, almost all at the vice president level, from Marketing, Finance, Transportation, Engineering, and Planning. My right-hand man was Dan Mazur, assistant vice president for planning, who had been a coal marketing executive with CR. Mazur had the right blend of smarts, patience, and negotiating skill to herd this high-level collection of egos and often-wrong-but-seldom-in-doubt convictions.

Deciding just how much and where to expand capacity is a tricky business. Railroad infrastructure is hugely expensive, and not easily moved if you make the wrong decision. It can take a couple of years to get new capacity in place, especially if there are environmental- or community-impact issues. Move too fast and you will have costly, idle capacity. Move too slowly and you will have a choke point that can impact much of your network. We liked to say that we wanted just-in-time capacity,

but while that makes a cute sound bite, getting there is very, very difficult.

Prior to our efforts, new capacity projects had bubbled up from the division level to the regional level to the vice president level, where the projects were selected for submission to the Finance Department. Once they passed that department's filter (return on investment, risk issues, etc.), the project was deemed worthy of consideration by the capital budget committee made up of the senior NS executives. In a good year, more money went to investment, while a bad year meant lower total spending.

The infrastructure team created a more open process in which projects were collected at the division level and were ultimately analyzed from a system perspective. This new process was useful because it looked at issues beyond the boundaries of a single division. For example, when we asked the superintendent of the Georgia division where his biggest choke point was, he said Cincinnati. Now, Cincinnati was over three hundred miles beyond the northern end of his division, but he said, "When Cincinnati is congested, the problems cascade down to my division." This broader look at the network found similar examples of why the narrow silo approach often gave the wrong answer. A side benefit of the new process was that once the infrastructure team gave its recommendations, the endless wrangling at the capital budget meetings ceased, and people could focus on the more strategic issues.

Goode then created a team to look at finding major operational savings—we needed some home runs. It was pretty much the same cast of characters as the infrastructure team, but by now we were all so comfortable with the team concept that we did not need a designated leader. Our first meeting was a wake-up call. Norfolk Southern had too many hump yards in service. Some argued that we should close Roanoke; others argued that the Sheffield, Alabama, yard be mothballed. It soon became clear that we simply did not have the information needed to make a good decision. Railroading is a network business: if you close yard A, what other yard or yards are going to handle the business? Likewise, if you change train schedules and/or the traffic that a train carries, there is a ripple effect. Our in-house network designers were months away from having a good working model.

The consulting firm MultiRail (now Oliver Wyman), of Princeton, New Jersey, had approached me earlier after being rebuffed by our transportation planners. I discouraged them at the time because NS had a very strong aversion to outside consultants (except in a crisis, such as the battle with CSX for Conrail, where there were no limits on the use of "outsiders"). The team decided that this was another crisis, and MultiRail was hired that very afternoon. They faced a difficult task—not only were our own transportation planners hostile, but the field operating officers were as well. Superintendents liked to do their own thing, and local dispatchers enjoyed the power of adding or annulling trains without system oversight. But thanks mainly to Mazur's sales ability, things never came to blows. In time, a new operating plan called TOP (for Thoroughbred Operating Plan) was implemented. Savings were achieved and the railroad ran better. Now, network planning models—which have been in-house for years now—are the standard tool for modifying system operations. The consultants put some high-powered talent into the project, including Carl Van Dyke, Jason Kuehn, and Rod Case. Though no smarter or more experienced than the NS people, they brought a much-needed new perspective—a new way of thinking about our network.

In a sense, it was a step back in time. When I started at the Southern, it operated a network of trains. (The premier train was number 153, which served most of the railroad through a hub-and-spoke operation.) If someone messed with the network, they would soon experience the wrath of Bill Brosnan. In the intervening years, the SR and NS had migrated to a less-rigid system, but with the implementation of the TOP plan, ad hoc railroading fell out of favor. Today the mantra is to run to plan, though staying on plan is a constant challenge even now.

ON TO NEW ENGLAND

The split of Conrail gave CSX the NYC line east of Cleveland, including the former Boston and Albany to New England. Essentially, when we sorted out who got what and who paid for what, CSX thought that it had bought a virtual monopoly in New England. After all, Guilford was running but a single round trip to Mechanicville, New York, where it connected with the Canadian Pacific (formerly the Delaware & Hudson). Conrail had made a deal with Guilford to pay Guilford its Mechanicville revenues, but Conrail would haul the traffic across the Berkshires and interchange the traffic with Guilford at Worcester, Massachusetts—essentially CR did the work and Guilford got the money. So Guilford basically opted out of the east–west trade before the CR split, and both CSX and I assumed that it would be only a matter of time before the line to Mechanicville would be inoperable or abandoned. The CSX hold on New England railroading would then be complete.

I had a different vision and thought NS should go to New England as part of its overall network. The more origin-destination pairs that a railroad can offer a customer, the better its chances of securing his business. Norfolk Southern was

Above, The NS New England expansion group at North Station before the Pan Am executive train departed, 2010. *Left to right*: Mike McClellan, David Fink Jr., John Friedmann, Jim McClellan, David Goode, Susan Goode, and Tim Mellon.

Right, A Pan Am executive train at Greenfield, Massachusetts, 2010. Years after both David Goode and I had retired, the Pan Am management invited some of the NS people who had made the New England expansion possible on a sentimental journey on the main line to Mechanicville.

The executive train approaches the east portal of the Hoosac Tunnel, 2010. For a railfan, no sentimental journey would be complete without a cab ride through this tunnel.

already at a slight disadvantage in Florida; it could reach the greater Miami market by working with the Florida East Coast, but it did not reach Tampa. Without service to New England, the NS disadvantage would be even worse. I knew NS could physically serve the market from both Binghamton, New York (east–west traffic), and Wilkes-Barre, Pennsylvania (north–south traffic). Both gateways had been active years earlier; after all, the Delaware & Hudson had a reason for calling itself the "Bridge Road." The challenge was to convince the D&H's current owner, the Canadian Pacific, to make a deal to haul NS traffic to Mechanicville, and then to convince Guilford to improve the service beyond that gateway to the Boston market and elsewhere. After talking to Guilford it appeared that a deal could be done if NS would pay to improve the clearances through the Hoosac Tunnel enough that "high-low" (a smaller international container married with a larger domestic box) could be accommodated. Without double-stack capability the route would never be competitive with CSX. Guilford estimated the cost to be $4 million. I went to Goode and asked for the money and the authority I needed. He had a good market sense and understood the stakes involved.

Long story short: after months of negotiating, a deal was reached with both the CP and Guilford. (Much of the heavy lifting was done by John Rathbone of NS—I was consumed with the STB case at the time.) The tunnel was improved and NS launched intermodal service to New England in 2001. Business expanded, and after I had retired, NS and Pan Am (the successor to Guilford) formed a joint venture called Pan Am Southern so that NS funds could be applied to improving the Mechanicville–Fitchburg, Massachusetts, route (beyond Fitchburg, Pan Am reaches the Ayer intermodal terminal over the tracks of the Massachusetts Bay Transportation Authority). Norfolk Southern then bought the south end of the former

Delaware & Hudson from the Canadian Pacific and now has its own railroad to the Albany area, with a joint venture beyond to Boston.

It took fifteen years, but now that the deal is done, NS has a solid presence in New England. Nothing is easy or fast in the railroad business, or so it seems. As an aside, it was my son, Michael (vice president for intermodal marketing at the time), who led the NS efforts to put together the terminals, the better track, and the better organization needed to make New England a success.

TIME TO GO

Norfolk Southern requires its board-appointed officers to retire at age sixty-five. I thought it was a fine policy until I approached that magic age, but rules are rules. I actually left a year before I had to, thanks to a very generous one-shot retirement program. It was time to leave anyway—my successor, Wick Moorman, had been chosen (he subsequently became CEO). Moorman would join me in meetings to get a feel for the challenges he would face. All fame is fleeting: when Wick was at a meeting with me and I presented a course of action, I noticed that most people in the room would look at Wick to get an idea of whether he agreed or not. Once people know that you will be gone by a certain date, they move on to find new alliances with new people.

After one of the board dinners there was a brief ceremony for me and several other vice presidents who were also retiring. We all collected our mementos and said farewell. And that was that. It had been a good run, and had turned out much better than I ever could have hoped. The best reward was that the industry that I loved so much had not only survived, but prospered.

An eastbound intermodal train rounds Horseshoe Curve as seen from the locomotive of a westbound intermodal train, 2008. I first rode this railroad when I was a student at Wharton and I spent much of my career trying to append this main line to the NS network. I still get a warm feeling every time I ride the line: one of my favorite rail lines is now part of "my" railroad. Retired or not, I still retain strong ties to NS.

The Southern Crescent arrives in Alexandria, Virginia, 1974. The Southern did not join Amtrak, and the Crescent became the darling of railfans nation-wide. Like the Canadian today, it was a throwback to a more elegant kind of journey by passenger train.

REFLECTIONS

WHEN I WAS IN HIGH SCHOOL, CIRCA 1955, MY UNCLE and I were stopped at a grade crossing in San Antonio. The northbound Missouri Pacific passenger train rolled by, a collection of mail and express cars punctuated by a solitary and virtually empty passenger coach. My uncle noted that "railroads were a dying business." Such was the opinion of most people at the time.

That opinion was close to the mark for the next two decades. Most passenger trains died and the Penn Central and some other freight carriers survived, thanks only to a massive infusion of taxpayer dollars. It was not a happy time and the future was very much in doubt. But a surprising thing happened on the way to oblivion. Railroads did not go the way of the stagecoach or, more recently, the rotary phone. Rail technology, born in the early nineteenth century, turned out to be remarkably resilient. Railroads streamlined and focused on those things that rail technology did best: the movement of traffic between high-volume origin-destination points.

It was a "rail renaissance," and that renaissance was anchored by new sources of traffic: western low-sulfur coal and international intermodal traffic in containers, and big, big trains often moving thousands of miles. More traffic meant more revenue and more earnings and with those earnings came the ability to rebuild much of the industry. No longer are there "standing derailments," and railways are well maintained; it is our highway network that now needs massive investment.

But nothing is forever. Just when it looked like the railroads were home free, along came the rapid decline in coal traffic. Coal has been the mainstay of much of the rail network for decades. New markets will have to be found and developed. There is certainly a lot of freight to move: take a ride on any major highway and that statement is obvious. But getting any substantial portion of that traffic onto the railroad will be hard.

Stand at Winslow, Arizona, and look west toward the San Francisco peaks. You will probably see two or three container trains, each with two hundred or more containers, tackling the Continental Divide.

How efficient is that!

But on the parallel interstate you will also see hundreds of trucks making their way across this high desert country: reefers, moving vans, flatbeds, tank trucks—mostly long-haul, but traffic that requires specialty attention in some form or

The Southern Crescent loading passengers at Alexandria, 1974.
What this image lacks in clarity, it makes up for in mood: the coach
porter ready to board passengers, the conductor standing a few cars
further up, and the families lying on the grass taking it all in.

My son and my daughter watching the Southern Crescent arriving in Alexandria on a summer evening, 1974. Going down to the station to see the trains was popular summer entertainment for us. The train "bug" took with my son, who is now a vice president at Norfolk Southern.

another. That's not something railroads do all that well these days.

Or drive any interstate in the eastern United States. There are wall-to-wall trucks handling the same variety of commodities, but with an added challenge: much of the traffic is short-haul, and the shorter the haul, the tougher it is for railroads to compete. Add to those challenges the fact that the US economy is getting more efficient. Cars are lighter, there are fewer McMansions, and so on. It's all good for the environment but it also means less "stuff" to move. And trucks and trains thrive on moving stuff.

My sense is that railroads are once again at a crossroads. Just as they were reinvented to create the rail renaissance, so must they be reinvented to find new markets. It will be tough because the available markets do not fit current rail technology or current marketing and operating strategies. But it's not an impossible dream. Compared to when I started my career, railroads are vastly more efficient. The infrastructure and balance sheets are the best in my lifetime. Passenger trains are wards of the government, so that huge financial burden has been shed.

Railroading has been around for almost two hundred years, which is quite a run when you think about it. So now we will get to see how the next generation of railroads adapt the technology for the markets of the future. It should be an interesting show.

I will close this book with a few images from my alma mater, the Southern Railway. The SR was a beacon in an often dark world in the 1970s. It opted out of Amtrak and ran its own class act, the Southern Crescent. The Crescent was very much a conventional streamliner of the post–World War II era, but it was perfectly maintained and squeaky clean, and it ran on time. So I spent many an evening down at the Alexandria, Virginia, station, watching the Crescent come and go. It was an uplifting experience—an affirmation that railroading could be great again.

The Southern Crescent heads into the sunset, the Washington Monument in the distance, 1978. The train had just come out of the tunnel by Virginia Avenue Tower. The Crescent exited the railroad scene in 1979, leaving only the Canadian to remind us of how things used to be.

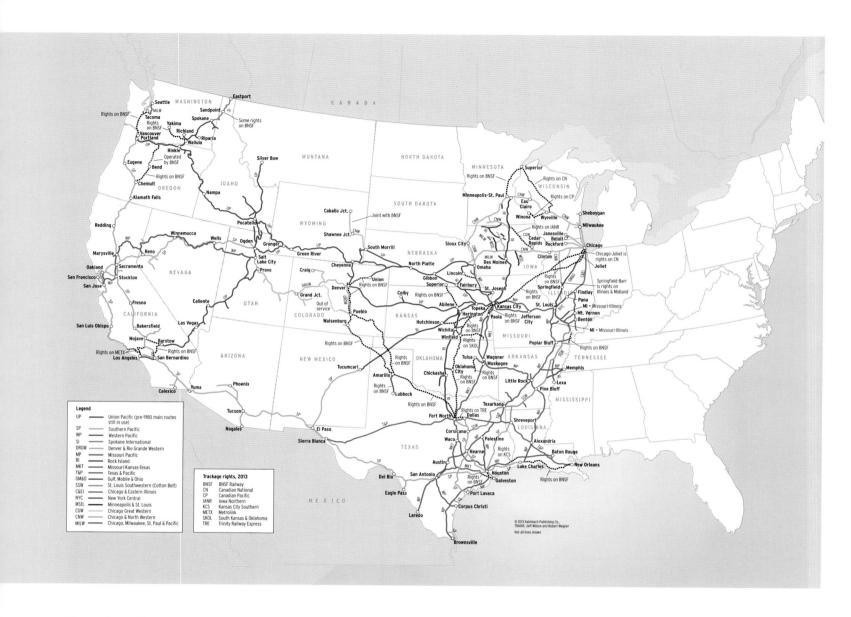

Legend

UP		Union Pacific (pre-1980 main routes still in use)
SP		Southern Pacific
WP		Western Pacific
SI		Spokane International
DRGW		Denver & Rio Grande Western
MP		Missouri Pacific
RI		Rock Island
MKT		Missouri-Kansas-Texas
T&P		Texas & Pacific
GM&O		Gulf, Mobile & Ohio
SSW		St. Louis Southwestern (Cotton Belt)
C&EI		Chicago & Eastern Illinois
NYC		New York Central
MStL		Minneapolis & St. Louis
CGW		Chicago Great Western
CNW		Chicago & North Western
MILW		Chicago, Milwaukee, St. Paul & Pacific

Trackage rights, 2013

BNSF	BNSF Railway
CN	Canadian National
CP	Canadian Pacific
IANR	Iowa Northern
KCS	Kansas City Southern
METX	Metrolink
SKOL	South Kansas & Oklahoma
TRE	Trinity Railway Express

© 2013 Kalmbach Publishing Co.,
TRAINS: Jeff Wilson and Robert Wegner
Not all lines shown

Above, The Burlington Northern Santa Fe. © 2013 Kalmbach Publishing Co., *Trains:* Jeff Wilson and Robert Wenger. Not all lines shown.

Facing, The Canadian National. © 2013 Kalmbach Publishing Co., *Trains:* Robert Wegner, Bill Metzger. Map research assistance provided by Greg McDonnell, Charles W. Bohi, Leslie S. Kozma, and Canadian National's Mark Hallman.

Appendix

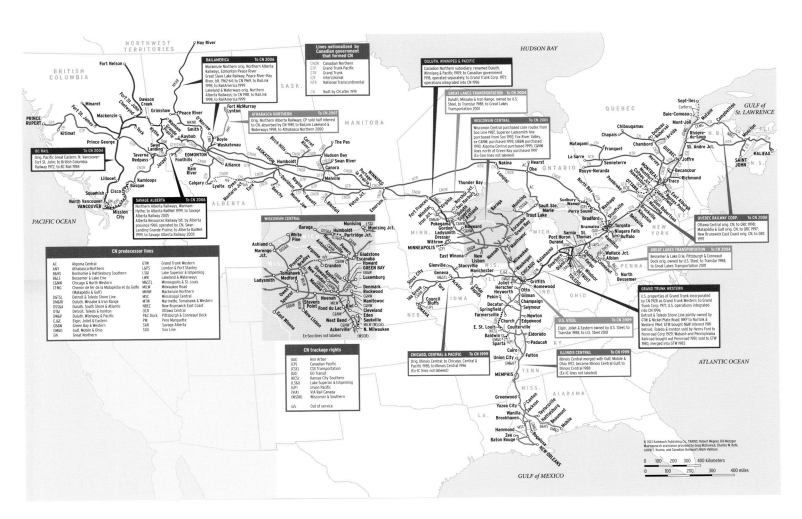

305

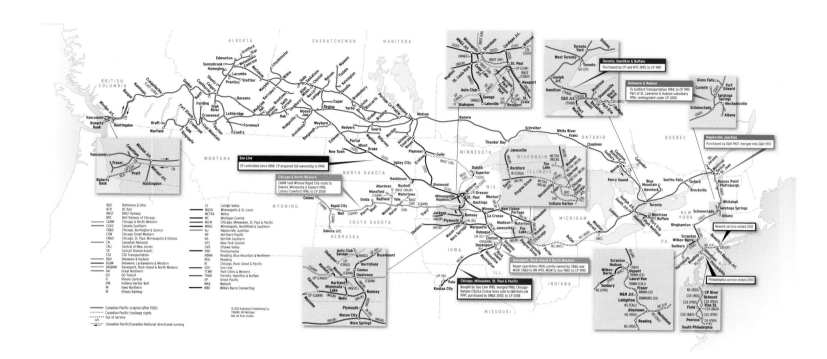

The Canadian Pacific. © 2013 Kalmbach Publishing
Co., *Trains*: Bill Metzger. Not all lines shown.

CSX. © 2013 Kalmbach Publishing Co., *Trains*: Robert Wegner. Not all lines shown.

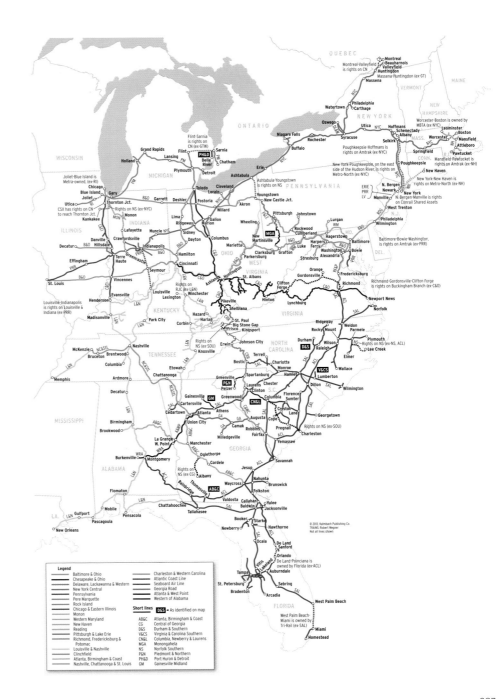

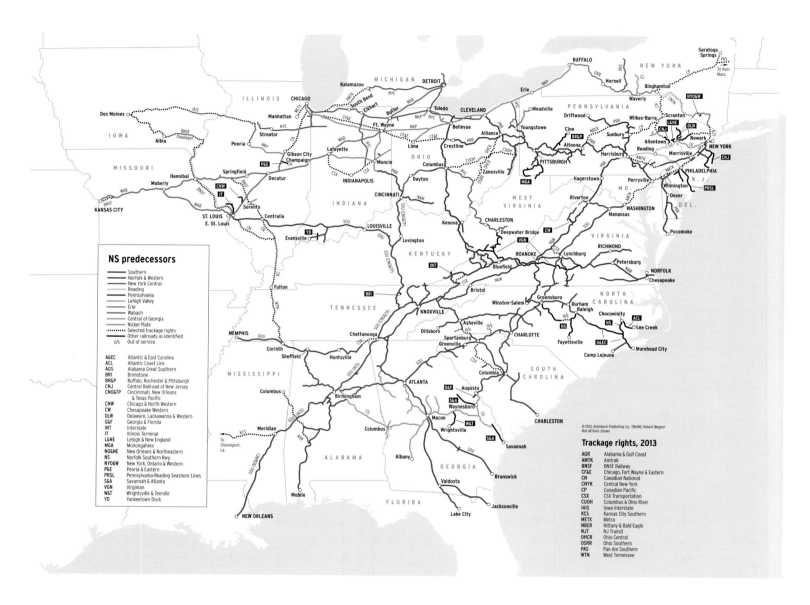

NS predecessors

——	Southern
——	Norfolk & Western
——	New York Central
——	Reading
——	Pennsylvania
——	Lehigh Valley
——	Erie
——	Wabash
——	Central of Georgia
——	Nickel Plate
••••	Selected trackage rights
——	Other railroads as identified
o/s	Out of service

A&EC	Atlantic & East Carolina
ACL	Atlantic Coast Line
AGS	Alabama Great Southern
BRI	Brimstone
BR&P	Buffalo, Rochester & Pittsburgh
CNJ	Central Railroad of New Jersey
CNO&TP	Cincinnati, New Orleans & Texas Pacific
CNW	Chicago & North Western
CW	Chesapeake Western
DLW	Delaware, Lackawanna & Western
G&F	Georgia & Florida
INT	Interstate
IT	Illinois Terminal
L&NE	Lehigh & New England
MGA	Monongahela
NO&NE	New Orleans & Northeastern
NS	Norfolk Southern Rwy.
NYO&W	New York, Ontario & Western
P&E	Peoria & Eastern
PRSL	Pennsylvania-Reading Seashore Lines
S&A	Savannah & Atlanta
VGN	Virginian
W&T	Wrightsville & Tennille
YD	Yankeetown Dock

© 2013, Kalmbach Publishing Co., TRAINS; Robert Wegner
Not all lines shown

Trackage rights, 2013

AGR	Alabama & Gulf Coast
AMTK	Amtrak
BNSF	BNSF Railway
CF&E	Chicago, Fort Wayne & Eastern
CN	Canadian National
CNYK	Central New York
CP	Canadian Pacific
CSX	CSX Transportation
CUOH	Columbus & Ohio River
IAIS	Iowa Interstate
KCS	Kansas City Southern
METX	Metra
NBER	Nittany & Bald Eagle
NJT	NJ Transit
OHCR	Ohio Central
OSRR	Ohio Southern
PAS	Pan Am Southern
WTN	West Tennessee

Norfolk Southern. © 2013 Kalmbach Publishing Co.,
Trains: Robert Wegner. Not all lines shown.

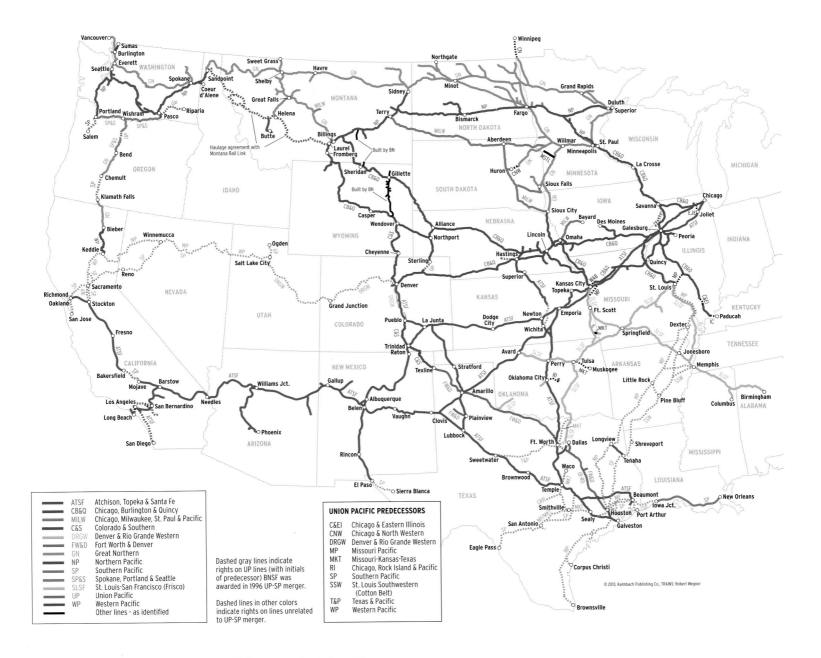

The Union Pacific. © 2013 Kalmbach Publishing Co., *Trains*: Robert Wegner.

Besson, Frank, 192
Biaggini, Benjamin, 96, 166, 242
Birmingham Special (Southern Railway, Norfolk & Western), *141*
Blanchard, Roy, 281–82
Blaze, Jim, 223
Blue Bird (Wabash), *15*
Bluebonnet (Katy), *88*
Blue Streak Merchandise (Southern Pacific), *166, 167*
Bond, Colorado, *101*
Boone, Jim, 220
Boston, Massachusetts, 184
Boston & Maine line, 6, 9, 17, 18, *110*, 218
Bredenberg, Rollin, 100
brick shippers, 145–46
Briggs, Dick, 185
Brinegar, Claude, 220, 221
British Columbia Railroad (BCOL), 113, *114*, *123*, 124
British Railways, 225
Broadway Limited (Pennsylvania Railroad), 4, *175*
Brosnan, Bill: and aggregate business, 146; and intermodal traffic, 255; leadership style of, 146–47, 251, 293; and management retreats, 138–40; and market research, 131; and modernization of SR, 12, 133; productivity emphasis of, 137, 138; reputation of, 142
Brown, Declan, 282
Buffett, Warren, 100
Burlington (Chicago, Burlington & Quincy [CB&Q]; the Q): Great Northern–Northern Pacific's joint ownership of, 53, 83; headquarters of, 61; reach of, *54*, 85; size and status of, *50*, 53; and Western Pacific (WP), 95; NAMED TRAINS: California Zephyr, 53, 85, *87*, *130*; Denver Zephyr, 53; Empire Builder, 53; Morning Zephyr, *50*; North Coast Limited, 53; Twin Cities Zephyr, 53; Zephyr Rocket, *71*
Burlington Northern (BN): and Amtrak, 192; creation of, 58, *60*, 61, 95; financial health of, 68; grain train of, *267*; intermodal traffic of, *60*; and line rationalization, 95; main line routes of, 53; and Pacific Northwest, 61; and Powder River Basin (PRB) coal, 89, *89*, 91, 104; Santa Fe acquired by, 98; and Union Pacific, *60*, 95

Burlington Northern Santa Fe (BNSF): Berkshire Hathaway's acquisition of, 100; and Canadian National merger proposal, 100; coal traffic of, 91, *97*, *274*; and crude-by-rail, 104; and Frisco's routes, 80; Great Northern main line acquired by, 104; intermodal traffic of, *97*, *104*; as major system in the West, 73, 95; and Montana Rail Link (MRL), *94*; and Norfolk Southern merger proposal, 100, 273–74, *275*; routes of, 53, *304*; transcontinental routes, *105*
Burlington–Rock Island Zephyr Rocket, *71*
Burwell, Ed, 251, 258, 262
business model of train industry, ix

Cairo line proposal, 241–42
California Zephyr (Burlington, Rio Grande, and Western Pacific joint operation), 53, 85, *87*, *130*
Canada, 17, 67
Canadian (Canadian Pacific), *110*, *117*, *118*
Canadian (Via Rail), *110*, *117*
Canadian National (CN): and BNSF merger proposal, 100; British Columbia Railroad acquired by, *114*, *123*, 124; and Chicago, 67; color scheme of, *111*, *112*, 113; and Conrail split, 283–84; corridor trains of, *111*; and difficulties posed by landscape, 122; diversified businesses of, 111, 113, 120; downsizing of, 120; elimination of inefficiencies at, 121; expansion of, 123–24; and financial forecasts for Railpax, 190; freight trains of, 111, *111*, 113, 283; as government-owned corporation, 113; Illinois Central acquired by, 67, 121, 124; intermodal traffic of, 123; long-haul trains of, 120; passenger services of, 111, 116, 120, 186, *188*, 188; privatizing of, 120–21; reach of, 111; route structure of, 124, *305*; size and status of, 111; NAMED TRAINS: Continental, 111, *116*, *117*; Super Continental, 111, *188*; Tempos, 120
Canadian Pacific (CP): and BNSF–Canadian National merger proposal, 100; and Chicago, 64, 109; color scheme of, 113; commuter services of, *108*; and Delaware & Hudson, 21, 123, 124; and difficulties posed by landscape, 119, 122; downsizing of, 120; elimination of inefficiencies at, 121; expansion of, 121, 123; freight trains of, *110*, 115, *125*; headquarters of, 120; intermodal traffic of, *106*, 119, 283; leadership of, 124 (*see also* Harrison, Hunter);

and Maine Central, 10; and Maritime Provinces, *109*; Milwaukee Road acquired by, 64, 67, 121; and Mount MacDonald Tunnel, 121; nonrail ventures of, 120; and NS's New England expansion, 296; passenger services of, *109*, *110*, 120, 188; route structure of, *306*; shield of, *109*; size and status of, 109; and Soo Line, 57, 64, 109; NAMED TRAINS: Atlantic Limited, *109*; Canadian, *110*, *117*, *118*; Rocky Mountaineer, *118*
Canadian railroading, 107–25; and difficulties posed by landscape, 119, 122; and diversification of businesses, 120; downsizing of, 120; expansions in, 121, 123–24; feeder line networks of, 115; and infrastructure costs, 115; major railroads of, 107, 109, 111, 113 (*see also* Canadian National [CN]; Canadian Pacific [CP]); regional railroads of, 113
Cannonball line, *15*
Capitol Limited (Amtrak), *52*
Capitol Limited (Baltimore & Ohio), 6
Cardinal (Amtrak), *11*
Carolina Special (Southern Railway), *135*, *143*
Carpenter, Pete, 278, 285
Carter, James, 68
Case, Rod, 293
Central of Georgia (CGA), *34*, 35, *36*, 170
Central of New Jersey, 4, *16*, 17, *217*, 218, 225
Central of Vermont (CV), *111*, 124
Central Railroad of New Jersey, 17, 18
Charleston & Western Carolina, 27
Chemical Manufacturers' Association, 98
Cherrington, Paul, 186
Chesapeake & Ohio (C&O): and coal, 12; freight trains of, 23; main line of, *11*; northward expansion of, 35; and NYC merger proposal, 14, 48; and passes for travel, 144; and rail-crisis proposals, 225–26; and Seaboard Coast Line merger, 43, 46, 242 (*see also* CSX); steam locomotives of, 12; NAMED TRAINS: Fast Flying Virginian, *144*; Sportsman, *11*
Chesapeake & Ohio/Baltimore & Ohio (C&O/B&O), 17, 18, 23
Chicago, Burlington & Quincy (CB&Q). *See* Burlington (Chicago, Burlington & Quincy [CB&Q]; the Q)

Denver Zephyr, 53, 54

Department of Transportation (DOT): and commuter services, 184; and freight traffic, 181, 219, 220; and high-speed rail service, 181; and Office of Management and Budget (OMB), 190–91; Orange Line Report (1974), 18, 68, 221–22, 224, 228; and Railpax plan, 186, 188, 189, 190–91, 194; work of author at, 73

derailments, 216

deregulation, 18, 20

Detroit Auto Club, 290–91

Dieffenbach, Phil, 235, 237, 243, 247

Dietz, Jim, 203, 205, 210, 223, 224

Dingell, John, 254

Ditmeyer, Steve, 186, 220

Dole, Elizabeth, 253, 254

Duluth, Missabe & Iron Range (DM&IR), 124

East Coast Champion (Atlantic Coast Line), 27, 29

Eastern Kentucky Railroad proposal, 243

Eastern railroading, 21, 47, 48. See also Southeastern railroading

economy of the United States, 302

Edell, Ed, 203

Edson, Bill, 205

electric engines and electrification, 4, 155, 160–61, 160, 173

Elgin, Joliet & Eastern (EJ&E), 124

Empire Builder (Amtrak), 83, 201

Empire Builder (Great Northern), 53, 83, 83, 198

Empire Corridor (Penn Central), 169

engineering experience of author, 239–40, 240

environmental hurdles in railroading, 265

Erie-Lackawanna line: bankruptcy of, 18, 218; and Conrail split, 282; freight trains of, 8, 13, 217; and government intervention and restructuring, 17; maintenance of, 13, 17, 217; merger of, 12, 14; and rail-crisis proposals, 225–26; secondary-carrier status of, 6; travel of author on, 171

ethanol, 68

express trains, 4, 132, 180

Fairbanks-Morse units, 13

Family Lines of SCL, 39, 42, 43, 51, 96

Fast Flying Virginian (Chesapeake & Ohio), 144

Fast Mail line, 74

Federal Express, 197

Federal Railroad Administration (FRA): and Conrail, 20; and financial issues in the Midwest, 68; and freight problems in Northeast, 219, 220; headquarters of, 179; Kansas City Southern's loan from, 102; and Office of Management and Budget (OMB), 190–91; and passenger services, 185; and rail crisis, 17; and Railpax plan, 186, 188, 189, 190–91, 194; work of author at, ix, 3, 179, 213

Final System Plan (FSP), 18, 222, 228, 233

Fink, David, Jr., 294

Finkbiner, Tom, 255–56

Fishwick, Jack: and Conrail bid, 254; and Crane, 244; and firewall against deficit railroading, 252–53; and railroad crisis in the Northeast, 225, 226; and SR/N&W talks and merger, 242–43, 244

Fleischman, Nancy, 245, 262, 273, 274–75

Flexi-Van system, 151, 161, 163–64

Florida East Coast (FEC), 33, 35, 144, 296

Florida Special, 27, 208

Ford Motor company, 57

Fox, Mike, 223

Frailey, Fred, 185

Frechette, Bill, 154

freight trains and traffic: and Amtrak, 198, 199; of Canadian National (CN), 111, 111, 113, 283; of Canadian Pacific (CP), 110, 115, 125; of Central of New Jersey, 217; of Chesapeake & Ohio (C&O), 23; and Chicago, 61; of Conrail, 19, 47, 212; control of, in East, 21; decline in, 4, 184, 214, 218; of Delaware & Hudson (D&H), 227; of Erie-Lackawanna line, 8, 13, 217; and government intervention and restructuring, 17–18, 218–19; and high-speed service proposals, 166–68; and highways, 12, 151; interference with, 184–85; of Lehigh & Hudson River, 218; of Lehigh Valley, 216; lighterage traffic, 154; and long-haul trains, 184–85; of Louisville & Nashville (L&N), 38; and Metro-North Commuter Railroad, 184; in Midwest, 53, 181; of Missouri Pacific (MP), 202, 236; and Montana Rail Link (MRL), 94; and nationalization threat, 179, 230; of New York Central (NYC), 6, 12, 154; and Nickel Plate

Road, 14; in Northeast, 12, 13, 151, 181; of Northern Pacific (NP), 84; and passenger services, 18, 181, 186, 189, 198; of Reading, 217; of Southern Pacific (SP), 77, 99; and track capacity, 214; of Union Pacific, 79, 80

Friedmann, John, 272, 273, 278, 294

Frisco (the St. Louis–San Francisco, or SLSF), 78, 80, 82, 83, 95, 144

Fullam, John P., 213, 220

Gallamore, Robert E., x, 186, 220, 224, 278

Garfield, Gene, 205–6

gas turbine locomotives of Union Pacific, 80

Gateway Western line, 102

GE engines, 161, 164, 165–66

General Motors, 17

Georgia & Florida (G&F), 35, 36

Georgian, 62

Georgia Railroad (Atlantic Coast Line), 31, 33, 143, 144

Georgia Railroad/West Point Route (GA/AWP), 27, 39, 236

Gessner, Jim, 147

GG-1 locomotives, 170, 171

Goode, David: and BNSF–Canadian National merger proposal, 100; and BNSF-NS merger proposal, 273–74; as CEO of NS, 261–62; and Conrail bid, 272; and Conrail integration, 289; and Conrail split, 48, 272–73, 281, 283; and inaugural double-stack train, 271; and infrastructure investments, 291–92; and merger strategies review, 274–75; and New England expansion, 294; and operational savings, 292–93; and John Snow, 276, 278

Goode, Susan, 294

Goodwin, Paul, 47

Gotham Limited, Pennsylvania Railroad, 2

Graham, Hal, 203, 205

grain transportation, 67–68, 115, 134

Grand Canyon line, 74

Grand Central Terminal, 160–61, 160

Grand Trunk Western (CN), 67, 124

Great Northern (GN): and Amtrak, 192, 194; ascendency of, 95; and Burlington, 53, 58, 83; main line acquired by BNSF, 104; and Northern Pacific, 83; passenger services of, 83; and quality of infra-

JIM McCLELLAN worked in the railroad industry for forty years. Along the way, he held positions at the Southern Railway, the New York Central, the Penn Central, the Federal Railroad Administration (twice), Amtrak, the US Railway Association, the Association of American Railroads, the Southern (again), and Norfolk Southern. He retired from Norfolk Southern as the Senior Vice President for Planning. An avid photographer and painter, Jim lived with his wife, Joanne, in Virginia Beach. Jim McClellan died on October 14, 2016, at the age of 77.